THE LAZARUS SYNDROME

THE LAZARUS SYNDROME

BURIAL ALIVE AND OTHER HORRORS OF THE UNDEAD

RODNEY DAVIES

BARNES
& NOBLE
BOOKS

NEW YORK

Contents

Acknowledgements

In addition to the staff at the new British Library, the Newspaper Library and the Guildhall Library, where the bulk of my research was done, I wish to thank Dr Stuart McDonald of the Laboratory of Human Anatomy at Glasgow University for sending me material about the electrical experiments of Professor James Jeffray; Michael Petch for lending me a computer and otherwise assisting me when my own machine unexpectedly failed; Brenda Collins, Joyce Harrison, Peggy Sullivan and Wendy Williams for their accounts of personal happenings beyond the ordinary; Diana Speight for suggesting the title; and John and Joyce Matthews of the Two Jays Bookshops at Edgware, from whom several helpful out-of-print volumes were obtained.

Thanks are also extended to Hugh Noyes for permission to use a few lines from his father's poem entitled 'The Burial of a Queen', and to Mick Brown for permission to quote from his article entitled 'Life After Death – Are We Closer to the Truth', which was first published in the *Telegraph* magazine on 27 March 1993.

However, despite every effort being made to contact all authors or publishers of copyright material, these proved impossible in some cases. My apologies are offered to those concerned.

This book is dedicated to all those many individuals who seemingly died but who later returned to life, whose unique and often terrifying experiences are recounted here.

Introduction

When I was a boy, living at home above the firm of undertakers and monumental masons that my stepfather managed, I shared my life with the appurtenances of the dead – that is, with coffins, gravestones, kerbstones, crematorium plaques, caskets, hearses, and a mortuary. And they all had their own noises and sights – the deep, insistent hollow-sounding buzz made by the circular stone-saw as it cut through slabs of marble or granite; the shriller whirr of the stone-grinding and polishing machines; the brisk yet monotonous chipping of epitaphs by the letter-cutters; the sawing, planing and hammering from the coffin shop; and the regular washing and waxing of one or other of the firm's hearses, an activity that was invariably followed by a coffin being brought from the mortuary and slid into the vehicle's rear end, in order that its occupant could be taken on that last journey which lies ahead of us all.

The hearses, manufactured by Rolls-Royce, were all big, black and elegant, and purred along majestically, shining with an unembarrassed splendour. When gaily decorated, both inside and out, with floral wreaths, they seemed more suited to a carnival procession than a funeral, especially as their drivers and the coffin bearers who accompanied them were such tall, jolly fellows, who looked sombrely sophisticated in their black suits, black ties and polished black shoes. And when my stepfather led the funeral procession he wore a top hat.

The finished coffins and the gravestones were also admirable. Made from natural materials whose intrinsic beauty was heightened by sanding and polishing, they were, in their own small way, works of art. The gravestones (or memorial stones) had their inscriptions carved by letter-cutters who had all served seven-year apprenticeships. Sometimes a particular gravestone's letters were brightened by being gilded, which was a silent job, but if they were leaded, the air would ring with the echoing sound of the rubber hammer, almost as if someone was impatiently banging a dinner gong. The workshops themselves were always a delight to visit, especially the coffin shop, notwithstanding its purpose. The wood shavings that gathered in cheerful piles under and around the trestles on which the coffins were made emitted a pleasant, fresh odour, which complemented the somewhat pungent smell of wood stain, while the coffin wax was as deliciously fragrant as any household polish. And when the shiny coffins had been lined with clean, luxuriously white quilted padding and had had gold-coloured metal handles attached to their outer sides, they looked almost welcoming.

Yet appearances can be deceptive, as I learned one day when a coffin-maker, the largest of the three employed, slyly asked me if I dared lie in the coffin he had just finished making. I had upset him some days before by accidentally breaking his wood plane, but I assumed that this had been forgotten and, not wanting to appear a coward, I clambered into the coffin and stretched out in it, grinning as I did so. To my surprise, the man then snatched up the coffin lid and, upbraiding me for being 'a meddling little so-and-so', lowered it down on top of me. To this day I can still recall its descending dark shape and the rapidly contracting strip of light surrounding it. I let out a scream of terror as the lid closed silently over me like a safe door, shutting me into an awful black-ness. I knew then that if the coffin-maker screwed the lid down I could never escape. But of course, that was not his intention, for he almost immediately raised the lid and set it back on the ground. Then he laughed and gave me his hand and pulled me, wide-eyed and trembling, out of the coffin. We were quits, but the experience not only taught me never to touch any of his woodworking tools again, it also gave me a brief encounter with the absolute horror of premature interment.

Nor can I forget how, when I happened to walk by the mortuary and someone had not properly closed its sliding door, I caught shocking glimpses of corpses, clothed in what appeared to be long, striped night-shirts, lying pale and still and seemingly asleep on the mortuary shelves. My bedroom overlooked that receptacle for the dead, and at night when I was in bed and the yard was dark and unnaturally quiet, the thought of those ghastly night-shirted figures brought a chill to my young heart. I feared that one of them might suddenly wake, climb down from its hard shelf, and somehow make its way to my bedside. To save myself from such a terrifying sight, I slept with the bedlocthes pulled up over my head. It was not until long aftewards that I discovered that my anxieties were by no means groundless, for some of the supposedly dead really are asleep, immobilized by trance, coma or catalespy, their condition misdiagnosed and their fate – to be buried, cremated or dissected alive – horrifying in the extreme. And while a lucky few do emerge from their death-like slumber in the mortuary or are even rescued from the grave, the majority of such unfortunates often only regain consciousness, if they ever lost it, when they are beyond help, facing death trapped in the confines of a long, narrow box.

Although death is, of course, the natural end of life, the final curtain, and we cannot escape it, no matter how much we might want to, none of us deserves to suffer a farewell that is part of everyone's worst nightmare. But far too many folk have done so, and in this book I examine their awful yet preventable plight.

However, let me add this warning: Do not read on if you have a nervous disposition; if you do, you might never allow yourself to fall sleep again.

And I want everybody to rest in peace.

1 The Signs of Death

So I knew that he was dying –
Stooped, and raised his languid head;
Felt no breath, and heard no sighing,
So I knew that he was dead.

From 'A Death-Scene' by Emily Brontë

Because the human body (like that of all other animals and, indeed, plants) is composed of microscopic living units called cells, which together number many tens of billions, each person's life, as we may call it, is necessarily the sum of these myriad parts. To put it another way, we are all both one and very many at the same time, which is why no one's life ends with the same abruptness with which, say, an electric machine stops working when its power supply is switched off.

Yet all those cells, if they are to continue living, must receive a constant supply of oxygen and glucose, from which, by chemical combustion, they produce energy. This process, known as respiration, simultaneously creates water and a waste gas, carbon dioxide, which must be eliminated. The blood, an iron-rich fluid which is pumped around the body by the heart, is the means by which these chemicals are taken to and from the cells. Hence when the heart, for whatever reason, stops beating, the cells it services are deprived of oxygen and glucose (and other food substances) and are subject to a build-up of carbon dioxide, which together gradually kill them. When enough cells die to cause a failure of the major organs, the body as a whole is said to be dead.

Brain cells are particularly susceptible to a lack of both oxygen and glucose. Strangulation, for example, by directly cutting off the air supply, quickly causes a loss of consciousness. Similarly, a fall in blood glucose (or hypoglycaemia) first produces disorientation and then, albeit more slowly, unconsciousness. However, although medical orthodoxy tells us that brain cells die if they are deprived of oxygen for between three and eight minutes, other factors may extend this period considerably. Drowning in cold water or suffocation under an avalanche for instance, which entail an accompanying drop in body temperature, can preserve the brain cells by reducing their oxygen (and glucose) need.

Other cells, such as those of the dermis of the skin, can remain alive for twenty-four or more hours after the heart has stopped beating and the person is beyond revival. Their continued activity may result, in men, in a noticeable post-mortem growth of facial hair, and sometimes, in both sexes, of the nails. This happens because there is a continuing slow exchange of gases between the dermal cells and the blood capillaries, which is sufficient to keep them alive.

Bone-marrow cells are even more tenacious of life; they can survive for over forty-eight hours after 'body death', thereby allowing a two-day delay in the taking of bone grafts. Yet even this incredible post-mortem longevity is exceeded by cells of the artery walls, which can stay alive for about three days. Hence death is not so much a sudden event as a process.

But clearly, if the body cells do not all die at the same time, it is very difficult to determine exactly when someone is truly (or irreversibly) dead. Brain-stem death, as determined by an electroencephalograph (EEG), which monitors brain activity, is now regarded as the prime indicator of death, even though the rest of the body may still be alive and can be kept that way artificially for an indefinite period. This is usually done when the person's corneas, kidneys, heart or other parts are needed as organ transplants. Hence in these cases an electronic machine, monitored by doctors in whose interest it is to pronounce death as soon as possible, becomes the ultimate judge. But the EEG is not, and cannot be, a completely accurate determinator of brain activity, and we cannot therefore know if the patient might have revived if more effort had been made at resuscitation. Nor do we know what, if any, pain is felt when that person, who is not of course anethaestised, is dissected, and what, if any, comprehension he or she may have of the event.

Dying, then, occurs gradually, which means that there is always an intermediate state, whose length varies, between life and actual death. It is during this period, called apparent death, when many of the so-called signs of death are evident, that resuscitation techniques, if applied with perseverance and determination, can be successful. But when apparent death is mistaken for actual death, this may result in premature dissection, or in premature burial or cremation, all of which are made even more horrible when the person concerned spontaneously regains consciousness. Such ghastly experiences have not only happened frequently in the past but regretfully still occur today. There is peace in actual death, but there may be none in apparent death.

Edgar Allan Poe stated the problem succinctly in his fascinating and pertinent short story entitled 'The Premature Burial'. He wrote:

The boundaries which divide Life from Death are at the best shadowy and vague. Who shall say where the one ends and where the other begins? We know that there are diseases in which occur total cessations of all the apparent functions of vitality, and yet in which these cessations are merely suspensions, properly so called. They are only temporary pauses in the incomprehensible mechanism. A certain period elapses,

and some unseen mysterious principle again sets in motion
the magic pinions and the wizard wheels.

Nowadays our familiarity with death is slight. This is partly
because people live longer and partly because they die less
publicly than they once did. In 1891, for example, when the
population of Great Britain was 29 million, an astonishing
671,498 people died from disease and other causes, whereas in
1996 when the population had more than doubled to 58.8
million, the number dying only totalled 625,640 people, or some
45,000 less than the 1891 figure. This tremendous decrease in
mortality has been brought about by the rapid growth of medical
knowledge and the discovery of effective medicines like antibiotics. Better housing and hygiene have also played an important
part. Infant mortality in particular has dramatically declined. For
while 14 per cent of children died before they reached their first
birthday in 1900, less than 1 per cent do today. Yet although far
more people now die when they are old, they increasingly do so
in hospitals and other institutions, away from their relatives and
friends. Indeed, it is a sad reflection on modern society that we
are often not there when our elders need us most.

By being shielded from the fact of death and from its sights, we
have come to believe that it is something abnormal and unpleas-
ant, rather than being the natural end to this journey we call life.
And whereas the dead were once laid out at home and kept there
until their funerals, which gave those who were not really dead a
chance to recover, nowadays they are kept in mortuary refrigera-
tors, which gives them no chance at all. For mistakes in this
regard still happen. Apparent death and actual death are easily
confused, even by those who are trained to distinguish them, our
doctors.

The two so-called signs of death with which we are all familiar, and which most of us regard as infallible indicators of the
condition, are lack of heart beat or pulse and absence of breath-

ing. Loss of facial colour, a fixed, glassy appearance of the eyes, the mouth falling open, body coldness and an absence of reflex actions and of sensibility are also apparently familiar signs of death. Yet while all of these do occur at death, they may also be exhibited by those who are still alive. Hence they are not irrefutable indicators, even when they appear together.

The famous anatomist Jacobus Benignus Winslow was the son of a Danish Lutheran minister. He planned to enter his father's church, but became a Catholic convert while on a visit to France in 1698, and afterwards settled in Paris, where he took up the study of medicine and went on to practise it. As a boy and again as a young man he had the misfortune to become very ill and seemingly to expire. Indeed, he narrowly escaped premature burial on both occasions. These two horrendous close calls led him to investigate the reliability of the signs of death, and to collect cases of people who had, like himself, wrongly been adjudged as dead. He noted

The Pulsation of the Heart and Arteries is sometimes so insensible, that we are very subject to be deceived, and believe the Person dead . . . . Respiration affords Marks no less precarious than those of the Pulse, since it is sometimes so languid, and as it were over-powered, that neither the Eye nor the Hand can discover the slightest Motion of the Breast . . . and on the contrary, the Paleness of the Complexion, the Coldness of the Body, and the Abolition of the external Senses, are very dubious and fallacious signs of a Certain Death.

Because a dead body no longer generates heat, which derives from the physiological activites of living cells, its internal temperature gradually cools from the normal 98°F to that of its surroundings. How quickly this happens depends upon the cause of death, the amount of clothing worn, the temperature of the surrounding air, the degree of exposure to wind, which has a cooling effect, and so on. A person's rectal temperatue may still be as high as 90°F fourteen hours after death. Skin coldness by itself is a very unreliable sign. After all, the skin of someone who is alive feels cold if it has been exposed to low outdoor temperatures or to wind, while if the hands of the toucher are cold, a cold skin, even that of a corpse, may feel comparatively warm. An unconscious person who has lain outdoors, particularly in winter weather, or has been lifted from water or mud, always feels cold yet may easily be resuscitated. More confusingly, the disease asphyxial cholera produces a corpse-like coldness in its comatose yet still-living victims, whilst fatal strokes, from which no recovery is possible, may be followed by a rise in body temperature, the perceptible warmth of which may last for as long as three days. Other examples of diseases that lead to a deceptive post-mortem rise in body temperature include yellow fever, rheumatic fever and smallpox.

Another so-called sign of death is the relaxation of the iris of the eyes (coincidently named by Jacobus Winslow), so that the pupils become larger, thereby contributing to the eyes' dark, fixed, staring look. However, if the person is short-sighted, his or her pupils will be larger than normal anyway, which thus negates their value as a diagnostic sign. Similarly, if a light is shone into the eyes of an apparently dead person, it will usually prompt an immediate reduction in the size of the pupils, which does not happen in someone who is actually dead. However, this pupil reflex is lost when a non-fatal dose of prussic or hydrocyanic acid has been swallowed. Also, if the cornea of the eye is touched lightly, it will normally cause an involuntary closure of the eyelids. Yet neither of these protective reflexes occur in someone suffering from catalepsy, which is, hardly surprisingly, often mistaken for death.

Few doctors anyway bother to check for the pupil or the eyelid reflex, as most regard a lack of heartbeat or pulse and an absence of breathing as sufficient indicators of death.

In former times it was recommended that the doctor's senses should always be aided where possible. Thus in order to detect slight movements of the chest, it was suggested not only that it should be bared, but that a watch glass filled with water should be stood on the xiphoid cartilage, which lies at the lower end of the sternum or breastbone. Better still Jacobus Winslow advises:

The Body ought not to be placed entirely on the Spine of the Back, but turned in such a Manner to one of the Sides, as that the Extremity of the Cartilage of the ante-penult Rib may be elevated as much as possible, and have the vessel containing the Water placed upon it, since it is much better disposed to render the slightest motion of the breast sensible than the *Xiphoid* or *Ensiform Cartilage*. ['Ante-penult' is an abbreviation of 'antepenultimate', and means the last rib but two, or the third from the bottom.]

A movement or trembling of the water in the glass, no matter how slight, reveals respiratory movements within the chest. However, a lack of movement in the water cannot be taken as an irrefutable sign of death because, as Winslow adds, 'it is certain from Experience, that a slow, gentle, and insensible Motion of the Diaphragm alone with the least Motion of the Ribs, is sometimes sufficient . . . to support and carry on Respiration'.

Many doctors would also try to discover if any breath, however faint, was escaping from either the mouth or the nostrils, although the former was regarded as the more reliable exit. This was done either by placing some teased-out cotton wool or a fine down feather on the mouth, and watching to see if it moved, or alternatively by holding a small mirror there, and noting if it misted over. Both results would show that exhalation was still occurring.

In Act IV, Scene V of William Shakespeare's play *Henry IV, Part Two*, Henry's son, Prince Hal, beautifully describes how a feather which had fallen on his dying father's mouth, seemed to show that he was dead.

> By his gates of breath
> There lies a downy feather which stirs not:
> Did he suspire, that light and weightless down
> Perforce must move. My gracious lord! my father!
> This sleep is sound indeed; this is a sleep
> That from this golden rigol hath divorc'd
> So many English kings.

Shakespeare's historical source, the chronicler Enguerrand de Monstrelet, records that King Henry IV suffered from epilepsy, a condition that can sometimes result in collapses mimicking death, which it evidently did on that occasion. But the monarch soon recovers, to find that his ambitious son has taken his crown from beside him and put it on his own head. He rebukes him angrily:

> Thou hast stolen that which after some few hours
> Were thine without offence; and at my death
> Thou hast seal'd up my expectation:
> Thy life did manifest thou lov'dst me not,
> And thou wilt have me die assur'd of it.

Jacobus Winslow observes that, where the misting of a mirror is concerned, 'almost similar vapours are discharged from the Mouth and Nostrils of a really dead Person, who is yet warm', while the lack of movement of a piece of cotton wool or a feather placed on or next to the mouth can happen 'because Persons not only alive, but also in perfect Health, may by checking their Respiration, frustrate the Ends of such precarious scrutinies'. Yet he fails to point out that because a mirror is made misty by the condensation of water vapour in the person's breath upon it, this only happens when the mirror is cooler than the breath. A mirror withdrawn from a doctor's pocket may not, therefore, immediately prove effective, because it has been warmed by his body heat.

Where a prankster is mischievously feigning death, Jacobus Winslow offers what must surely be the definitive way of catching him or her out. His method has a similar rousing effect on someone who is in a trance. 'We ought to irritate his Nostrils,' he remarks, 'by introducing into them Sternutatories, Errhines, Salts, stimulating Liquors, Synapisms, the Juice of Onions, Garlic, and Horse-radish, or the feathered End of a Quill, or the point of a Pencil.' A sternutatory, like the other substances and objects mentioned, is something that prompts sneezing, although Winslow does not mean that everything listed should be thrust into the nostrils together (which would probably terminate the life of a genuinely comatose person!), but rather that one or other of them should be so used.

It may seem strange that such an assault on the nose should be necessary to catch out a person pretending to be dead, since the heartbeat or pulse would surely be detected by a half-competent doctor, but there are some people who can will their vital functions to reduce themselves to the extent that they seem to die.

St Augustine mentions one such person in Book XIV, Chapter 24 of his monumental work entitled *Concerning the City of God Against the Pagans*. The man, a presbyter named Restitutus in the diocese of Calama, apparently 'could at his pleasure deprive himself of all sense' and thereby lie as if he was dead. In this state he felt no discomfort or pain when pinched or pricked, and he was once burned but without knowing it, only becoming aware of the pain of the burn when he recovered himself. Indeed, the depth of his trance was such that, 'he did not breathe at all, and he would say, that the voices of men, if they spake louder than ordinary, were heard by him, as if they were at some great distance from him.'

Another example was Marie Isabeau, a young servant

employed, coincidentally, by the Paris surgeon Jean Devaux (1649–1729), a colleague of Jacobus Winslow and the author of several medical works. Like an Indian Fakir, Marie Isabeau was able to slow her heart and respiration rate to such an extent that she not only fooled Jean Devaux into thinking she was dead, but actually allowed herself to be placed in a coffin and carried to the graveyard, not once but three times. This morbid deception was almost certainly intended to attract attention, and was preferable to risking actually killing herself by slashing her wrists or swallowing poison. However, crying wolf almost rebounded on her, as Dr Walter Whiter relates in *A Dissertation on the Disorder of Death*.

So determined was she in doing justice to the perfection of her art, that at the third time of the exhibition, *she remained under the semblance of Death, till the bearers were actually letting her down into her grave.* According to the sequel of the story, when she *really died,* as it is expressed, her friends kept her unburied for the space of six days, a most extraordinary time in the customs of France, that the delusion, if any such should be practised, might flatter as little as possible the vanity of the artist.

The equally remarkable physiological self-control of Colonel Townshend, a retired army officer, was described for posterity by another contemporary of Dr Winslow's, Dr George Cheyne (1671–1743), in his celebrated work entitled *The English Malady*. Dr Cheyne attended the colonel during his final illness, and he was able to investigate the man's unusual talent fully. Colonel Townshend, a resident of Bristol, had for many years suffered from a painful kidney complaint, and when his condition deteriorated, he had himself carried on a litter from Bristol to the Bell Inn at Bath, where he and his servants took rooms, in order to receive treatment from both Dr Cheyne and his colleague, Dr

Baynard. The two doctors, along with Colonel Townshend's apothecary, Mr Skrine, visited the sick man twice a day for a week, at the end of which, his illness showing no improvement, Colonel Townshend took leave to describe to them the strange ability he had acquired.

> He told us ... that [by] *composing himself, he could die or expire when he pleased, and yet by an effort or somehow, he could come to life again;* which it seems he had sometimes tried, before he had sent for us. We heard this with surprise .... We could hardly believe the fact, as he related it, much less give any acount of it, unless he should please to make an experiment before us, which we were unwilling he should do.

Despite the medical men's reservations, or perhaps because of them, Colonel Townshend resolved to demonstrate his strange skill, not least because they would then be able to verify it. This is what happened next:

> He composed himself on his back, and lay in a still posture sometime: while I held his right hand, Dr Baynard laid a hand on his heart, and Mr Skrine held a clean looking-glass to his mouth. I found his pulse sink gradually, till at last I could not feel any, by the most exact and nice touch. Dr Baynard could not feel the least motion of his heart, nor Mr Skrine the least soil of breath on the bright mirror he held to his mouth; then each of us by turns examined his arm, heart, and breath, but could not by the nicest scrutiny discover the least symptom of life in him.

Thus by using what are still the standard tests for death, the two doctors and the apothecary were completely unable to detect any sign of life. Indeed when Colonel Townshend had lain apparently lifeless for half an hour, they concluded that their worst fears had come to pass and that he had in fact died. Then, however, he again surprised them.

As we were going away, we observed some motion about the body, and upon examination, found his pulse and the motion of his heart gradually returning; he began to breathe gently, and speak softly. We were astonished to the last degree at this unexpected change, and after some further conversation with him, and among ourselves, went away fully satisfied as to all the particulars of this fact, but confounded and puzzled, and not being able to form any rational scheme that might account for it.

Notwithstanding the fact that they occurred in the early years of the eighteenth century, these two famous cases reveal how unreliable the apparent absence of heartbeat and respiration are as indicators of death, and more significantly show that where death is concerned, a speedy diagnosis is always inappropriate. Hence although modern medical opinion says that if the heartbeat, pulse and breathing stop for at least an hour, and if there is no response to external stimuli and no demonstrable reflexes, the person is brain dead (a condition that permits the removal of organs for transplantation), neither the time limit nor the lack of responses make the diagnosis certain.

Indeed, one warning which comes through time and time again from medical writers of previous ages, is that, except when a person is the subject of irrefutable death, as with beheading (although even this, as we shall see, is not instantaneously fatal), no one should be dissected, buried or cremated until he or she has not only received prolonged attempts at revival but has lain apparently dead for at least six days, or until putrefaction has begun.

Another sign of death is the stiffening of the limbs, a condition known as rigor mortis, which is caused by the muscles losing their flexibility. In life, movement at a hinge joint like the knee happens when the flexor muscles behind the thigh contract, thereby exerting an upward pull on the rear of the tibia, while the extensor muscles, those at the front of the thigh, simultaneously relax and are stretched, so allowing the leg to bend at the joint. When the reverse occurs, the limb is straightened. However, when neither of the muscle groups can be stretched, as happens in rigor mortis, the limbs cannot be flexed, extended or even rotated at the joints without using force. Thus when a person dies with bent limbs or with a turned head, clenched hands, etc., rigor mortis holds him or her in that position.

As a trainee undertaker, my stepfather once had to help with the laying-out of a man who had died at home in bed. The dead man's legs were bent up at the knees, and my stepfather was told to straighten them. But rigor mortis had set in, and when he pushed down hard on the knees, the corpse correspondingly sat up and leaned against him, which caused him to scream loudly and nearly gave him a heart attack. Life with the dead is not always a bundle of fun!

The time taken for rigor mortis to manifest varies quite considerably. In one study involving ninety-two corpses, for example, it was found that whereas half developed the condition within four to six hours of death, twenty-one took over eight hours, of which ten took between ten and thirteen hours. And while rigor mortis's onset is gradual and variable, it is not permanent; indeed, the condition usually does not last above twenty-four hours. More confusingly, in very hot weather it may not happen at all. These variations make it a troublesome indicator of death, especially as it may easily be confused with the limb rigidity of catalepsy. A similar stiffening or spasm of the muscles is a symptom of tetanus, as is evident from its popular name of lockjaw.

When a limb stiffened by rigor mortis is forcibly bent or

extended, the bones remain loose at the joint. Thus if an arm in rigor is wrenched up from a corpse's side, it will drop back beside the body on being released. However, if a limb stiffened by catalepsy or tetanus is bent or straightened, it will remain in the position to which it is moved.

Limb rigidity is also encountered in someone who has been frozen, although if the bones are forcibly moved at the joints a distinctive cracking noise is heard, which is caused by the ice crystals in the joint grating together. A frozen person also feels hard all over, unlike someone who has died without being frozen, and one can only press one's fingers into the skin with some difficulty. Moreover, the depressions left behind when this is done only fill out very slowly, if at all. An ordinary corpse's skin, however, remains pliant even though rigor has developed in the muscles, and finger impressions (which of course result from the tissues beneath being compressed) gradually fill out, although much less rapidly than those made in the skin of someone still alive.

In addition to the tests for death mentioned above, there are a number of others that are broadly chemical in nature, although none is entirely trustworthy. Such tests can only be done by trained professionals with the right chemicals and equipment, which limits their use, and they are rarely employed unless there is real doubt about the primary signs, which there seldom is, even though their reliability is questionable. Moreover, because the body's cells may continue living for twenty-four hours or more after a person's heart has stopped beating, such tests give erroneous results if carried out too soon.

If a visible vein in the arm is blocked by the pressure of one's thumb and the blood is expressed from it towards the heart using the fingers of the other hand, the vein will not refill when the thumb is removed if the heart has ceased to beat. This test only reveals a lack of heartbeat and not irreversible death, as it may be possible to restart the heart with massage or electric shocks. It is also often difficult to carry out when the arm veins are hidden beneath subcutaneous fat.

An old test, recommended by Winslow and by others before him, is to burn the skin, say of the hand or arm, with a candle flame or other intense heat source. Nowadays a lighted cigarette would do. Dead skin will only char, whereas living skin will give rise to a water blister. But again, this test only indicates life in the skin dermis, which may not necessarily reflect its continuation in the heart or brain. And the test is very painful to those who may be suffering from catalepsy. However, it would certainly bring a modern-day Marie Isabeau to her senses!

The pain of a burn can also sometimes rouse the genuine apparently dead person. Dr Peron-Autret, the author of *Buried Alive*, cites the case of Luigi Vittori, a musketeer in the Vatican Guard of that much-troubled pontiff Pius IX, who once became seriously ill with asthma. He was taken to hospital and given treatment, but he none the less died – or at least so it seemed. However, one young doctor had doubts and impulsively held a candle flame to the end of his nose. Luigi's sudden scream and the reflex jerk of his head conclusively demonstrated that he was still alive. With that settled, he was soon restored to health and was eventually able to continue with his career as a musketeer, albeit with a livid burn scar on his nose!

When a hypodermic needle is pushed into the skin and fat of a living person, the narrow aperture it makes usually closes up immediately when the needle is withdrawn. This does not happen with dead skin, as it has lost its elasticity. But if a small quantity (about 2 cc) of ether is subcutaneously injected into living skin, a jet of the vaporized chemical follows the needle's removal. However, this fails to occur if the cells of the dermis are dead. The subcutaneous injection of a similar quantity of ammonia, known as Monteverdi's test, produces a characteristic red flush in the skin if the dermal cells are still alive. There is no change in skin colour if they are dead.

Lastly, the Icard test, devised in 1905 by Dr Severin Icard, which is now better known as the florescin test, requires the injection of a coloured but otherwise harmless solution of florescin into a vein of the arm. If blood circulation is still continuing, no matter how intermittently, the entire skin will turn yellow, while the eyes become a brilliant emerald green. These startling colour changes, which make the person resemble a large, exotic frog, happen within twelve hours if he or she is still alive. They do not occur if the person is dead. And fortunately, the colours eventually fade and disappear, which is just as well as the subject might otherwise prefer to remain unreanimated!

It is usual for the contents of the bladder and the bowels to be expelled during the hours following death, but because this also happens with those who are unconscious for any length of time, it cannot be accounted a reliable indicator of death. The same can be said of the expulsion of mucus from the nose and mouth. The arteries of a corpse also become empty of blood, while the blood itself loses liquidity as it coagulates. People often ask for an artery (the carotid artery is a popular choice) to be cut after they die, so as to make sure that their demise is real and not apparent, although the slicing of an artery is not without its hazards, as if they are still alive, the resultant loss of blood would certainly finish them off. However, that is doubtless better than being interred or cremated alive.

Putrefaction, or bodily decay, is the most certain sign of death, and those concerned about how easily mistakes are made have long argued that no apparently dead person should be buried, cremated or dissected until putrefaction has started. They reason that when no decay is seen, recovery may still be possible, whereas once putrefaction has begun, it is not.

Yet, bodily decay can happen in life. It is called gangrene or necrosis and it may develop around an untreated wound infected with soil bacteria, for example, or in a body part that has for some reason been deprived of its blood supply. Gangrene of the feet and lower legs is a health risk faced by diabetics, particularly those who smoke and do not exercise, and it may require the amputation of the affected parts. And if the hands and feet are tied too tightly they may subsequently become gangrenous.

Putrefaction following death begins in the alimentary canal and is brought about by saprophytic (or 'putrid-eating') micro-organisms, notably bacteria and protozoa, which naturally occur there. These live upon, and help to digest, our food, which is of course dead organic matter. Hence when the cells in the lining of the intestines die, the saprophytes continue their job and digest those too, so that in this regard we eat ourselves after death. The saprophytes in due course also spread to and attack the other internal organs. But the intestinal cells may take two or three days (or sometimes longer) to die, and this accounts for the delay in the external evidence of putrefaction, notably a discoloured skin. The bacterial and protozoal activity generates much foul-smelling, ammoniacal gas, which swells up the abdomen like a balloon, and which, when death has occurred by drowning, will give the corpse sufficient buoyancy to float to the surface. The microbial activity is also encouraged by the internal temperature of the abdomen, which remains warm longest, whereas more external chambers like the mouth and nose, which likewise contain many micro-organisms, are subject to faster cooling, particularly if the corpse lies outside or in water, and which necessarily slows their metabolic rate and thus the decay of these cavities.

According to Dr Deschamps, in a memoir presented to the French Academy of Medicine in 1843, the incontrovertible sign of putrefaction, and thus of death, is the development of a greenish-blue colour in the skin of a corpse's stomach or belly. This spreads evenly across the stomach, and its position makes it easily distinguishable from skin discoloration elsewhere that may be due to other causes. It usually appears on the third day after death, but if the external temperature is low, four or five days may pass before it becomes apparent.

The changes undergone by a dead body which is protected from the predations of carrion-eaters and flies, as it is when it is enclosed, without being embalmed, in a coffin and buried, are decribed by Dr Charles Clay in the following passage, taken from an article which appeared in *The Medical Times*:

> From the sixth to the eighth day, the backs of the hands and the soles of the feet whiten, and the face becomes softer and of a faded white. About the fifteenth day the face swells, and is reddish; a green patch is observed in the hollow pit, at the point of the breast bone; the inside of the hands and feet are quite white and wrinkled; the surface of the chest reddish. From the twenty-sixth day the face becomes darker, eyelids and lips swollen, neck green, and a dark spot as large as a hand, edged with green, on the centre of the chest; genitals distended with gas; hands and feet have the appearance of being parboiled; lungs distending the chest. About the fortieth day the skin detaches itself, and first at the connection of the hand with the wrist. At two months' end the body is covered with slime; face brown and enormously swelled; lips swollen and separated; teeth exposed.

When a corpse is left outside, however, its smell is highly attractive to bluebottles and other dipterous flies. The odour, which is subtle at first, begins when the subject is still alive, thus making him or her an object of great interest to *Musca* species, like the smells emanating from a butcher's shop or a domestic kitchen. But while flies will feed on any kind of organic matter, including faeces, corpses offer them an ideal place on which to lay their eggs. These hatch into larvae, colloquially known as grubs or maggots, within twenty-four hours. The favourite places for egg-laying are cavities like the mouth, nostrils and ears, which offer the maggots protection from birds and other predators, and also give them, so to speak, a head start. The larvae eat hungrily into the corpse's flesh, helping to break it down and thus playing an essential part in the natural cycle of decay. Five days later, having increased their size several times, the maggots transform themselves into hard-coated, relatively immobile pupae, the next reproductive stage, from which, in a further three or more days, depending on the temperature, a new generation of adult flies will emerge.

Any corpse lying outdoors, whether human or animal, not only attracts flies but also a number of much larger scavenging animals. We are perhaps most familiar, through television, with those of the African plains, like vultures, jackals and hyenas, which are always on the lookout for a free meal of dead meat, and which will quickly tear apart and devour a corpse. The fleshy parts of an entire buffalo, for example, can be eaten by a flock of vultures in three or four hours, leaving the bones for the hyenas. The natural scavenging habits of the vulture are made good use of by the Parsees of India, who place their dead in walled mortuary towers constructed in high places, where they are eaten by the large birds. Hyenas will even dig up and devour bodies that are buried uncoffined in shallow graves.

In Britain, the scavenging animals are smaller but no less efficient. A human corpse left in a wood or field will soon attract birds like magpies, starlings, ravens, and the aptly named carrion crow. Body-strewn battlefields in the past drew flocks of ravens and carrion crows, whose unsavoury eating habits, black colour and harsh cawing earned them an unlucky reputation, as well as the once common buzzards and red kites, whose hooked bills make short work of human remains. Such birds first peck or rip out the eyes, which are not only invitingly open but are of particular gustatory delight to them. The lips and ear lobes, being plump and fleshy, form the next item on the menu, followed by other exposed areas of the face and neck. Foxes and badgers will eat dead human flesh, although a cadaver is most likely to attract rats, which soon get under the clothing and eat their way into the chest and abdominal cavity for delicacies like the heart, lungs, liver and kidneys.

The activities of these feathered and furred creatures run parallel to those of the bacteria, protozoa and fungi, which attack the corpse both inside and out, and the dipterous maggots, ants, woodlice, beetles, slugs, earthworms and other macroscopic invertebrates, which together produce a frantic rush of squirming activity, carried on within a ghastly odorifous cloud of putrefaction. The feeding goes on until only the bones remain, although even these will eventually be cracked open for their nourishing marrow.

We can only feel sorry for the man whose apparent demise Emily Brontë poetically describes in 'A Death-Scene', the last verse of which is quoted at the beginning of this chapter. Named Edward and called by her 'my dearest friend', it seems that Miss Brontë did him no favour by so hastily judging him to be dead. We can only hope that he received a second and more qualified opinion, or it may well be that he later regained consciousness, only to find himself inescapably buried in that damp moorland soil, to face the most ghastly and unbelievably awful death of all.

2 Apparent Death

As we have seen, a person who is apparently dead lacks the signs of life that would ordinarily distinguish him or her from a corpse. Such signs may be indiscernible simply because their rate has been greatly reduced or they have become very intermittent, or alternatively they may be entirely absent. A lack of heartbeat or breathing would normally result in actual death, yet occasionally, as for example when someone has been frozen or otherwise cooled, he or she remains in a state of suspended animation, from which resuscitation is possible. Likewise, those desperate terminally ill souls who try to cheat death by having themselves cryogenically frozen in liquid nitrogen immediately after their hearts stop beating are effectively held in suspended animation, from which they hope to be revived one day, when a cure for their particular ailment has been found.

We are nowadays familiar with the restarting of stopped hearts by massage or applied electric shocks, and with the restoration of breathing by mouth-to-mouth resuscitation. Yet, reanimation may also occur spontaneously, so that a person who has apparently died may come to life again. In such cases, of course, it is only the more obvious life activities like the heartbeat and breathing that may have stopped; activity still continues, albeit at a reduced rate, in the body cells. Everyone passes through this intermediate state at death, for it is part of the gradual running down of the body.

The physical appearance of someone apparently dead is so accurately and delightfully described by one of the characters in William Shakespeare's celebrated romantic tragedy *Romeo and Juliet* that it seems the bard may have had first-hand experience of the condition. The subject certainly fascinated him, for apparent death also plays a part, as we have noted, in *Henry IV, Part Two*, as well as in *Pericles, Prince of Tyre*. Shakespeare probably also came across instances of apparent death and of premature burial in his background historical reading, as well as hearing about cases in his own day, which would have been discussed with great interest, if not alarm.

In *Romeo and Juliet*, following Capulet's insistence that Juliet must wed Paris, a wealthy suitor, her friend and adviser Friar Laurence suggests a means by which she can avoid the marriage. She must, he says, swallow a potion that will seemingly kill her. He explains that after she has drunk it,

> . . . through all thy veins shall run
> A cold and drowsy humour, for no pulse
> Shall keep his native progress, but surcease;
> No warmth, no breath, shall testify thou liv'st;
> The roses of thy lips and cheeks shall fade
> To paly ashes; thy eyes' windows fall,
> Like death, when he shuts up the day of life;
> Each part depriv'd of supple government,
> Shall, stiff and stark and cold, appear like death;
> And in this borrow'd likeness of shrunk death
> Thou shalt continue two-and-forty hours,
> And then awake as from a pleasant sleep.

Juliet drinks the potion, apparently dies, and is entombed in the family crypt. But unfortunately the Friar's letter informing Romeo of the deception is delayed, and Romeo arrives at the crypt believing she is really dead. After gazing upon her beautiful face, he drinks the poison he carries with him and dies, where-upon Juliet, suddenly waking to find his corpse beside her, takes Romeo's dagger and stabs herself to death. Thus Friar Laurence's ingenious plan goes horribly wrong.

Overdoses of prescribed drugs like sleeping pills, anti-depressants and tranquillizers, or of over-the-counter headache remedies like paracetamol, often washed down with several alco-holic drinks are among the commonest causes of misdiagnosed death today. Similarly, overdoses of heroin, cocaine, ecstasy and other illegal drugs, whether taken accidentally or intentionally, can also be misleading. The deep unconsciousness these substances produce and the associated reduction of heartbeat and breathing rate, may lead a doctor to misread the signs and certify death when in fact the person is still alive.

Such a mistake was made recently following the attempted suicide of a 61-year-old Cambridgeshire farmer's wife, who had tried to kill herself with an overdose of prescribed drugs. Australian-born Daphne Banks lived with her husband of forty years, Claude, in their out-of-the-way farmhouse at Stonely, near Kimbolton. An epileptic, she had become increasingly depressed during the previous two years, partly because of the loneliness of farm life, which was made worse by the fact she could no longer drive because of her epilepsy, and partly by her increasing lack of communication with her husband. So when she was left alone by him on New Year's Eve, 1995, she felt she had nothing to look forward to in the coming year and decided to end it all. Thus at 10.30 p.m. she hurriedly wrote 'Goodbye' on the back of an enve-lope, which she left on the kitchen table, and then went up to the spare bedroom. There she swallowed a handful of epilepsy tablets, sleeping pills and anti-depressants.

Claude found her lying pale and motionless in the spare bed when he returned to the farmhouse accompanied by two friends, at about 12.30 a.m. Her skin was cold. Shocked and distressed he immediately telephoned for an ambulance, and then put a call through to her doctor, David Roberts, who arrived first, shortly after 1 a.m. The doctor examined Daphne and declared her to be dead. So the ambulance was sent away, and after Dr Roberts had notified the police of her sudden death, a firm of undertakers was contacted to remove her corpse. The undertaker and his assistant arrived at 3.38 a.m., and took the supposedly dead woman to the mortuary at Hinchinbrooke Hospital, in nearby Huntingdon.

One of the men was 61-year-old Ken Davison, who had known Claude and Daphne Banks for several years. He was upset by what had happened, and at the mortuary his distress prompted him to stand contemplating Daphne's still form. It was then that he made a startling discovery. 'I noticed that she had a vein in her right leg which seemed to twitch,' he said. 'I looked at her again and her chest started going in and out. Then I heard her snore. I told the mortician the lady was still breathing but I don't think he believed me. So I said, "Actually, I've heard her snore twice."'

Mrs Banks was immediately rushed to the hospital's intensive care unit, where the staff managed to revive her. She remained under close observation there for three days, after which she was transferred to a general ward, where she stayed for another five days before being allowed home to her relieved and delighted husband. The couple have now left the farm and moved into a modern house in Stonely village, where they are trying to rebuild their lives.

Daphne Banks is one of the few who can honestly say that she came back from the dead. But most hospital mortuaries now have refrigeration units in which the dead are placed in order to delay putrefaction and keep them fresh. Had Mrs Banks been put in the one at Hinchinbrooke morgue immediately she would not have recovered sufficiently to start snoring and would very probably either have died there or been dissected alive at her autopsy.

A 19-year-old French pharmacy student named Eric Villet, a resident of Orléans, had an almost identical encounter with death in November 1990. Like Daphne Banks he was also suffering from depression, and after a heated argument with his girlfriend one Friday afternoon, he decided to kill himself. So he drove 25 miles to the Côte-de-Coeur forest, parked off the road, and swallowed what he thought was a fatal mixture of anti-depressant, barbiturate, sedative, and beta-blocker tablets, which he washed down with swigs from a bottle of whisky.

He soon lapsed into unconsciousness, but luckily he was found a couple of hours later by some deer hunters, who hurriedly called an ambulance. When it arrived, the crew spent nearly half an hour trying to revive him with heart massage and other resuscitative techniques, but without success. A local doctor, Anne-Christine de Guillebon, was then summoned to the scene, but on failing to find any vital signs she declared him to be dead. Eric was taken to the mortuary at Blois, where mortician Didier Gallet was waiting to put the cadaver into the refrigeration unit along with the other bodies, prior to going off duty.

But Eric Villet's luck again held out. For the observant Gallet suddenly noticed his Adam's apple move. 'I was stunned,' he noted later. 'Nothing like it has ever happened to me before. And I've worked at the morgue for seventeen and a half years!' Eric was rushed to hospital, where emergency recuperative procedures were started. He was still alive, but only just. His heart rate had plummeted to twenty beats a minute, his respiration to four breaths a minute, and his temperature to only 80°F. He remained in a coma for three days, but finally pulled through and went on to make a complete recovery. He was certainly very fortunate, because had he remained at the mortuary and survived the weekend in cold storage, he would have undergone an autopsy on the following Monday. Hardly surprisingly, Eric now realizes that life is to be lived, not foolishly thrown away.

A few years earlier, on 17 March 1981, another would-be suicide was saved from a premature autopsy by an alert under-taker. Earlier that day 32-year-old Jacqueline Rosser, a divorced mother of two from Stroud, in Gloucestershire, was found by police lying slumped in her bedroom. Several empty drug bottles lay near her. Dr Graham Voss was called to the house; he examined her but found no vital signs, and pronounced her dead. Once permission had been granted by the coroner to move the body, Mrs Rosser was put in a coffin and driven by hearse to Gloucester mortuary, 10 miles away. On opening the coffin when she arrived, the undertaker happened to notice that the expression on her face had changed, and looking closer he saw that she was still breathing. She was rushed to Gloucester Royal Hospital, where after a spell in intensive care she was allowed to go home.

In view of these cases, it is hardly surprising to read of what happened to an elderly eighteenth-century gentleman, who took more opium than he should have done and paid a dreadful price. The incident was recorded in *The Gentleman's Magazine* of December 1786. Its author, Mr R.W.E. of West Bromwich, explains that he took up his pen . . .

to relate the extraordinary appearance of a skeleton, whose coffin lid was broke open by a labourer, in digging the foundation for a vestry intended to be built at the east end of West Bromwich church; the body and head was turned on its right side, with the left elbow pressing hard against the lid of the coffin, apparently as if struggling after burial. It seems not improbable but the body of the unhappy man was buried in a trance, and on the best information I could get, it was the body of an old lawyer in the said parish of the name of Whitehouse, and what strengthens my conjecture in the above matter, was his frequent use of large quantities of opiates during his last illness. He died about the year 1764.

We can only commiserate with poor Mr Whitehouse, who suffered a death that is almost too terrible to contemplate, premature interment. His grim end, which inadvertently came to light twenty-two years after his burial, underlines the danger faced by those who use drugs in excessive amounts.

Opium, which is obtained from the opium poppy (*Papaver somniferum*), became an increasingly popular anodyne in the eighteenth century, its use reflecting the growth of English sea trade with India and the Orient. As the principal ingredient of such popular nostrums as Godfrey's Cordial, it was taken to relieve pain, combat sleeplessness, reduce anxiety and generally calm the spirits, and had the added advantage as far as the opium traders were concerned of being addictive. Indeed, opium's popularity continued into and through the nineteenth century, until legislation was finally introduced to ban its importation and use. Godfrey's Cordial was widely administered to fractious children, which led one worried eighteenth-century physician to complain: 'I am persuaded that the sleep it produces has proved the sleep of death to thousands of children.'

Another person who was inadvertently buried alive was Frederick Leider, a citizen of New Philadelphia, Ohio, who attempted to kill himself with morphine, a derivative of heroin, in October 1890. The physician who examined his comatose body likewise misread the signs, and certified him as dead. But he was still clinging on to life, and woke up to find himself trapped underground in a coffin. The following report in *Sunnyside* magazine explains how this was discovered.

Fred. H. Leider, who took an overdose of morphine, October 25th, and was supposed to have died, was buried October 27th. His brother, who could not get to the funeral, came and wanted to see his body. When the coffin was opened it was found that the supposed dead man had been in a stupor,

and had come to life in the coffin. His face was scratched
and the glass in the coffin broken.

I do not know why there was glass in Frederick Leider's coffin,
but the fact that it was broken and had presumably caused the
scratches on his face reveals that he struggled to free himself
when he regained consciousness. Such self-inflicted injuries
acquired by those awakening in the awful darkness of a buried
coffin are commonly reported. Indeed, they are often the most
obvious way to tell that a person has been prematurely buried.

Drugs cause their malign effects by acting directly upon the
brain. They not only alter the subject's perceptions of reality but,
when taken in large enough quantities, have a negative influence
upon the medulla oblongata or brain stem, which controls the
heartbeat, breathing and other important body activities. And
some, like morphine, also lower the blood pressure. Together
these physical changes, along with an accompanying sedative
effect, can result in coma, which is sometimes mistaken, as the
above cases demonstrate, for death.

However, coma is most commonly produced by head injuries,
bacterial infections like meningitis, and cerebral strokes. Those
affected are unresponsive to stimuli which would, in normal
circumstances, rouse them, such as loud sounds, pinpricks and
bright light. Depending on its cause and the amount of damage
done to the brain, a coma may be brief in duration or last for
weeks or months, sometimes even for years. Those in a coma can
of course be kept alive by life-support machines, without which
they would starve to death.

When a patient remains in a coma for a month, he or she is
classified as being in a persistent vegetative state. Should the
coma last for a year, and there is no recordable brain activity,
medical staff have the option of switching off the life-support
equipment. Yet proving that a person's brain is *not* working is
more difficult than showing that it is still functional, and the

problem is made even worse by the fact that an apparently unconscious person, who does not react to stimuli, may nevertheless know what is going on around him.

Such was the condition of Mark Newton, who lapsed into a coma following a freak diving accident in December 1990, when he was on holiday in South Africa. He surfaced too quickly from a deep dive and damaged his lungs, which in turn deprived his brain of oxygen. Medical tests indicated that he was almost brain dead. Yet not only was the diagnosis wrong, but Mark was not even unconscious. Indeed, during the six months he remained in the coma he was aware of everything that was said to and about him; and he even thought he was having conversations with the people who spoke. He was saved from death when his mother refused to allow the doctors, who thought he was a hopeless case, to switch off his life-support equipment. Her belief in him proved entirely right, as Mark emerged from his coma shortly after his twenty-fourth birthday on 9 June 1991. He is now back in England, making a new life for himself in a wheelchair, and he recently completed a business administration course. 'I was very lucky,' he admits. 'I don't even want to think about what could have happened.'

Indeed, Mark Newton could have undergone a far more horrific end than simply having his life-support equipment turned off. For if he had been diagnosed as entirely brain dead, with no hope of recovery, then he would almost certainly (with his parents' permission) have been dissected to provide organs for transplantation. And because this would have been done without anaesthetic, Mark would literally have suffered a fate worse than death.

Two other psychophysical conditions that may lead to premature interment, cremation or dissection are trance and catalepsy. They both produce a death-like immobility, yet differ in that while catalepsy (or catochus) is characterized by a rigidity of the limbs, which may be confused with rigor mortis, this normally does not occur in trance. However, a hypnotist may suggest to an entranced subject that his or her muscles are rigid, in which case the trance becomes catalepsy.

Dr Walter Hadwen, the Vice-President of the Association for the Prevention of Premature Burial, was once called to the bedside of a 17-year-old girl who had fallen into a cataleptic seizure, but whose parents feared she was dead. He made these observations about the strange stiffness of her limbs when giving evidence before the Home Office Committee on Coroners and Coroners' Law in 1909:

I had lifted the wrist from the bed in order to examine the pulse, and was struck by the fact that upon releasing it the forearm remained suspended and continued in a state of suspension for some considerable time. I then put other limbs in various positions, placed the body in absurd postures, when, to the amazement of the onlookers, such positions were maintained, and apparently would have been maintained indefinitely. At the close of the sixth day I noticed a light sign of consciousness. I told her to sit up, and she did so, and opened her eyes vacantly.

Catalepsy is nervous in origin and is typically produced by acute mental exhaustion, whereas trance often has a physical cause, which may be a serious physical illness like influenza, cholera or plague, or an accidental or self-inflicted injury, although it is sometimes induced by hysteria. The nervous origin of catalepsy explains why its seizures are usually quite short, lasting for only as long as the mental fatigue, with about a fortnight being their maximum length. Trance, by contrast, can last much longer, and in extreme cases may endure for months, even years. Indeed, it is probable that the old stories of people falling asleep for many years, like that of the Seven Sleepers, refer to persistent trance states. Greek myth, for example, tells of Endymion, beloved of Selene, who still lies entranced in a cave on Mount Latmos in Caria, and of Epimenides the Cretan, one of Greece's seven wise men, who supposedly fell alseep in a cave on Mount Ida for about forty years. The Greeks also believed that during such a trance, the person's soul or double could separate itself from his or her body and go wandering about the world.

Both trance and catalepsy may result in loss of consciousness, although this is more likely to happen in the former state. When people fall into a religious or mystical trance, they remain aware but are detached from their surroundings, and may experience transcendental revelations. However, ordinary trance is characterized by amnesia or loss of memory, which stops the patient from remembering any details about what has happened to him.

One of the most famous and interesting cases of trance happened to Arabella Churchill in her old age. The elder sister of John Churchill, Duke of Marlborough, the victor of the famous battle of Blenheim and other Continental engagements, Arabella had been mistress of James, Duke of York, subsequently King James II, by whom she had four bastards. When the liaison ended she married Colonel Charles Godfrey, who through the influence of the Duke of Marlborough became Comptroller of the Household to William III.

When her brother died on 16 June 1722, Arabella was heartbroken. The 74-year-old woman, described as being 'a tall creature, pale-faced, nothing but skin and bone', became ill and was confined to bed for several weeks. But one Sunday, feeling somewhat better and hearing the ringing of the chapel bells, she resolved to leave her bed and attend the service. So she rose and commenced dressing, helped by her maids, but then suddenly collapsed and lay so still she was thought to be dead. The screams of the women brought her husband to the room, and he ordered that she be put back in bed and kept warm. Doctors were sent for and upon examining Mrs Godfrey and finding no heartbeat, pulse or respiration, they opined that nothing could be done for her as she was certainly dead.

However, Colonel Godfrey, having had experience of soldiers who had apparently died but then spontaneously returned to life, wanted to be quite sure that his wife was dead before burying her. So he had her watched by alternating pairs of women, who were told to continue their vigil until she either woke up or showed irrefutable signs of being dead.

The days went slowly by. Arabella remained motionless and apparently dead, although she did not start to decay, which is perhaps why her husband, despite being advised by concerned friends to have her buried, refused to give up hope. Then on the following Sunday, when the chapel bells were again ringing, she suddenly awoke from her trance, looked around the room with some astonishment, and asked why she hadn't been wakened earlier, as she had intended going to chapel. She remembered nothing about her collapse and had no idea that she had been lying in bed for a week. And Colonel Godfrey, not wishing to alarm her with the news, ordered that it should be kept secret from her. This was done, and Arabella apparently never learned that she had so strangely lost a week. She lived for several more years, dying only in 1730.

Another well-known figure to fall into a week-long trance was Benjamin Disraeli, the Earl of Beaconsfield, who achieved fame as a novelist and distinction as a politician and statesman, twice becoming Prime Minister of Great Britain. He originally trained as a lawyer and went into practice in 1825, but wrote in his spare time. Indeed, the following year the first volume of his first novel *Vivian Grey* was published, and was acclaimed by both critics and readers. However, overwork coupled with 'a singular disorder', as his biographer J.A. Froude delicately puts it, brought on 'fits of giddiness, which he described as like a consciousness of the earth's rotation'. Not long afterwards, he adds, 'he fell into a trance, from which he did not completely recover for a week'.

Disraeli's doctors recommended the curative effects of travel abroad, and a spell on the Continent did prove beneficial to him, if not entirely restorative.

Disraeli made use of this experience in his novel, *Venetia*, which was published in 1837. The lovely Venetia, who is brought up in rural isolation by her mother, collapses from shock when she discovers who her father is. 'This is not sleep; it is a feverish trance that brings no refreshment,' says the surgeon who attends her. The 15-year-old girl lies unconscious for four days, when 'the medical attendants observed a favourable change in their patient . . . . The crisis had occurred and was past; Venetia had at length sunk into slumber.' And when the symptoms of the disorder reappear some years later, Venetia is taken to the Continent by her mother to help her get over it.

Towards the end of his life the famous Victorian character actor Benjamin Nottingham Webster was overcome by a death-like trance that also lasted for seven days. Yet unlike Arabella Churchill, and presumably Benjamin Disraeli, he did not lose consciousness, so that he remained aware of what was going on around him. He related the frightening incident to John Coleman, who included it in his autobiographical *Fifty Years of Active Life*.

I lay in a trance for a week, during which, though I was speechless and motionless, I was perfectly conscious. The dear old doctor came to see me two or three times a day, and I tried every time he spoke to answer him, but I could neither speak nor move. At last one night, having felt my pulse and examined me more carefully than usual, I heard him gasp, 'Poor old Ben!' Then he turned to say to the housekeeper, 'It's all over! You'd better lay him out.' I listened in speechless horror, for I saw myself already in my coffin and buried alive! I was somewhat reasured when the old girl said stoutly, 'Dead! He's not dead! Do you'd think he'd die without saying goodbye after all these years?'

Indeed, the housekeeper was so convinced that Ben Webster, as he was known to all, was still alive, that when the doctor went downstairs to inform Ben's secretary of his sad demise, she lifted the actor's head and managed to pour a spoonful or two of 'J.J.', a family cure-all made of hot whisky sweetened with sugar, down his throat. As the liquid did not choke him, he presumably must have swallowed it. She also rubbed some of the potion on his supposedly lifeless chest.

The lifting of his head and the rubbing of his chest, perhaps even the drinking of the 'J.J.', evidently brought Ben out of his trance, for he suddenly opened his eyes, sat up, shouted 'Where's that doctor?' and stepped out of the bed. On being informed that the physician was in the downstairs drawing-room, Ben pulled a sheet from the bed, wrapped it around himself, and somewhat unsteadily descended the stairs. He found the doctor and the secretary lamenting his loss over a steaming bowl of punch. The sudden sight of the white-faced 'dead' man wrapped in a white sheet had the pair leaping up with cries of alarm, upsetting the punch, and they were only persuaded it was not Ben's ghost when he swore at them for their clumsiness and at the doctor for his mistaken diagnosis. Then he laughed heartily, called for another bowl of punch, and together they celebrated his resurrection!

The related state of catalepsy may sometimes be an early symptom of epilepsy, although it is most frequently caused, as I have said, by acute anxiety and mental exhaustion, which somehow prevents nerve impulses travelling from the brain to the voluntary or skeletal muscles. It can affect people of any age, either awake or asleep, although it most commonly happens during sleep. When the person is awake, he or she may lose consciousness. When catalepsy happens during sleep, the person may awake to find that he or she has completely lost the power of movement. This is why it is often called sleep paralysis.

What then is catalepsy like for its victims? I can answer that question from my own experience, having suffered four attacks during the autumn of 1974, when I was living in Montreal. That summer had been an unexpectedly difficult one for my wife and myself, as a result of outside factors. A construction boom was then taking place in downtown Montreal, and the battle between avaricious developers and those trying to save the wonderful old mansions and other private homes from demolition was reaching its climax. My wife and I, as immigrants to Canada, were concerned about the situation yet did not feel it was any of our business. Our attitude changed when our landlord decided to sell the attractive greystone terrace in which we had our apartment for development. We decided to fight the eviction and hopefully save the building.

It was a decision that plunged us into a maelstrom of protest. And the huge task of organizing petitions, holding rallies and fund-raising street parties, dealing with the press, seeing lawyers, and coping with all the assorted weirdoes that crawled out of the woodwork, ostensibly to offer their help and support but in reality to fill a void in their own lives, while still working at our own jobs, was exhausting and ultimately futile. For we lost our ill-advised and legally mishandled court case, and within a few weeks our home had been flattened and turned into what we had all along suspected, a car park.

I mention these events simply to convey a sense of the uncertainty and strain that we had been under. And it was the resulting mental exhaustion that apparently brought about my attacks of catalepsy. They occurred in the night when I was asleep, usually at about three o'clock in the morning. Their onset woke me up although at first I felt nothing out of the ordinary, except that I was lying on my back. But when I attempted to move, even to open my eyes, I found to my horror, that I was completely unable to do so. Despite every effort, I could not move a muscle. Yet my mind was completely unimpaired. So I was fully aware of my situation, which made things worse because the more I tried to move but failed, the more alarm I felt. On one occasion, after making great efforts to turn over, I thought that I had at last managed to do so – I was even aware of the bedclothes rising and moving with me. But I found that it was only an hallucination and that I had not moved at all.

However, while I thought that I might be permanently paralysed, it fortunately never crossed my mind that I might be mistaken for dead and buried alive.

Nevertheless, despite recovering from a couple of seizures, the onset of the next was still frightening, as there was no way of knowing if I would be released from it. I would emerge quite spontaneously from these bouts, as far as I could tell, after about half an hour, either by simply finding, without any warning, that I could move again, or by dropping off to sleep again and discovering, when I woke up, that they had gone. And what a relief it was to know they had!

In 1807 or 1808 a combination of acute anxiety and a self-inflicted injury led a maid at an inn at Uppingham, in Rutland, called Mary, to become cataleptic, and she narrowly escaped being buried alive. She had been stealing from the inn's owner with some regularity, but while she was suspected of the thefts, she had been neither caught in the act nor found with any of the purloined goods. Then one Wednesday afternoon a new calimanco petticoat went missing. Mary's room was searched, and the petticoat and other stolen articles of clothing were found hidden in a chest. Shaking with fear, she was locked in another room pending her appearance before the local magistrate on the following day. This was, however, forestalled by a sudden dramatic development. *The Royal Leamington Spa Courier* reported that:

The next morning the terrible discovery was made that she had cut her throat with a knife, which was lying under the bed. She was found stiff and lifeless, although still warm. A surgeon was sent for immediately, who pronounced the wound to be too slight to be dangerous, and on examination of the body, considered her to be in a state of catalepsy, produced by unusual mental excitement. All sorts of restoratives then known to the faculty were, of course, immediately applied, but without any result. The body lost but little of its warmth and the colour never left the cheeks. The eyes were nearly closed, and the jaw seemed set fast.

Later that day the girl's worried parents, who lived in a nearby village, arrived and sat by her bed to watch for any signs of returning life. However, after spending the night beside her but observing no change in their errant daughter, the couple became increasingly impatient and the next day (Friday) ordered a coffin, for delivery on the Saturday afternoon.

They proposed to take the body therein to their residence in the village from whence they came, and, after waiting there a reasonable time, to bury her in the churchyard. Still, there were no changes sufficient to justify such a course, there not appearing the least symptom of decomposition. On the contrary, the colour of the cheeks and a certain degree of warmth still existed.

The landlord of the inn did not object to the idea, even though Mary had not yet been charged with theft, which suggests that he was either half-convinced she was dead or perhaps just wanted to get rid of her. After all, news of her strange predicament had spread and was drawing all sorts of people into the inn to look at her, many of whom were undesirables. He even promised Mary's parents the use of a horse and cart to transport the coffin.

The next night passed and Saturday morning came, but without any change in Mary's condition. She had now been in the grip of catalepsy for more than forty-eight hours. It began to seem as if she would not recover and would be taken away inside the coffin and perhaps even buried.

About eleven o'clock, however, the father and mother were still quietly and patiently watching the body, when all of a sudden, without any premonitory symptoms, the girl raised herself up, and in a sitting posture opened her eyes and called for water; which was soon procured, and she drank copiously.

The account does not say if Mary was conscious during her cataleptic seizure, but it seems probable that she was for at least part of the time. She might therefore have heard her parents talking about taking her home in a coffin and in due course burying her, which would have been frightening in the extreme. However, she was doubly lucky: having avoided a premature burial, the landlord of the inn decided not to charge her with theft, which was then a capital offence. So she returned with her parents suitably chastened, to a life of rural anonymity, and the coffin was sent back unused to the undertaker.

There are two early accounts of people who developed catalepsy and were coffined. One, a woman, was saved from premature burial by the sweat her acute fear produced on her face, while the other, a man, was unlucky enough not only to be buried for about four days, but to die when exhumed.

The first, which was related by the Revd Walter Whiter and others, happened to the maid of an unnamed German princess, who had been confined to bed with a vaguely described yet none the less significant nervous complaint for several days. She then apparently died, was removed from her bed and placed in a coffin, where she remained until the day of her funeral. But then, as hymns were being sung and the lid of the coffin was about to be placed over her and nailed down, perspiration was noticed on her face and neck. Next, her hands and feet gave a convulsive jerk. Then, to the further astonishment of those present, colour returned to her lips and cheeks, and a few minutes later she opened her eyes and gave 'a pitiable shriek'. She had been released from the iron grip of catalepsy at literally the last moment.

What I find particularly interesting about this case is the degree to which the sense of horror felt by the woman at her immobility matched my own.

She said it seemed to her, as if in a dream, that she was really dead; yet she was perfectly conscious of all that happened around her in this dreadful state ... She tried to cry but her soul was without power, and could not act on her body. She had the contradictory feeling, as if she were in her own body, and yet not in it, at one and the same time. It was equally impossible for her to stretch out her arm, or to open her eyes, as to cry, although she continually endeavoured to do so. The anguish of her mind was, however, at its utmost height, when the funeral hymns began to be sung, and when the lid of the coffin was about to be nailed on. The thought, that she was to be buried alive, was the first one which gave activity to her soul, and caused it to operate on her corporeal frame.

The second case, which dates from the early years of the eighteenth century, is altogether more tragic. It was told to Dr Jacobus Winslow by a fellow surgeon named Jean Bernard, who witnessed the event as a young man. Apparently the youthful Bernard was with his father and several other onlookers when an exhumation took place at a cemetery in the Parisian parish of Riol. They watched as the coffin containing the body of a Franciscan monk, who had been buried three or four days earlier, was frantically dug up. The reason for this hurried activity became apparent when the coffin was raised from the grave (which was a shallow one) and wrenched open, for the man within was found to be still alive. His bruised and bloody arms revealed that he had been struggling to free them from the cords that held them by his side.

Bernard eventually learned that the exhumation had been ordered by the head of the monastery where the monk had resided, following his receipt of a letter from an old friend of the monk, who, on learning of his death, had written to warn the abbot that, as he was prone to cataleptic seizures, great care should be taken to make sure he was really dead before burying him. Unfortunately, in accordance with the common practice of the time, the monk had been quickly interred. Thus warned, the abbot ordered his immediate exhumation, but the poor man died shortly after his coffin was opened, another victim of precipitate interment and its accompanying terror, hopelessness, thirst and exhaustion – one of the most ghastly deaths known to man.

The narrator in Edgar Allan Poe's short story, 'The Premature Burial' claims that, like the monk, he is prone to cataleptic attacks, and Poe, through him, makes several interesting observations about the condition, although he exaggerates by claiming that catalepsy can maintain its hold on those it afflicts for weeks – even for months. However, he rightly points out that the seizures lengthen with repetition, and that they can, in some instances, result in premature burial, which is why those who know of a person's cataleptic tendency can play a vital part in helping to prevent such a tragedy. Poe writes:

> Very usually he is saved from premature interment solely by the knowledge of his friends that he has been previously subjected to catalepsy, by the consequent suspicion excited, and, above all, by the non-appearance of decay.... The unfortunate whose *first* attack should be of the extreme character which is occasionally seen, would almost inevitably be consigned alive to the tomb.

The depth of seizure can vary, to the extent that at its most profound, catalepsy may be accompanied by a general loss of sensitivity, although this rarely happens. Reflex movements are also prevented by the rigidity of the muscles, including the eyelid blink reflex that is otherwise apparent when the conjunctiva is touched, and such a lack of response can easily be mistaken for death.

Shortly before he died the Scottish physician James Braid (1795–1850), who investigated the trance state of hypnotism, previously known as mesmeric sleep, described the agony experienced by a cataleptic woman at Manchester Royal Infirmary, where she was examined somewhat robustly by Dr John Mitchell and others. The woman's catalepsy was so intense that her jaws remained locked together, preventing her from being given food or drink for an astonishing fourteen days. Braid remarks:

> The only visible signs of vitality were, a *slight* degree of animal heat, and the appearance of moisture from her breath when a mirror was held close to her face. Every variety of contrivance and torture was resorted to by various parties who saw her, for the purpose of testing the degree of her insensibility, and for determining whether she might not be an imposter, but without eliciting the slightest indication of activity of any sense . . . . Nevertheless she *heard and understood all that was said and proposed to be done, and suffered the most exquisite torture from various tests applied to her!*

But while this physical abuse was very painful and distressing for the woman concerned, we can imagine how much more terrible it would have been for her if she had been certified as dead, put into a coffin, and buried alive.

3   Laying-out and Mortuary Resuscitation

> O Death, rock me asleep,
> Bring me to quiet rest,
> Let pass my weary guiltless ghost
> Out of my careful breast.
>
> From an anonymous poem entitled 'Death'

In addition to apparent death resulting from a drug overdose or from trance and catalepsy, there are, as I have already said, a large number of physical injuries, traumas and diseases that may result in a similar torpidity, when the heartbeat and breathing become imperceptible or temporarily absent, and which may therefore be mistaken for death. Such crises include those that lead to apparent sudden death, like angina pectoris, heart attack, heart failure, aneurysms, low blood pressure, head injury, falls and similar accidents, acute shock or stress, fright, intense excitement, lightning strike, electric shock, heatstroke, drowning, diabetic coma, choking and strangulation, hanging, gunshot wounds and epilepsy, from all of which the subject may sometimes be successfully revived.

To these abrupt apparent deaths we may add those that typically follow serious illnesses such as eclampsia, bleeding ulcers, tetanus, cholera, tuberculosis, pneumatic fever, smallpox, typhus and bubonic plague. And even a protracted illness may be suddenly ended, or seemingly ended, by a heart attack, stroke or some other thrombo-embolic incident, or from a secondary infection or an internal haemorrhage.

The following recent cases are examples of people who have been mistakenly certified as dead and taken either to a mortuary or to a funeral home, and who have shown signs of life either there or while on the way there. They illustrate the point that while there is no certainty in life, there is often little even in death.

Late on the evening of Sunday, 14 April 1996, widow Maureen Jones, a 59-year-old diabetic, fell into a hypoglycaemic coma while she was undressing in the bedroom of her cottage at Thwing, Humberside. As their name suggests, such comas are caused by low blood sugar, which in this case probably resulted from Mrs Jones skipping her evening meal. They are not normally life-threatening and a comatose diabetic, if left unattended, will in most cases eventually regain consciousness as sugar is released into the blood from the liver. However, in Mrs Jones's case her coma was so profound that she had not woken from it by the following day. Indeed, it was her failure to answer telephone calls from her eldest son, Neil, at lunch-time on Monday that alerted him to the fact that something might be wrong. He went to her cottage and, to his dismay, found his mother lying unconscious on her bed, clad in her underclothes. Because it was not the first time she had had such a collapse, he telephoned the local GP clinic at Hunmanby, some 4 miles away, and apprised them of the situation.

On receiving Neil's call, Maureen Jones's physician, Dr Marion Meeson drove straight to the cottage. To his surprise, his examination of the prone woman failed to reveal any sign of heartbeat, pulse or breathing, and at 4.30 p.m. he pronounced Mrs Jones to be dead. The shocked Neil notified the police and contacted a funeral company to come and remove his mother's body. Half an hour later a hearse was waiting at the door as police constables Kevin Smith and Phil Shrimpton, having answered what appeared to be a routine sudden-death call, took a last look around the bedroom. Then PC Smith noticed a most uncorpse-like movement.

'I suddenly saw her leg twitch,' he said. 'I had to take a step backwards. She appeared to be in some kind of coma but she was obviously alive.' He shouted to his colleague, and the two police-men immediately began giving Mrs Jones heart massage. 'We were unsure about telling the family straight away because our main concern was keeping the woman alive,' added PC Smith. 'But eventually we called her son and asked him to speak to his mother in the hope that hearing his voice might help to save her.' The officers knew that their joint efforts were successful when they heard Mrs Jones gasp for breath. She had been brought back from the dead! And after a short stay in a Scarborough hospital, she made a full recovery.

The risk of a doctor making a diagnostic mistake is perhaps greater when the apparently dead person is very old, as dying is something that is associated with age. As a result the physician, perhaps unconsciously, may not be quite as careful as he or she would with somebody younger. And yet the elderly are just as capable of making remarkable come-backs from the brink of death as anyone else.

A case in point is that of Mrs Agnes Tomblin of Leicester, a 94-year-old widow who collapsed at home in November 1987 and was found apparently dead on the floor by her home help. The shocked carer immediately rang Mrs Tomblin's doctor, who came around right away. He carried out an examination, but found no signs of life and certified Agnes Tomblin to be dead. Her son Peter was told the news, and later said: 'I didn't check myself, because you expect a doctor to be right.' A hearse was called and Mrs Tomblin was taken in a coffin to the Ginns and Gutteridge funeral home. But not long after her arrival there, a sharp-eyed undertaker's assistant noticed that she was still breathing. She was rushed to Leicester Royal Infirmary, where she eventually recovered sufficiently to be allowed home. Peter Tomblin tells me that her first words on regaining consciousness were 'Pass me my book and spectacles.' But strangely, what makes her resurrection particularly piquant is that one of her nephews was then a surgeon at the same hospital. Mrs Tomblin was soon afterwards placed in a retirement home, where she lived happily for a further two years, only dying in June 1989, aged 96.

An even more startling case of geriatric revival happened at the end of September 1996 in Zamora, in Spain. A 101-year-old woman named Micaela Velasco collapsed at home and was certified dead by her doctor. She was taken in a coffin to the local funeral home, but when undertaker Francisco Heredero and his assistants began preparing her for burial, they were stunned to notice a sudden movement of her lips. 'We all had this sensation of total shock,' he gasped. 'Then we found she really was alive.' An ambulance rushed her to hospital, where the tough old bird not only amazed staff by making a full recovery, but was soon well enough to be released into the care of her daughter.

There is little excuse for such diagnostic errors in view of the fact that it has been known since at least 1777 that 'even in old age, when life seems to have been gradually drawing to a close, the appearances of death are often fallacious'. The writer of these words, William Hawes, goes on to quote the case of an elderly woman who was believed to be dead and spontaneously returned to life.

Not many years since, a lady in Cornwall, more than eighty years of age, who had been a considerable time declining, took to her bed, and in a few days seemingly expired in the morning . . . But one of those who were paying the last kind office of humanity to her remains perceived some warmth about the middle of her back, and acquainting her friends with it, they applied a mirror to her mouth; but, after repeated trials, could not observe it in the least stained; her under-jaw was likewise fallen, as the common phrase is; and, in short she had every appearance of a dead person. All this time she had not been stripped or dressed, but the windows were opened, as is usual in the chambers of the deceased. In the evening the heat seemed to increase, and at length she was perceived to breathe.

At the other end of the age scale, a four-month-old baby named Nathan Lee Oates is unique in having been snatched from the hands of the Grim Reaper by the two-tone sound of a police siren. The drama began for Nathan's mother, 34-year-old Sheffield resident Rita Oates, on the morning of Sunday, 12 May 1974, when her baby suddenly started choking and gasping for breath. Mrs Oates ran to a neighbour, who immediately offered to drive both her and the infant to hospital. As they set off another neighbour, John Taylor, rang the police, and two officers, patrol car driver PC Ron Calvert and his partner PC Mick Basford, who were fortunately in the area, went in pursuit of them. When they caught up with the neighbour's vehicle, they found the frantic mother clutching what appeared to be a dead child, for baby Nathan had ceased to breathe and showed no other signs of life.

PC Basford gently took Nathan from her and transferred him to the patrol car, then he and PC Calvert sped off towards the Sheffield Children's Hospital. Although Nathan seemed to be dead, PC Basford none the less laid him across his lap and began to massage his little body, hoping that he might be able to bring him round. Nathan showed no response until PC Calvert, encountering heavier traffic, switched on the patrol car's siren. This prompted the child to start gasping for breath again!

'Then after being sick in the car,' reported PC Basford, 'his breathing became more normal. But we all thought he was dead when we picked him up. It's amazing!'

The miraculous resuscitation of her baby delighted his

distraught mother, who had feared the worst. 'I believed Nathan was dead when I handed him over to the police,' she said later. 'Then when I got to the hospital a few minutes after them, they told me he was alive and would be all right. I heard them switch on the siren, and I'm very glad they did.'

Nathan was kept overnight at the Children's Hospital but was allowed to go home with his relieved parents the next day. And while the mystery of his choking fit was never entirely cleared up, it is believed that he may have inadvertently swallowed a marble.

Another astonishing, but all too brief, return from the dead happened just over two years earlier, on Thursday, 13 April 1972. The unfortunate victim was a 36-year-old woman named Ruth Young, of Wallasey in Cheshire. She was travelling with her two-year-old son Craig on the upper deck of a bus, when the boy accidentally fell down the stairs and then rolled off the platform on to the road. Unthinkingly, Mrs Young dashed down the stairs after him and jumped from the moving bus, only to fall heavily on to the road herself, knocking herself out and sustaining severe head injuries. The child, however, only had cuts and bruises. Mrs Young was rushed to the Victoria Central Hospital, where she was admitted to the intensive therapy unit and attached to the resuscitation equipment. Yet none the less, her heart stopped beating, and she was certified as dead.

However, because the attention of the intensive therapy unit's staff was temporarily diverted by another emergency case, Mrs Young was left lying where she was. Then one hour later, to everyone's surprise, the heart monitor suddenly showed signs of cardiac activity. Ruth Young's heart had begun to beat again! Unfortunately she remained critically ill and although she made it through the following day, she finally died on Saturday, 15 April.

Another fall with a frightening, yet ultimately happier, aftermath happened to a French lady in January 1890. The woman, a resident of the seaport of Brest, in Brittany, travelled by train to

Paris, a journey of about 350 miles. When the train finally pulled into Montparnasse Station, she descended from her compartment, but while walking along the platform, she suddenly fell over and lay quite still, although it is not known whether she had tripped or fainted. A doctor who was at the station waiting to board another train ran to help her, and when he failed to detect a heartbeat or pulse, he declared her to be dead.

Hearing of the accident, the station authorities instructed two of their own first-aid stretcher-bearers to carry the body of the unfortunate woman to a Paris morgue, which was then the normal destination for anyone deceased and homeless (as she technically was, not being a resident of the city), and from where many corpses were later sent to local teaching hospitals to be dissected. However, as the stretcher-bearers were crossing the nearby Place du Paris de Notre Dame, the 'certified corpse', much to their alarm, suddenly sat up and asked for a drink. After they had recovered from their shock, the men continued on to the Hôtel Dieu hospital, where the lady received liquid refreshment and also the medical assistance she needed, and in due course completely recovered her health and senses.

Another equally startling recovery also happened in Paris in the nineteenth century. As in the Nathan Oates case, a loud noise woke the supposed corpse, who later in life became a celebrated dancer. In 1836, 21-year-old Zaire Martel, who performed under the name of Madame Nathalie, suddenly collapsed on stage while playing the part of Azurine in the fairy ballet *La Fille d'Air* at the Folies Dramatiques. There was a doctor in the house and he examined her and, to everyone's astonishment, pronounced her dead. She was taken to an undertaker's, where she was dressed in grave clothes and put into a coffin, which was left open. And there she remained motionless and seemingly dead, for two days, during which she was visited by many weeping mourners who came to pay her their last respects.

However, when the time came for the funeral, the undertaker

placed the coffin lid over her and prepared to nail it down. On his very first hammer blow, Madame Nathalie woke with a start from the lethargy into which she had fallen and cried out, alerting the startled man to the fact that she was not dead. She was given restoratives and, after only a few days' rest, was strong enough to return to her stage role. Zaire Martel lived for another forty-nine years, only actually dying in 1885. But what is perhaps oddest of all, considering the manner of her arousal, is that 'martel' means 'hammer'.

David Morgan Adams, a well-known Labour MP, had a similar close call with death as a young man at the turn of the century. After having served aboard ships that took him as far afield as South America, he returned to his native South Wales, but lack of work and hunger prompted him to enlist in the 69th Welsh Regiment, which was preparing a draft of men to go to India. David had only been in training for two weeks when he contracted pneumonia. He received the best treatment available, but it was not enough to prevent his steady decline and apparent death. He later wrote of the incident:

Doctors stood round my bed, shook their heads mournfully, and declared that life was extinct. My heart had stopped beating. I was removed to the Welsh Regimental Depot mortuary and then stretched on a slab in company with other corpses. Later, the same day, an RAMC sergeant came to prepare my body for the post-mortem. But – as I learned later – the man drew back with horror when he discerned signs of life. Panic-stricken, he fled from the dimly-lit building to inform his amazed superiors that the 'dead' man was breathing again!

David Adams was hurriedly returned to his hospital bed and was fortunate enough to make a full recovery. He later completed his training and was shipped with his regiment to Trimulgherry, in the southern state of Madras, India, where he found that an outbreak of cholera had caused many fatalities among the troops already stationed there. So having just escaped the Grim Reaper in Wales, he spent the first few weeks of his three-year stay in India tending the sick and helping to bury the dead!

During the Second World War, a soldier in the Welsh Guards named John Elwyn Jones, was captured by the Germans when retreating with his regiment to Dunkirk, after having fought in France for several months. He was sent to the prison camp at Bedzin, in Poland, where he met 17-year-old Celin Maria Grygiel, known familiarly as Celinka, who had been interned for having slapped the face of a German soldier. He and the pretty teenager had many surreptitious nocturnal meetings, with John climbing over barbed-wire fences, risking being shot, to visit her. They soon fell in love, and when John proposed to her, she accepted. On Christmas Eve, 1943, the couple went through a do-it-yourself marriage ceremony, conducted by one of Celinka's girlfriends. They were both deliriously happy despite their grim, hostile surroundings.

But their happiness was not to last, for on the following day one of the German guards, who was consumed with a malevolent jealousy, had them separated. Not long afterwards John was moved to another camp 300 miles away, from which he eventually escaped and joined a group of Polish freedom fighters. Celinka, however, became seriously ill, having previously contracted tuberculosis, and, desolate at their parting, she rapidly weakened, then suffered a collapse, and was pronounced dead by a camp doctor. She was taken to the mortuary, and laid out for burial.

When John first learned through the grapevine that Celinka was still held at the Bedzin camp, he trekked across the country to see her, and if possible to organize her escape. However, he was captured before he could put his mad plan into action, and all his hopes crumbled when, at the next camp he was sent to, he was told that Celinka had died.

But amazingly, she had not. Having lain for several hours in the Bedzin mortuary, waiting to be buried, she suddenly woke up. The startled attendants hurried her to the camp hospital, where she was brought to a full recovery and eventually cured of her tuberculosis. She remained at the prison camp until it was liberated by the Allies in 1945, yet she was still not free, for she became trapped behind the Iron Curtain, in Russian-occupied Poland. And John, believing she was dead, had no reason to search for her. They never saw each other again, and although Celinka had a son by another man in 1950, she did not marry. Indeed, she lived until 1990, but tragically it was not until 1997, after mourning her loss for over half a century, that John Elwyn Jones discovered that she had not died all those years before.

Celinka recovered and survived, but things did not work out quite so well for 49-year-old Thomas Brennan of Huddersfield, Yorkshire, when he suffered a heart attack at his home in April 1978. A West Yorkshire ambulance crew answered his wife's frantic 999 call, but by the time they arrived Mr Brennan was apparently past help, as all their tests showed him to be dead. In such situations, ambulance crews were instructed to notify the police and so pass the responsibility on to them. Thus nothing further was done for the deceased man.

The police in due course contacted an undertaker to remove the body. He placed Thomas Brennan in a coffin and drove him to the mortuary at Huddersfield Royal Infirmary. However, when he arrived there, a doctor happened to notice Mr Brennan's eyes were moving. Unhappily, it proved too late to revive him, for despite every effort he died not long afterwards.

This case led to a revision of the rules given to ambulance crews. Indeed, West Yorkshire coroner Philip Gill pointed out that 'establishing the existence of life or death is a difficult operation to perform with certainty and requires more equipment than an ambulance crew carry with them'. Nowadays ambulance crews must take every unconscious person to hospital unless he or she is incontrovertibly dead – that is, by being decapitated or otherwise grossly injured, partly decomposed, or certified dead by a doctor. However, as we have seen, the pronouncements of doctors are by no means always completely reliable.

Michel Delepine certainly had cause for complaint in this regard when he mysteriously collapsed at his home in Dour, south Belgium, on Wednesday, 16 March 1988. The doctor who was called by his alarmed father Alfred examined Michel, but quickly concluded that nothing could be done for the 33-year-old, as he was dead. He accordingly issued a death certificate. Yet astonishingly, several hours later when Michel was at a funeral home, the undertaker halted his preparations to bury him because he thought his corpse was too supple to be dead. The worried man contacted another doctor for a second opinion, but he confirmed the vedict of his colleague. Hence Michel Delepine, according to two doctors, was as dead as a doornail.

However, the undertaker, who had seen many more corpses than they had and who knew that Michel Delepine should be showing signs of rigor mortis if he was really dead, was still unconvinced. So he telephoned for an ambulance and had Michel taken to the local hospital. There he was given emergency resuscitation treatment and, to his grieving family's delight and relief, eventually recovered consciousness. On waking, the first words Michel said were, 'I'm cold.' He is now fully recovered and glad to be alive, especially as he knows how close he came to being prematurely interred.

The determination of death is further complicated by the fact that it has been claimed that body movements can sometimes occur after a person has actually died. Such post-mortem motions are blamed on the spontaneous contraction or relaxation of muscles, or on the build-up or the release of gases, and may erroneously suggest that the person is still alive. Physicians who doubt whether premature burial ever occurs, also consider them to be the reason why exhumed bodies, for example, are occasionally found in a position different from that in which they were buried. Indeed, their reality seems to have been recognized by no less a personage than Sir Walter Raleigh, who wrote in his poem 'The Ocean to Cynthia':

> But as a body, violently slain,
> Retaineth warmth although the spirit be gone,
> And by a power in nature moves again,
> Till it be laid below the fatal stone.

However, because death is a process rather than a single event, movements of this type are more likely to be caused by a sudden upsurge in vitality prior to the dying person's actual demise, rather in the manner of a guttering candle, which having burned down to its holder suddenly flares up brightly before extinguishing itself.

This may explain why a Mr Masters unexpectedly interrupted the coroner's inquest into the sudden death of an elderly man named Freeman, which was being held in London on Wednesday, 27 December 1843. Mr Masters burst in, protesting that Mr Freeman was still alive, for after the inquest jury had examined his supposedly dead body, he had gone to look at it himself and had 'felt the neck and upper part of the body, which was warm. That whilst doing so, he saw the deceased's lips and chin move, and the woman who was there saw the same.' Despite these excited assurances, a subsequent examination of Mr Freeman showed him to be dead. Thus the old gentleman may well have expired on the cold slab of the mortuary, another victim of medical incompetence.

Similarly, following the certified death of the manager of a public house at Wavertree, Liverpol, in September 1908, his corpse was placed in a coffin in his bedroom and exposed to the view of his family and friends. Immediately prior to his funeral, as his widow and a few intimates were saying their last goodbyes, 'the eyes of the dead man were seen to open, and his arms to move. A panic followed. Some of the women fainted, and the others rushed hysterically from the room.' Two doctors were summoned to see if he really was still alive, but their examination proved negative. Although it was suggested that 'the only explanation of the scare is that the watchers saw one of those muscular movements not unknown after death', it seems more likely that the manager had lain entranced in his coffin and had finally managed to move, only to exhaust himself fatally in the process.

We are fortunate in Britain to have eradicated mass killers like bubonic plague, smallpox, cholera and typhus, which were once endemic. During epidemics of these diseases, the infected were often mistakenly buried alive. This happened not only because of the difficulty in distinguishing the dead from the merely comatose, but because those given the task (notably during epidemics of the plague) were frequently uneducated, slipshod and grasping. And in the general state of alarm, people wanted the dead consigned to the grave as quickly as possible to avoid contagion.

Indeed, Giovanni Maria Lancisi, the well-known Italian doctor and anatomist, who was responsible for the health of three popes, Innocent XI, Clement IX and Innocent XII, noted: 'In the Time of Plague Things are transacted with such Disorder and Precipitation, that Little Care is taken to distinguish those who are really dead, from such as only appear to be deprived of Life.'

Plague is actually a disease of rats caused by the aptly named *Yersinia pestis*, a type of bacteria. The primary host is the black rat, which thrived in the overcrowded and unhygienic towns and cities of pre-nineteenth-century Europe, and the infection is passed to humans, and of course from rat to rat, by the rat flea, *Xenopsylla cheopsis*. There are two forms of the illness: bubonic plague, so called because one of its symptoms is painful swellings known as buboes in the lymphatic glands; and pneumonic plague, which infects the lungs but produces no lymphatic swellings.

Both have a mortality rate of about 80 per cent. The dreadful outbreak of bubonic plague, known as the Black Death, that swept Europe in 1348–50 killed one third of the inhabitants. During the seventeenth century there were epidemics in England in 1603, 1625, 1636, 1640–7, 1665 and 1679. That of 1665, known as the Great Plague, killed about 100,000 people in London alone (out of an estimated total city population of 460, 000). One anonymous poet pertinently wrote about it:

> We laught at all diseases else, for they
> Like small guns but one a time doe slay
> This like a Canon teares whole Troups away.

The hopelessness and resignation felt during plague epidemics was described by the French essayist Michel de Montaigne, who witnessed the effects of *la peste* in the province of Guienne, where he had his chateau, in 1573. He noted:

Generally, every one renounced all care of life; the grapes, the principal wealth of the country, remained untouched upon the vines; every man indifferently prepared for and expected death, either tonight or tomorrow, with a countenance and voice so far from fear, as if they had come to terms with this necessity, and that it was an universal and inevitable sentence ... Some, who were yet in health, dug their own graves; others laid themselves down in them whilst alive; and a labourer of mine, in dying, with his hands and feet pulled the earth upon him.

This pitiful behaviour was occasioned by the dread of either being left unburied, and so made prey to the beasts and birds of the countryside, or being unceremoniously tipped naked into a plague pit. And such desperate acts were by no means exceptional. During the English epidemic of 1625, for example, which killed over 41,000 Londoners, a refugee from the city, one Richard Dawson, discovered that he had already contracted the infection when he reached his native Cheshire 'and perceyveing he must die at yt time arose out of his bed and made his grave, and caused his nefew John Dawson to cast strawe into ye grave, which was not far from ye howse, and went and laid him down in ye said grave and caused clothes to be layd upon him and soe dep'ted out of this world'. It is plain that living burials must often have resulted from these DIY interments. And such was sometimes the speed of death, or at least collapse, that bizarre happenings like the following described by the same anonymous poet occurred:

> Here a man brings his shovell and his spade,
> In ye churchyard he digs a pit,
> But dyes as soone as he has finisht it.
> And falls into ye grave he for another made.

Once *Yersinia pestis* has been passed by the rat flea to a human host, there follows a short incubation period lasting from two to ten days, when the bacteria multiply rapidly in the bloodstream, which carries them in turn to the internal organs. The course of the infection thereafter varies from person to person. Some start to shake violently, become nauseous and are wracked by vomiting, which may be sufficiently debilitating to kill them. Others, perhaps the lucky few, become increasingly tired and will, if not forcibly kept awake, fall into a profound lethargy, in which they may remain until they die. The latter stand the greatest chance of being interred alive, as the trance state resembles death and can easily be mistaken for it.

For most, however, the next stage is the onset of intense headaches, which may cause fits, and these are followed by fever and sweating. Sleep is now dangerous, as death may occur during it. Hence anyone feverish must likewise be kept awake. The bacteria then invade the lymphatic glands, causing hard visible swellings in the groin and armpits, and sometimes behind the ears, which are very painful. If these buboes break and eject their poisonous contents, recovery follows, but if not, the doctor in attendance may cut them with a knife to bring about the same effect, which is not only painful but exposes the patient to secondary infection.

In the final stage of bubonic plague red or dark spots appear all over the skin, which are surrounded by a blue, or sometimes a black, ring. These are ominously known as 'the tokens' and signify imminent death. Yet the tokens are sometimes not preceded by any of the other symptoms, and are the first signs that the patient is doomed. No cure is possible once they become visible.

The Elizabethan poet and playwright Thomas Nashe was obliged to stay out of London when the city suffered a serious outbreak of plague in 1592–3, and he expressed the helplessness of those who were infected in a song entitled 'In Plague Time' which is sung by a character in his play *Summer's Last Will and Testament* and includes the verse:

> Rich men, trust not in wealth,
> Gold cannot buy you health:
> Physic himself must fade,
> All things to end are made.
> The plague full swift goes by.
> I am sick, I must die.
> Lord, have mercy on us!

The plague that ravaged the town of Dijon, in Burgundy, France, in 1558, was so virulent that pits had to be dug to hold all the dead, who were tipped into them from carts at night. According to Dr John James Grafft, one Nicolle Lentillet, a young married woman, was infected by *la peste* for several days before falling 'into a Syncope so profound, that she was taken for dead'. What happened to her next was particularly gruesome.

[She was] buried in a Pit with other dead Bodies; the next
morning after her interment she returned to Life, and made
the strongest Efforts she could to get out, but her Weakness
and the Weight of the Bodies with which she was covered,
rendered her incapable of executing her Design. In this situation she remained for Four Days, till the Grave-digger coming
to inter other Bodies, took her up and carried her to her own
House, where she recovered a perfect state of Health.

Another incident that occurred in Burgundy during a plague
epidemic (which may have been the same one, although my
source, Nathaniel Wanley, does not mention the date) happened
to a member of the aristocratic Taloriedi family. The young man
in question, having apparently died of the infection, was not
dumped into a plague pit (only the poor ended up in those), but
was placed in a coffin and carried off to the family sepulchre,
which stood about 4 German miles from his home, by some of his
farm workers. Having started late and not hurried on the way, the
workers were obliged to stop for the night at a barn, outside which
they lit a fire. The rustics then had a shock, however, for they . . .

perceiv'd a quantity of fresh Blood to drain through the chinks
of the Coffin; whereupon they opened it, and found that the
body had been wounded by a Nail, that was driven into the
shoulder through the Coffin, and that the wound was much
torn by the jogging of the Chariot he was carry'd in: but withal,
they discover'd that the natural heat had not left his breast.
They took him out, laid him before the fire; he recover'd as out
of a deep sleep, ignorant of all that had pass'd.

The youth in question had clearly lapsed into the early,
comatose stage of plague, from which he would probably not

have recovered before being buried alive, had not the accidental piercing of his shoulder disclosed that he was alive. Wanley says he afterwards married and fathered a daughter, who in due course also married and presented him with a grandson, named Sigismundus, who became the chief pastor of St Mary's church in Basel.

Daniel Defoe records in *A Journal of the Plague Year* that during the Great Plague of 1665 a poor man who made his living by playing the pipes one night got drunk at a public house in Coleman Street. When the inn closed, he was carried out and laid on a nearby stall to sleep off his intoxication. Later that night, however, the ringing of the dead-cart's bell prompted some people dwelling in an adjacent alley to bring out the body of a family member who had died of the plague, which they placed on the stall beside the piper.

The men who droved the dead-cart, thinking both men were dead, put them into the almost full conveyance, and in due course added a few more corpses on top of them. But when they arrived at the plague pit the piper suddenly woke up and, realizing the horror of his situation, frantically thrust his head out from between the bodies, and by calling out managed to alert the driver to his presence. The truth of this remarkable narrow escape is confirmed by the account given in the memoirs of Sir John Reresby, although he claims that the piper played his pipes when he woke up, which sounds somewhat unlikely. A statue of the lucky piper, carved by Caius Cibber, is to be found at Welcombe house, near Stratford-on-Avon.

Interestingly, Kenneth Henry Cornish, surgeon to the Royal Humane Society, writing in 1884 about the danger of premature interment during epidemics of cholera, another highly infectious disease, mentions the cases of 'a grave-digger at Toulon, buried a few weeks ago as dead of Cholera, when he was only drunk; and those of two men later on nearly buried as dead of Cholera at Omergues, and only saved by the caution of the grave-digger'.

However, as he gives no other details it is difficult to understand how it was discovered that the Toulon man was only drunk at the time of his burial, unless he managed to alert those above ground by shouting.

Cholera, like bubonic plague, is a bacterial disease, although it is spread, not by fleas, but by the drinking of contaminated water, or less often by eating infected food. It is thus a type of food poisoning. Water becomes contaminated by exposure to human sewage bearing the cholera organism, while food acquires it from flies that have walked on human faeces or from unwashed hands. The first recorded outbreak took place as recently as August 1817, at Jessore, in the Indian state of Bengal, from whence it spread to Europe and elsewhere. There were serious epidemics in the British Isles in 1831–2, and also in 1854 and 1866. The 1832 epidemic killed sixty-four people at Bicester, in Oxfordshire. One victim was a young boy named John Hudson, who was prepared for burial and placed in a coffin. Fortunately his grandmother, on taking a last look at him, happened to notice a slight movement of his face. He was immediately removed from the long wooden box and, upon receiving medical attention, soon recovered. He lived for another seventy-eight years, only dying in 1910.

It was the German bacteriologist Dr Robert Koch who first discovered (in 1883) that cholera is caused by a microbe, and not, as some workers had previously thought, by either bad air or electrical disturbances. After a short incubation period, the patient experiences abdominal pain, severe vomiting, and diarrhoea, the loss of body fluids causing muscle cramps. The diarrhoea then worsens, the motions passed being only a thin milky liquid, the so-called 'rice-water' symptom. The resulting weakness leads to collapse, which is characterized by a low, almost imperceptible pulse and by cold hands and feet, which together mimic death. This is when premature interment is most likely. Moreover, if treatment with antibiotics is not available, about 70 per cent of those infected die at this stage.

Typhus, by contrast, is an acute virus infection that is spread from person to person by body lice. It therefore flourishes in crowded, dirty, unhygienic conditions, such as once existed in gaols, asylums and slave ships, and in those urban districts inhabited by the poor. Indeed, one of its several alternative names is 'gaol fever'. Typhus was first described in 1546 by the Italian physician Girolamo Fracastoro, best known for his pioneering work on syphilis, but the disease did not appear in England until 1643.

The onset of typhus is marked by a sudden rise in body temperature to 102°F. Three or four days later the temperature may reach 107°F. On the fifth day the fever is often accompanied by a rash of reddish blotches on the chest, abdomen and wrists. During the second week, the patient experiences weakness and delirium, and has a feeble pulse. If consciousness is lost, the symptoms may be mistaken for death, even though the body still feels warm. However, while death can happen at this stage, the patient may also recover even without medication.

Typhus was a particular scourge of prisons during the eighteenth century, where it ended the lives of far more felons than the hangman. Many of those infected, however, were prematurely buried, for no time was wasted on those who were unconscious and seemingly without a pulse. But as prison reformer John Howard discovered, a surprising number of seemingly dead prisoners recovered when they were washed under the prison pump, and afterwards went on to make a full recovery.

In his report *The State of Prisons in England and Wales*, pubished in 1784, Howard notes:

I might mention as an evidence of the advantage of Baths in prisons, that I have known instances where persons supposed to be dead of the goal-fever, and brought out for burial; on being washed with cold water, have shown signs of life, and soon recovered. Even persons with the small-pox have found advantage by the cold bath.

The benefit of washing was probably as much due to the rubbing and the movement of the body parts as to the shock of the cold water. Physical manipulation helps to stimulate the heart, the blood circulation, and breathing. And the blood, by thus carrying more oxygen to the brain, will bring about a return to consciousness. But for this renewed activity to be self-sustaining the body temperature must be raised to normal, which is why a revived patient had to be quickly dried and warmed.

It is interesting to note in this regard that the Arabs always wash their dead in a brisk, thorough manner, which suggests that they have long known the restorative effects that such vigorous treatment can have on those who are not really dead. The adopted Bedouin H.R.P. Dickson gives this vivid account of the work of the body-washer or *ghassal* in his classic work *The Arab of the Desert*:

> The body-washer places the nude body on a large wooden table and pours water over it in quantities. Then with a gauntlet of coarse wool which he puts on his hands, he scrubs the corpse all over with soap and water, sousing it over and over again with copious douches of water. After this procedure he dries the body well and dresses it up in its new white cotton shroud, or perhaps assists members of the family to do this.

Yet as burial happens next, and always within twenty-four hours of death, in accordance with the teachings of the Koran, washing has to have an immediate effect to prevent someone still alive from being buried. Such a surprising restoration happened in 1973, during the washing of 53-year-old Murat Muletia, who had collapsed and apparently died while suffering an epileptic seizure. His best friend Imam Abdullah happily took on the ritual of washing him, yet Abdullah was so shocked when Muletia groaned and sat up after he had thrown a bucket of cold water over him, that he had a heart attack and fell down dead. Indeed, their roles were now strangely reversed, for the next day Abdullah was not only immured in the coffin intended for Muletia, but the latter helped to bury him1

Washing was also a potent restorative, as John Howard noted, in some apparently fatal cases of smallpox, a fact confirmed by Dr Charles Clay, who writes in *The Medical Times* that 'there cannot remain a doubt that the sudden change of temperature produced by washing and laying out, as practised after death, with the cool air admitted by open windows, had often resuscitated individuals supposed to be dead from smallpox'.

Smallpox was a virus disease with a high mortality rate, particularly among young children. But while it was once common, it has now been eliminated worldwide, the last case occurring in 1977. It was transmitted by droplet infection and by contact with excrement or the skin crusts of infected persons. The disease began with headache and backache, followed by fever and sometimes by delirium, which were accompanied by, or succeeded by, a skin rash that spread from the extremeties to the middle of the body. By the sixth day the livid spots became the characteristic pus-filled blisters; these burst and formed crusts six days later, and the sites were permanently marked by ugly pitted scars. Many Europeans in the eighteenth century had disfiguring smallpox scars on their faces, although they were generally left out by flattering portrait painters.

Dr Clay gives the following interesting example of someone who, supposedly dead from smallpox, was revived by washing:

The daughter of Laurens the American president [Henry Laurens, president of the Continental Congress from 1777 to 1778], was laid out for dead, after an attack of smallpox, when the washing and cool air restored her to life; the father had so great a dread of premature interment in consequence of this, that he willed his body to be burnt at his death by his friends;

It was, however, just as possible to commit the same mistake in the burning as in the interment.

There was a smallpox epidemic in Gloucester as late as 1896, and during it an infected child, believed to be dead, was taken from his hospital ward to the mortuary. Yet the following morning, a gardener walking beside the mortuary was alerted by the sound of crying to his revival. The boy was hurriedly returned to the hospital, where he made a full recovery. The case, however, was hushed up to save the hospital authorities any embarrassment.

One of the most touching recoveries from apparent death caused by smallpox happened in the eighteenth century to Owen Manning, who for nearly forty years was vicar at Godalming, Surrey, where he researched and wrote his estimable *History and Antiquities of Surrey*. When he was an undergraduate student at Queens' College, Cambridge, he contracted the disease, went into a rapid decline, and seemingly died. He was therefore laid out, and his parents were informed of his death. Preparations for his funeral were also begun.

However, when Owen Manning's father arrived in Cambridge, he went into the room where his son's body lay to take a last look at him. He was struck by the colour remaining in his face, and he impulsively put his arm around him and raised him somewhat, saying: 'I will give my poor boy another chance.' To his astonishment he noticed the eyelids flicker, which told him that his son was not as dead as he was supposed to be. A medical student named Heberden, who was a friend of Owen's was immediately called to the room, and he used his skills to return him fully to life.

Astonishingly, there was another occasion when Dr Heberden, as he became, saved Owen Manning's life. For a year or so later (probably in 1740, when he graduated), having developed epilepsy, Owen had a fit while walking beside the river Cam and fell into the water. When he was pulled from the river, he showed no sign of life and was again thought to be dead. However, Dr Heberden ran to the scene and managed, by giving artificial respiration, to restore him to life.

4   Drowning and Hanging

In water once too long he dived,
And all suppose him beat,
He seem'd so cold – but he revived
To have another heat,
Just when we thought his race was run,
He came in fresh – th' Undying One!

From 'The Undying One' by Thomas Hood

One remarkable case of recovery in which smallpox played a part, although it was not the cause of the patient's apparent death, is given by Dr (later Sir) William Watson in the appendix of his *Account of a Series of Experiments, Instituted with a View to Ascertaining the Most Successful Method of Inoculating the Small-pox*, published in 1768. It was brought to Dr Watson's attention by his friend, the surgeon and apothecary Mr Osborne, of Clerkenwell in London, whose ministrations successfully revived the person concerned.

In the third week of November 1741, a poor 23-year-old woman named Jane Brown contracted smallpox. She was fortunate enough, however, to be taken into the care of a nurse who specialized in treating the indigent, who lived at Islington, close by the New River. She soon developed the second stage of the disease and became delirous. When the nurse stepped out at about noon on 21 November to do some shopping, she left her bed, ran out of the house and through the back garden to the New River, into which she threw herself.

The area was quiet and rural at that time, and Islington was still a village. However, Jane was noticed some time later, floating face down, by an old man walking along the opposite bank of the river. He crossed the river as fast as he could and made his way to an ale-house called the Crown, the nearest inhabited building, where he raised the alarm. As the hostelry stood some way from the river, Jane's face must have been submerged for at least half an hour, possibly longer. She certainly showed no sign of life when she was eventually pulled from the water and laid on the bank. It was assumed by those at the scene that she was dead, and no attempt was made to revive her.

There was a long delay in moving her body because, having drowned herself right on the border between Islington and Clerkenwell, both parishes wanted the other to pay for her removal and burial. Yet it was eventually decided that she should be taken to the workhouse in the parish of St James, Clerkenwell. A coffin was therefore brought to the spot by the parish grave-digger William Stevens, assisted by a bearer named Thomas Bull, who together placed Jane's wet corpse in it. They then hoisted the coffin up on to their shoulders and set off towards St James's. On the way, they had an accident which proved to be extraordinarily lucky for the woman.

As they were bringing her in a coffin across the fields to Clerkenwell, Bull's foot, it being frosty weather, slipped from under him; and he not being able to recover himself, let her fall to the ground. While they were lifting her up again on their shoulders, they fancied they heard a faint groan, which was related to the people, when they brought her to the work-house.

Nevertheless, the workhouse staff were of the opinion, after having viewed her body, that she was dead. She was therefore removed from the coffin, placed upon its lid, and left under an open arch at the entrance to the infirmary, where corpses were always placed prior to burial. However, not long afterwards she showed another sign that she was still alive.

While some people were looking at her with much attention, they discovered some little motion of her upper lip; and as this seemed to corroborate the former circumstance of her supposed groaning, the master of the workhouse ordered her to be removed into one of the wards, and put to bed; and, besides, directed Mr Osborne to be sent for.

The workhouse master was more careful than might at first appear to have been necessary, for neither groaning nor twitching, nor indeed both together, always mean that a person is still alive. A groan or similar noise can be produced when air is forced from the lungs of a cadaver, and such compression might have happened to Jane's chest when her coffin was dropped, while muscles can twitch or flicker at intervals for an hour or more after death. The continued life of the muscles in this way may be even more dramatic, as the following example given by the editor of *The Lancet* indicates. 'Short of cadaveric decomposition there is no certain sign of death, much less an absolute criterion which can determine the precise moment of death. In some cases of somatic death – e.g. after decapitation – the heart, once termed *ultimum moriens*, has been known to beat for many minutes.'

When Mr Osborne arrived at the St James's workhouse infirmary, he found few grounds for optimism. Jane felt extremely cold, she had no perceptible pulse, nor was she breathing, and her stomach was distended with water. And more than three hours had gone by since she was pulled from the New River. None the less, he set to work to attempt to revive her. He first, and somewhat oddly, gave her a spoonful of warm water impregnated with spirit of hartshorn, an aqueous solution of ammonia. The fact that she did not choke on it meant that her swallowing reflex was functional. He next, and more effectively, rubbed her vigorously with coarse cloths, and then rolled her 'backwards and forwards upon her stomach and sides'. Both would have warmed her and helped to stimulate her heart and lungs. These motions most noticeably brought 'an odd croaking noise' from her, then a sudden release of wind and water from her mouth. She was turned immediately on her stomach, with her head over the side of the bed, so that the vomited water cascaded on to the floor.

With her pulse now detectable and her breathing resuming, she was demonstrably alive and showing signs of staying that way, although still very weak. She was placed in a warm bed and kept well covered, and by eight o'clock that night she was not only able to turn herself over, but had managed to drink a little broth and eat some bread. Her temperature was also normal. Yet while she had survived the drowning, she was still infected with smallpox, the course of which resumed the following day, when pustules began erupting all over her body. But Jane had a charmed life, for she successfully recovered from this affliction, and was discharged 'perfectly well, and at her own request, on December 12, 1741'.

Deaths by drowning, whether accidental or intentional, are still frequent, although very often the victim can be successfully revived. As recently as 5 April 1996, for example, a three-year-old girl who had been out walking her dog near a pond at St Helens, Merseyside, decided to take a swim in it. So she undressed herself, carefully folded her clothes and left them on the bank, and went into the cold water. It was not long before she got out of her depth and into serious difficulties. Fortunately, a passer-by who had earlier noticed her walking the dog, became worried for her safety when he later saw the dog on its own, and called the police.

When two policemen arrived to look for the girl, they eventually caught sight of her floating face down in the pond, some 20 yards from its edge. One of the officers, PC Kevin Smith, swam out to retrieve her, but when he brought her to the bank she seemed lifeless, cold to the touch and without a detectable pulse. An ambulance was called, and while the policemen waited for it to arrive, the second officer, PC Paul Gibson, wrapped the girl in his police jacket and gave her the kiss of life. His prompt action was effective, for by the time the ambulance arrived, she was showing signs of life. She was then rushed to Whiston Hospital, whose emergency care had her breathing unaided within hours. The girl went on to make a full recovery, and the policemen were commended for their fast, appropriate action.

In both these cases, the victims' faces were under water for at least half an hour, but there are several instances on record of people being successfully revived after having been wholly submerged for a much longer period. One of the most remarkable and well attested occurred in the eighteenth century, at Tronningham, Sweden. The details of the incident were recorded by Dr Joel Langelot, who presented them to a German academy.

The person concerned was a 65-year-old gardener at the Royal Palace at Tronningham. His misadventure began when he tried to help a man who had fallen into the nearby lake. In doing so he rather foolishly walked out on the ice, which broke under his weight and precipitated him into the water. Its depth there was about 18 feet, and the gardener, who was unable to swim, sank straight to the bottom, where his feet became trapped. He was unable to free himself because the coldness of the water almost immediately robbed him of the power of motion. Dr Langelot reports: 'This man informed me, that all his limbs first became still with cold, and that he had afterwards lost all sensation, till he felt his head struck violently with a crook, by those who were searching for him.'

Incredibly, the searchers with the crook, which was used to pull him out once they had located him, did not find him until fully sixteen hours had gone by, during which time he partly lost consciousness, although he thought he heard the sounds of bells being rung in Stockholm. His survival for such a length of time may have been due to air trapped in his mouth, for Dr Langelot adds:

> That as soon as he had been taken out of the water, a great bubble of air issued out of his mouth, which without doubt kept him from being suffocated, and that his ears were filled with water; that they began by wrapping him up exactly, from head to foot in a sheet, and that in this condition they warmed him gradually before a gentle fire, the Swedes knowing by experience that drowned persons are not recoverable when exposed too soon to the open air.

If such a prolonged submergence sounds impossible, it is not the longest by any means. The record may be held by another Swede, who met her watery fate, if not her end, in the early years of the seventeenth century.

In about 1604 (the exact year is uncertain), a young girl named Margaret Lasdotter, of Dalia province, fell into the water of a fjord, where she sank and remained submerged, it is said, for three days. She was finally discovered by searchers, who resuscitated her in a similar way to that used on the royal gardener. She nearly drowned on two subsequent occasions, although she was found more quickly both times. M. Tilasius, the keeper of the Royal Library of Stockholm, who knew her well, recorded these happenings. Margaret finally died in 1672, at the advanced age of seventy-five years.

An even longer (and altogether more incredible) submergence in water was also said to have happened in Sweden. Lawrence Jona, of Boness, in the parish of Pithovia, fell into water when he was seventeen years old and was supposedly not pulled out until seven weeks had gone by. He survived this ordeal and lived to the age of seventy. The rector who gave the sermon at his funeral was the source of the story (which was recorded for posterity by a passing traveller named Peter Burmann), although he may merely have been repeating local exaggerations.

Even if some of these periods have been exaggerated the victims would still have been submerged for considerable lengths of time. They indicate that anyone who is brought out of water apparently lifeless should be regarded as recoverable, unless he or she has started to putrefy. This is particularly true of drownings that occur in cold water.

Indeed, according to Dr Martin Nemiroff, an assistant professor of internal medicine at Michigan University's medical centre, immersion in cold water prompts a diving reflex action in humans and other air-breathing mammals. This helps survival underwater by cooling the body and by reducing the blood flow to non-essential body parts like the skin, muscles and stomach, which can tolerate a lack of oxygen for up to one hour. At the same time, blood flow (and the oxygen it carries) is maintained to the brain and the heart, which are vital to bodily survival. And since Dr Nemiroff's definition of cold water applies to temperatures of 70°F or less, almost all drownings in British and northern European lakes, rivers and seas fall into this category.

Dr Nemiroff studied thirteen cases of drowning in cold water, of whom all the persons concerned remained underwater for much longer than four minutes, which is popularly regarded as the maximum length of time that anyone can stay submerged and be successfully revived. Of these, nine were successfully revived without brain damage or other physical impairment.

An 18-year-old college student named Brian Cunningham, for example, survived being trapped in an upturned car, which was submerged in a semi-frozen pond, for 38 minutes. When he was brought to the surface, he was blue with cold and without a detectable pulse. He was of course thought to be dead, but he fortunately gave an involuntary gasp on the bank, and resuscitation was immediately started, and kept up for fifteen hours, until he finally regained consciousness. Brian eventually made a full and complete recovery, and he even returned to school one week later.

Another case of apparent drowning investigated by Dr Nemiroff is similar to that of the three-year-old St Helens' girl mentioned above. The victim, a two-year-old boy, fell into Lake Michigan and was found by a power-boater floating face down in the cold water more than twenty minutes after he disappeared. When he was brought to shore by the boat owner, the boy's mother gave him mouth-to-mouth resuscitation and chest massage, while the man drove them to a hospital. Her son revived before they reached the hospital and was eventually released none the worse for his experience.

These amazing rescues prompted Dr Nemiroff to advise, 'Even if the body looks lifeless, the victim still may be recovered. I would not stop resuscitation before the victim has been brought to hospital.' And in addition to mouth-to-mouth resuscitation, he recommends massage to stimulate the heart and the circulation, and a gradual warming of the victim's body. The latter is most effectively done by allowing the person to breathe, when possible, pure oxygen that has been heated to a temperature of about 110°F.

The ability to revive drowning victims after long immersion is confirmed by the amazing recuperative method possessed by John Jeremy, of Stillwater, Minnesota, who used it to restore to life about 500 people who had at different times been pulled, apparently lifeless, from water. Indeed, his talent in this regard earned him the sobriquet of 'Fisherman'. He was not only able to resuscitate those who had just been drowned, but also people who had been in the water for some time. His method was a family secret that had been passed on to him by an uncle, who had restored some 1,000 drowned people to life, and who had received it from his father.

John Jeremy was offered large sums of money to reveal the method, but he jealously kept it to himself. His fame led to him being called out to all parts of the United States, and even to Canada. Before he died in 1926, aged only forty-one, having no children of his own, he handed on the secret to his 12-year-old nephew George Lawrence. And he has been reviving drowned people with it ever since.

Perhaps the most bizarre method of resuscitation from drowning was performed at Passy, in France, on 24 July 1757. A 21-year-old waterman fell into the river there, stunning himself as he did so, and was carried by the current out to the middle of the river, where he remained submerged for half an hour before he could be rescued. He was taken to a nearby house, but everyone thought he was dead, until:

> A physician happening to come by, blew up a great quantity of tobacco-smoke by the *anus*, with a straw, and blew also the same smoke plentifully into his mouth and nostrils: the man very soon gave signs of life, very slight indeed, but sufficient to encourage the good Samaritan to proceed . . . [and] in a short time the patient recovered so far as to be able to speak [The *Annual Register*].

One cannot help but observe that it was fortunate the physician had a straw with him and was thus not obliged to perform mouth-to-anus resuscitation!

In normal circumstances, because those pulled unconscious from water are cold, morbidly pale, swollen, with imperceptible pulses and no breathing, they are easily mistaken for corpses. And there is an increased risk of such a mistake being made when large numbers of people are involved, particularly when the medical personnel are not very well trained. This was the case in India in November 1997, when an overcrowded and speeding school bus which was crossing the Yamuna river in Delhi, skidded, smashed through the side-barrier and plunged 30 feet into the sluggish, dirty water below. Aboard were 120 children aged between six and fourteen, twice the number the bus was permitted to carry. The many drowned and injured were sent to the inadequately staffed Bara Hindu Rao Hospital, where two of those believed dead, who were carried off to the mortuary, later recovered and survived.

Hanging kills in a similar way to drowning, by asphyxia – that is, when the victim falls only a short distance, as was in the case with executions in the old days. The weight of the body pulls the noose tight around the neck, and thus throttles the victim. But it is not the only factor. Loss of consciousness and death can also result from a combination of asphyxia and a stoppage of the blood supply to the brain, or alternatively, if the carotid veins are closed by the tightened rope but not the arteries, from cerebral hyperaemia. The following description of the hanging of Thomas Athoe, the Mayor of Tenby, who was executed for murder along with his son, also called Thomas, at eleven o'clock on the morning of Friday, 5 July 1723, at St Thomas's-Watering, in Surrey, suggests that the latter condition may have contributed to his death: 'When they were ty'd up, by the Executioner, old Athoe cover'd his Face first, and after he was turn'd off, he bled very much at the Nose ... Old Athoe was about 58 Years of Age, and his Son wanted one Day of being 24 Years old, at the Time of their Deaths.'

The speed with which a hanged felon lost consciousness and died also depended upon a number of variables. These included the length of the drop, the weight of the person, the diameter and suppleness of the rope, and the placement of the noose knot or ring, through which the remainder of the rope slipped. When the hangman was sober and skilled, he would do a quick and effective job, but when he was neither, as was often the case, then the victim might not be dead when he was cut down. And even when two felons were hanged together by the same executioner, the demise of each could be entirely different. For example, when

John Hawkins and George Simpson were executed at Tyburn in May 1722 for the robbery of the Bristol mail coach, Hawkins had a far harder time dying than his colleague:

> Being in some Confusion [Hawkins] was turned off and died, not without prodigious Difficulty and Struggling, contrary to his Friend, who was more composed before he died, and more easily lost his Breath . . . The same Day that Hawkins and Simpson were hang'd at Tyburn, their Bodies were carried to Hounslow-heath, and there hang'd in Irons on a Gibbet erected for that Purpose [*Select Trials at the Sessions-House in the Old-Bailey*, as above].

The type of rope used for hangings was usually made out of hemp. This is a somewhat stiff material, which meant that, if the rope was thick and not very pliable, it might not close tightly around the criminal's neck. And the rope had to be supplied by the condemned man's family, who, if they were poor, would not want to spend money on something they would not see again. So they tended to buy rope of inferior quality, which explains why poor criminals often took longer to die and why the fortunate few who survived hanging came from their number.

The desire for a speedy death made silk the preferred material, although such expensive ropes could only be afforded by the well off. In his diary for 27 February 1662, Samuel Pepys records that one wealthy wrongdoer actually fashioned his own, in order to be certain of a rapid exit from the world.

> It seems one Dillon, of a great Family, was, after much endeavours to have saved him, hanged with a silken halter this Sessions (of his own preparing) not for honour only, but it seems, it being soft and sleek, it do slip close and kills, that is, strangles presently; whereas, a stiff one do not come so close together, and so the party may live the longer before killed.

Old-fashioned hanging seldom compressed the trachea or windpipe, which is what happens when someone is throttled. Rather, when the ladder or cart was pulled out from under the felon, his downward movement and sudden mid-air arrest would jerk the noose up over the larynx, tightening it around the upper throat, forcing open the mouth and simultaneously pushing out the tongue. The effect is the same, however, for the windpipe is blocked and breathing cannot occur. As we have seen, there would often be some kicking and struggling. There was also an involuntary opening of the bowels and the bladder, so that a hanged man messed his pants, if he hadn't messed them before. But of more interest to the female spectators who thronged to public hangings, many of whom belonged to the gentry, was the associated erection of the penis, and sometimes the ejaculation of semen.

While the law required that the criminal should be hanged by the neck until he (or she) was dead, the estimation of when that occurred was not easy, particularly in the crowded and noisy circumstances of the execution. For while the hanged person was obviously alive if he was still struggling, once he lost consciousness and went limp, it was impossible to tell when he died, or if indeed he was actually dead. The length of time that the felon remained suspended by the neck was left to the discretion of the hangman, who estimated when death had occurred. His judgement could only be a rough one, however, based on experience, although in most cases it proved good enough. Everyone was left dangling for at least five minutes, but sometimes for much longer. The weather, the mood of the crowd, the wishes of the relatives, who might press money into the hangman's hand for a quick recovery of the corpse, and the number being executed were all factors that might reduce or increase the length of the condemned person's swing.

There was no discrimination where hanging was concerned; women were strung up for the same offences as men, unless they were pregnant. Many women who committed capital crimes therefore either made sure, or pretended, that they were in that condition. The imposters were usually discovered by knowledgeable midwives, but it was always worth a try.

Women, however, ran the risk of being hanged if they had a miscarriage, for it could easily be mistaken for a self-induced abortion; and abortion, or child-murder as it was considered, was a capital offence. A miscarriage that was made into a double tragedy by the subsequent hanging of the mother was recorded by William Harvey in folio 492, quoted by Percivall Willughby. He describes how, 'in the Protector's dayes', one pregnant girl, a village simpleton who was being looked after by two female friends that slept with her, one night slipped out from between them to relieve her stomach ache by emptying her bowels.

[She] hasted to a ditch side, where did run a small rivulet of water, there, supposing to ease her belly-ach, instead of a naturall stoole, an abortion came from her . . . But the women, her attenders, missing her, did arise to follow her, and they met her nigh, coming towards the house. They asked her where shee had been; shee said, That her belly did ake, that shee went to the ditch to grunt, that something was come from her, and that it lay on the bank.

What lay on the bank was 'a very small child', and the local coroner therefore had the girl arrested and put in jail. At her trial, Harvey himself spoke in her defence, but in vain. The jury found her guilty of aborting the infant, and the 'judge condemned her, and shee was, afterwards, hanged, for not having a woman by her, at her delivery'.

Another case of a girl being hanged after her miscarriage also happened 'in the Protector's dayes', but what took place afterwards suggested to all that the sentence was an offence against God. The girl was Anne Green (born 1629) who worked as a servant for Sir Thomas Read at Duns Tew in north Oxfordshire, and who, in the summer of 1650, was made pregnant by one of Sir Thomas's sons, an event which was, as it still is, something of an occupational hazard for serving-maids.

In the fourth month of her pregnancy, Anne, who was by all accounts a sprightly lass, rather overdid things when turning malt, and her exertions brought her into labour. Without realizing what the consequences might be for her, she took herself off to the 'House of Easement', as the lying-in establishment was pleasantly called, where she soon gave birth to a dead child 'scarce half a Span long, and of what Sex not to be distinguished', which likewise 'fell from her unawares'.

Although she had 'a woman by her, at her delivery', as Harvey recommended, she was nevertheless immediately suspected of having induced the birth. She was therefore arrested and sent to Oxford, where she was imprisoned in the castle. And she was there tried for the murder of her bastard child, before Serjeant-at-law Umpton Croke, and the verdict going against her, she was condemned to hang and afterwards to be dissected.

The execution, which was carried out in the castle yard on Saturday, 14 December 1650, was a difficult one, and Anne was sorely treated by those present, perhaps because of the detestation that people felt for child-murderers, which she was believed to be. She was left hanging, it is recorded, for half an hour, and because there was still some doubt about her death, some pulled on her legs, others beat her on the breast, while one of the soldiers, who was named Oran (or Orum), struck her several times in the stomach with the butt of his musket. She was then cut down and conveyed in a coffin, with the rope still around her neck, to a nearby house, where her dissection was scheduled to take place. This was to be carried out by a distinguished group of Oxford anatomists and physicians, who included Sir William Petty, Dr Ralph Bathurst and Dr Thomas Willis, all of whom were associates of William Harvey.

Having brought Anne Green into the room where she was to be opened, her bearers noticed, to their alarm and amazement, that she was still breathing. Some of them now felt sorry for her and, not wishing her to be dissected alive, tried to save her from such a fate by ending her life. A man named Mason stamped on her chest, while Private Oran hit her again with his musket butt. Fortunately, the arrival of the dissectors put a stop to this well-meant but rough treatment. Discovering that their subject was not dead (they heard, it was said, 'a small Rattling in her Throat'), they immediately set about trying to revive her. She was put to bed, along with another woman to keep her warm, bled from a vein, and various poltices applied to her head, neck, chest and stomach. And because she had survived execution by the grace of God, the anatomists applied for her to be pardoned.

It took her several hours to regain consciousness, although she was awake and speaking again before the end of the day. On Sunday her pardon was granted, which effectively meant that she was not guilty of murder. The news of her revival from death spread like wildfire through the town, bringing out many thousands of excited people to view her, for she was a living miracle and an example of God's justice. Yet when questioned about what it was like to be hanged, Anne said she recalled nothing of the event. 'Nor was she sensible of any Pains that she could remember, but, which is most observable, she came to herself, as if she had awakened out of her sleep; not recovering the use of her speech by slow degrees; but in a manner altogether, beginning to speak just where she had left off on the Gallows.'

It is interesting to note that this continuance of conversation, when she was revived, from the point at which it ended when she was hanged, also happened in the case of Arabella Godfrey, who woke from her week-long trance still wanting to go to chapel. However, while Arabella had no awareness of being unconscious, Anne's loss of memory extended back to just before she was brought out of Oxford castle. 'She neither remembered how the Fetters were knock'd off, how she went out of Prison, [nor] when she was turn'd off the Ladder', which was perhaps fortunate for her.

Anne Green later married and settled in Steeple Barton, a village lying a couple of miles south of Duns Tew, where she reportedly lived in good repute among her neighbours. She remained something of a celebrity and was visited by various people of note from time to time, one of whom was William Derham, the rector of Upminster in Essex. He mentions her revival from hanging in his book entitled *Physico-Theology: or, a Demonstration of the Being and Attributes of God, from his Works of Creation* (1713), and records that 'I myself saw her many years after, after that she had (I heard) born divers children'. In fact Anne gave birth to three children, and she survived her hanging by several years, only dying in 1659.

The question of whether hanging is painful or not has been argued about for centuries, if not for millennia. Anne Green could certainly remember no pain, and it was generally believed by physicians of the time that there was none, for they assumed that once a felon was 'turned off' he lost all sensation and could therefore experience no suffering. This was certainly the view of those doctors with whom Samuel Pepys dined at the Chyrurgeon's Hall on Thursday, 27 February 1662, just before he spent an enjoyable afternoon watching the corpse of a seaman, hanged for robbery, being dissected. He noted: 'All the Doctors at table conclude, that there is no pain at all in hanging, for that it do stop the circulation of the blood, and so stops all sense and motion in an instant.'

But of course the hanged did not always immediately become senseless, or for that matter have their circulation stopped so abruptly, and it is evident that John Hawkins, mentioned above, who 'had a far harder time dying than his colleague', was both conscious and presumably in agony for some time.

Moreover, although Anne Green had no memory of feeling any pain, it is interesting to note the recollection of John Smith, otherwise known as 'Half-hanged Smith', a burglar and highwayman who was found guilty of two robberies in the early years of the eighteenth century. He was hanged at Tyburn on Wednesday, 12 December 1705. But after he had been swinging limply from the 'Tree of Death' for about fifteen minutes, a messenger unexpectedly arrived bearing a reprieve. Smith was immediately cut down and taken to a nearby house, where to everyone's amazement he was restored to life. And when he was later asked what his 'feelings' were when he was swung into space, he gave the following enlightening reply:

> When I was turned off, for some time I was sensible of a very great pain, occasioned by the weight of my body, and I felt my spirits in a strange commotion, violently pressing upwards: which, having forced their way to my head, I, as it were, saw a great blaze of glaring light, which seemed to go out at my eyes with a flash, and then I lost all sense of pain. After I was cut down, and began to come to myself, the blood and spirits forcing themselves into the former channels, put me in a sort of pricking or shooting of such intolerable pain, that I could have wished those hanged who were bringing about my recovery.

There is thus no doubt about Smith's pain. But while Anne Green may have forgotten her suffering at the moment of her hanging, it is nevertheless strange that she felt none, as Smith did, when she revived.

John Smith did not regard his reprieve and resurrection as a second chance to do something good and useful with his life. For the following year, he was again arrested and tried for burglary, but was acquitted on a point of law. He still did not learn his lesson. He was afterwards caught committing another burglary, and was sent to gaol to await trial. But amazingly, his prosecutor died and he was released. Smith really did lead a charmed life! Then he went to sea, lured by the idea of making his fortune afloat, possibly as a pirate, and was drowned when his vessel capsized in a storm.

Another woman accused of child-murder who suffered the supreme punishment yet revived afterwards, was Margaret Dickson (colloquially known as 'Half-hangit Maggie'), a Scotswoman from Musselburgh, near Edinburgh. In her case, the pregnancy went the full term, and the infant was born dead. She was tried for, and found guilty of, its murder; the jury no doubt believed that, having been made pregnant by a lover and then abandoned by him, while her husband, a sailor, was away at sea, she had decided to smother the fruit of her unfaithfulness before the latter returned home.

She was hanged in Edinburgh's Grass-market in 1727. When she was cut down from the gallows, her corpse was placed in a coffin and driven on a horse-drawn cart to Musselburgh for burial, accompanied by a small crowd of relatives, friends and various ghoulish spectators. The distance to Musselburgh is only about 4½ miles, but by the time the party reached the hamlet of Peffermill 2 miles from Edinburgh, their throats were dry and they accordingly stopped at the wayside inn.

With the noise of the turning wheels, the creak of the cart, and the horses' hooves temporarily arrested, and with most of the group inside the inn, a startling sound was noticed coming from the coffin.

One of them heard a noise like something scratching on the inside of the lid. They immediately broke it open, when to their surprize they found the body moving, and a gardener being present, opened a vein, and in a few hours she [Margaret Dickson] recovered so as to be able to speak, and next day walked home to Musselburgh.

95

She had therefore been still alive, albeit unconscious, when she was nailed up in the coffin, and her apparent return from the dead had perhaps been helped by the jolting of the cart and the cries of those walking alongside her.

But Margaret was dead in Scottish law and could not be made to suffer the same punishment again, a ruling which also applied to her marriage; this was annulled by her execution. Hence her sailor husband, James Wardlow, whom she married at Inveresk on 7 November 1721, was free, if he wished, to turn her out of the house and take a new wife. Hardly surprisingly, all Musselburgh was eager to know what he would do when he returned home not long afterwards. According to the romantic version of the story, he not only forgave Margaret for cuckolding him but believed her innocent of murder, and to make things entirely right between them, he remarried her at Inveresk church. However, my search of the Inveresk church records show that while a Margaret Dickson did marry there on 3 June 1728, the man with whom she tied the knot was William Cockburn. Hence if she is the same Margaret Dickson, James Wardlow did in fact wash his hands of her. Whatever the true story, Margaret lived until 1752, a quarter of a century after her miraculous resuscitation.

Not long afterwards, on Monday, 26 July 1736, a rogue named Reynolds was hanged at Tyburn. He had been convicted of turn-pike levelling (throwing down the toll barriers which had been erected across many of the nation's roads to pay for their upkeep), which unluckily for him was only made a capital offence the previous year. The tolls hit the poor, who were least able to pay them, hardest and turnpike levelling was therefore a form of political protest, which traced its origins to the Levellers of the preceding century, who wanted to 'throw down' all class divisions and social barriers.

Reynolds was thus hanged for his crime instead of going to gaol. Not being earmarked for dissection, he was then placed in a coffin which had been brought to the gallows' site. But as the lid of the coffin was being nailed down, he recovered sufficiently to push it aside and make an effort to sit up. This brought a roar of delight from the crowd, who quickly made it known that if the hangman thought he was going to have a second try at finishing Reynolds off, he could think again. He demurred, and the revived felon was taken off to a nearby house for relief. He first vomited up some blood, and was then given a glass of wine to drink. Rather than acting as a restorative, however, it had the opposite effect, and the turnpike hero died a few minutes after swallowing it.

Four years later, on Monday, 24 November 1740, a 19-year-old thug named William Duell (sometimes spelled Duel or Dewell) was hanged at Tyburn, for the rape, robbery and murder of Sarah Griffin, in Acton. He was strung up along with four other felons, two male and two female, who had together carried out several burglaries and other crimes, on the familiar Triple-Tree gallows. Duell's punishment also included being dissected, and once he had been cut down from the gallows he was carried immediately to the Barber-Surgeons' Hall, which stood on the site of the present Barbican. The surgeons there were entitled to four corpses a year from Tyburn, all of which were felons who had committed the worst sorts of crime.

However, hanging five convicts one after the other proved too much for Derrick, the hangman, whose concentration wavered somewhat. As a result William Duell was not as dead when he was cut down as he should have been. This came to light at the Barber-Surgeons' Hall, where he was stripped and laid out on a board. One of the attendants, in order to prepare him for the anatomists, set to work washing the grime and faeces from his body. The cold water and the rubbing had a stimulating effect on Duell and roused him from his stupor; he began to breathe again and show other life signs. A surgeon was summoned, who according to *The New Wonderful Magazine*, 'bled him, and took several ounces of blood from him, and in about two hours he came so much to himself as to sit up in a chair, groaned very much, and seemed in great agitation, but could not speak.'

This was by no means an everyday happening, and much excitement and interest was generated by Duell's return to life. He was kept at the Barber-Surgeons' Hall until midnight, then conveyed to Newgate gaol, where he had to be held until it was ascertained that he actually was William Duell. He was much improved on the following day: he not only regained his voice and his appetite, but asked to see his mother, Hannah. His revival made him into something of a celebrity, and crowds thronged the gaol on that and subsbequent days to stare wonderingly at him. He would doubtless have signed autographs had he been able to write.

He did not receive a pardon, however, for while he could not be hanged again for the same offence, there was no doubt about his guilt. The killer was instead given the same sentence as that received by those who were reprieved from the gallows: he was transported for life.

Similar mistakes were made by hangmen elsewhere in Europe, and it is perhaps pertinent to quote one case mentioned by the surgeon John Bell, which happened in Italy, probably in the early sixteenth century.

> There was a robber, (says Benivinius) one Jacobus, who having been taken down from the gibbet apparently dead, but really having in him the remains of life, was laid carefully, recovered, was perfectly restored, betook himself to his old ways again; and so in the natural course of things came round to his old mark the gallows, and was this time very thoroughly hanged.

What is equally astonishing about this robber, apart from his evident stupidity, was the discovery, when he was dissected after his second hanging by Benivinius (or, rather, Benivenius, which is the Latinized surname of the Italian surgeon Antonio Benivieni, who published *De abditis nonnullis ac mirandis morborum et sanationum causis* in 1507), that his heart was 'not covered, but (refertum pilis) crammed with hair'. The possession of an internally hairy heart was, in ancient times, considered to be a sign of courage and vigour (although not presumably, of longevity), for several brave souls were found to have one. These include Aristomenes, a Messenian general who was killed by the Spartans in 671 BC, and, less obviously, a rhetorician named Hermogenes (died AD 161), whose heart, in addition to being hairy, was found, perhaps not surprisingly, to be grossly enlarged.

Yet the days of recovery from hanging were numbered, a change that was brought about by the use of a trapdoor and, with it, a long drop beneath for the person being executed. Trapdoors had been in use for some time for the rapid removal of people from theatrical stages, and someone had the bright idea of employing them to send criminals into eternity. After all, a felon turned off a ladder or a cart with a rope around his (or her) neck often suffered slow strangulation, which was not always fatal, whereas the sudden opening of a trapdoor with a long drop below resulted in a quick fall and a broken neck when the end of the rope was reached. This rendered him instantly unconscious, and quickly, if not equally instantly, dead. The method was not only much faster and more humane, but seemingly mathematically exact, because the force necessary to break the average neck was soon determined, and by combining it with the weight of the criminal and the speed of his downward movement, the exact length of the drop required to kill him without pulling off his head could easily be calculated.

For best results the hangman's slipknot, which was soon replaced by a ring, was sited at the side of the neck, beneath the jaw, thereby exerting a sideways leverage on the neck when the end of the rope was reached. Such force suddenly applied typically snaps apart and separates the second and third cervical vertebrae, breaks the spinal cord, and tears the various ligaments and blood vessels of the region. This results in immediate unconsciousness and in the complete paralysis of the body's voluntary muscles. Respiration also ceases, although the heart may continue to beat for up to fifteen minutes, until its muscles, deprived of oxygen, falter and stop, and then die.

The successful breaking of an average neck requires a force of about 1,260 foot pounds. Such pressure is exerted on the neck when someone falls the requisite distance before suddenly reaching the end of the rope. The length of the drop required to produce this force is determined by dividing the weight of the felon (in pounds) into 1,260. For example, for a 13-stone (182-pound) man, one would divide 182 into 1,260, which gives an answer of 6.9. This is the distance in feet that he would need to fall to bring about a successful snapping of his neck. A lighter, 8-stone (112-pound) woman, by contrast, would have to fall 11 feet 3 inches to bring about the same result (1,260 divided by 112 gives 11.25). Longer falls in either case might result in the head being torn from the body. Modern hangmen are usually equipped with books of tables to allow them quickly to determine the correct drop needed for criminals of any weight.

The first person hanged with the help of a trapdoor was Laurence Shirley, the fourth Earl Ferrers, of Staunton Hall, Leicestershire. He shot John Johnson, his elderly land-steward, in a fit of aristocratic rage on Friday, 18 January 1760. Earl Ferrers was executed on Monday, 5 May, at Tyburn, and afterwards anatomized at Surgeons' Hall. Yet despite the success of the long drop method of hanging, it took many years to spread to all parts of the kingdom, and even longer to travel around the world. Indeed, there was some resistance to it, many believing that vicious felons should be made to suffer before they died.

Czarist Russia was certainly behind the times. Hanging was employed as a punishment for both murder and robbery in towns and cities throughout that huge country. Its inefficient use led to numerous mistakes being made, none of which was more bizarre and cruel than the following case. In the mid-nineteenth century, a provincial governor named Von Rohren was obliged to attend the execution of a Jewish robber, who was hanged by the neck until dead in accordance with the law. Yet when the felon was cut down and a doctor came to certify his death, it was found that the man's thick and bushy beard, which the hangman had failed to push out of the way, had saved him from being properly strangled. He was still alive, although unconscious, and the doctor thought that he would revive in about five minutes.

This astonishing development put Governor Von Rohren in a quandary. If he allowed the robber to recover, he was not permitted to hang him again; yet, on the other hand, he was obliged to carry out the execution fully. What should he therefore do? In the face of this difficulty, the governor showed great, if not wholly admirable, presence of mind. He simply ordered that the man be put in a coffin and buried before he woke up, thereby solving the problem at a stroke. And thus it was that another poor unfortunate came to be buried alive.

Von Rohren's action was distressingly similar to that of the impatient Irish husband mentioned by William Hone, who, writing of the events which happened on 15 July in his *Every-Day Book*, records that 'on this day in the year 1743 died, "in earnest", the wife of one Kirkeen, who was twice at Dublin ready to be buried; but came to life to her loving husband's disappointment, who fearing the like accident immediately put her into a coffin, had it nailed up, and buried her the next day.' To which Hone appends the following poem:

> As wrapp'd in death-like sleep Xantippe lay,
> 'Twas thought her soul had gently stole away;
> Th' officious husband, with pious care,
> Made no delay her funeral pile to rear:
> Too fast, alas! they move the seeming dead,

101

With heedless steps the hasty bearers tread,
And slipping thump the coffin on the ground,
Which made the hollow womb of earth resound;
The sudden shock unseal'd Xantippe's eyes,
O! whither do you hurry me? she cries;
Where is my spouse? – lo! the good man appears,
And like an ass hangs down his dangling ears;
Unwillingly renews his slavish life,
To hug the marriage chain, and hated wife.
For ten long tedious years he felt her pow'r,
At length 'twas ended in a lucky hour;
But now the husband, wiser than before,
Fearing a fall might former life restore,
Cries, 'Soft, my friends! let's walk in solemn measure,
Nor make a toil of that which gives us pleasure.'

While the death penalty has been abolished in Great Britain and elsewhere in Europe, hanging is still often used as a means of committing suicide. Suicides invariably employ the old-fashioned, short-drop method, often not even raising their feet off the ground, thereby bringing about their deaths, to all intents and purposes, by strangulation.

The attempted suicide of a 53-year-old woman, known as patient M.A.S., in 1883 is interesting in this regard. Her apparent death by self-inflicted hanging was reversed by prompt treatment, and her mental condition, which had previously been depressed, was greatly improved by her experience. Her surprising revival was reported in *The Lancet* by Dr Ernest White, the Senior Assistant Medical Officer at the Kent Lunatic Asylum, where the woman had been undergoing treatment for melancholia or depression.

M.A.S. was admitted to the Kent asylum on Tuesday, 3 October 1882, having become depressed and suicidal three months earlier. She had already made several unsuccessful attempts on her life, and she made another one on 10 October, when she tried to strangle herself with a stocking. Soon afterwards, she threw herself down a flight of stairs. Then, on Thursday, 4 January 1883, she attempted to strangle herself with an apron.

In the following months, thanks in part to the alert staff and in part to an amelioration of her condition, no further suicide attempt was made. But on Friday, 30 November of that year, she managed to slip herself into the bathroom of her ward, unattended by a staff member. There she hurriedly ripped up her clothing and underclothes to make an improvised rope, looped it around her neck and around the rung of a ladder positioned against one of the walls, and went limp. She was found hanging there about eight minutes later by a fellow patient, who raised the alarm, and she was cut down by staff two or three minutes after that. She was apparently quite dead. Dr White makes these observations on her lifeless condition:

> She was pulseless at the wrist and temples. There was no definite beat of the heart recognisable by the stethoscope. There was absolute cessation of all natural respiratory efforts, complete unconsciousness, total abolition of reflex action and motion, and galvanism with the ordinary magneto-electric machine failed to induce muscular contractions. The urine and faeces had been passed involuntarily during or immediately subsequent to the act of suspension.

The 'total abolition of reflex action and motion' applied equally to M.A.S.'s pupils, for while they were widely dilated, they showed no diminution of size when exposed to light, nor was there closure of the eyelids when the conjunctiva was touched. And lack of these reflexes, particularly the pupil reflex, as we have seen, is generally regarded as a reliable sign of death.

None the less, the junior assistant medical officer, J. Reynolds Salter, began immediate artificial respiration, using a manual method named after its inventor, Sylvester. This was continued, apparently unavailingly, for ten minutes, when a slight contractual twitch of the diaphragm was noticed, while a stethoscope revealed a rapid, asynchronous yet scarcely detectable beating of the heart. M.A.S.'s legs were raised and massaged towards her torso to promote circulation. The Sylvester artificial respiration method was continued, but another half-hour went by before further spontaneous contractions of the diaphragm occurred, and natural respiration did not establish itself until 5.45 p.m., and then only haltingly. Rather more bizarrely, the patient was then slapped with wet towels, which evidently had a positive stimulating effect because fifteen minutes later artificial respiration was no longer required. The still-unconscious woman was then cleaned and dried off, and put into a warm bed.

It was not until 11 p.m. that the pupils of her eyes started to contract in response to light, and she did not begin to come around until 5 a.m. By 9 a.m., notes Dr White, 'she was semiconscious, very drowsy'. Progress was maintained during the following few days and she took nourishment along with various prescribed nostrums, like ether in digitalis solution. On 6 December she was returned to her ward. By 12 December she was still experiencing muscular pains, although her general bodily health was good. But most surprising of all was the positive change in her mental condition. Dr White comments:

A curious fact in connexion with this case is that since this attempt at suicide she has steadily improved mentally, has lost her delusions, is cheerful and employs herself usefully with her needle. She converses rationally, and tells me she recollects the impulse by which she was led to hang herself, and remembers the act of suspension; but from that time her memory is a blank, until two days subsequently, when her husband came to see her and when she expressed great grief at having been guilty of such a deed.

104

Like the cases of drowning mentioned earlier, these short-drop hangings demonstrate that the human body is remarkably resilient to suffocation, in other words to lack of oxygen, which can be borne for far longer than supposed, and often does not have the rapid and irreversibly fatal effect it is popularly supposed to have. Thus no unputrefied hanged person should be regarded as dead until prolonged and vigorous restorative methods have been tried. There is always a chance that he or she may surprise all by 'returning from the dead'.

As we have seen, there are several cases of people who have survived being hanged for half an hour or more, but is there one that rivals in length the three-day submergence of Margaret Lasdotter described earlier? The answer, astonishingly, is yes. Indeed, the hanging in question exceeds the length of Margaret's immersion by two days. Hence it comes as no surprise to learn that the incident was, and indeed still is, regarded as a miracle.

The hanging took place at Bonn, in Germany, probably in September 1605, although the exact date is uncertain. The victim was a young Englishman named John Johnson, who was employed by his uncle, John Peterson, a merchant, at Antwerp. Mr Peterson had taken John with him to Frankfurt to attend the city's annual fair. When the fair ended, John was sent back to Antwerp ahead of his uncle, who had some other business to attend to. John returned via Bonn, where he stopped overnight at an inn. However, while he slept, the owner of the inn, who had stolen money and other valuables from another guest, planted it on the sleeping Englishman by concealing it in his purse.

The following morning, the unsuspecting John rose early and set off before anyone else was out of bed. But his departure marked him out as the thief when his fellow guest discovered that he had been robbed. The man, along with the thieving host, quickly organized a pursuit, and the Englishman was soon over-taken and stopped. A search of his purse revealed the stolen property and, despite vigorously protesting his innocence, John was immediately brought to trial, found guilty of the crime, and sentenced to be hanged. Moreover, the Bonn judge, angered by John's refusal to admit to the crime and by his blasphemous prayers to God to reveal his innocence by means of a miracle, ordered him to be strung up straight away.

Five days later, John Peterson, having completed his business in Frankfurt, came to the same inn on his way home, and was upset to learn that a young English guest at the inn had recently been hanged for theft. He was even more distressed at the description of the youth, who sounded very much like his beloved nephew. He therefore hurried to the gallows, where his worst fears were realized: the hanged man was indeed John Johnson. Seeing him, the uncle fell to the ground, overcome with grief. What happened next is almost beyond belief, for his nephew was not dead. The historian G.B. Harrison records that:

The young man there hanging spake to him, declaring that God had placed a stool under his feet, albeit unperceived by others, and that an angel fed him these five days. So the merchant went straightway to the magistrates who forthwith caused the young man to be taken down, who was then in perfect health, although he had hanged five days.

John was re-examined by the magistrates, who, awed by the miracle of his survival, listened with fresh and unprejudiced ears to the account of his innocence. The landlord of the inn was then summoned to appear before them, and when he clapped eyes on the man he thought was hanged, the wonder of it made him confess to his wrongdoing. He was therefore condemned to death, as a thief and a perjurer, by being burned alive. An apology was given to John, along with a compensation payment of 3,000 guilders, taken from the landlord's estate. He returned to Antwerp with his uncle, where he remained happily for many years, and prospered.

5   Burial Alive

Spirit of Earth! thy hand is chill:
I've felt thy icy clasp;
And, shuddering, I remember still
That stony-hearted grasp.

From 'The Three Guides' by Anne Brontë

It stands to reason that if some people, despite being medically certified as dead, spontaneously revive when they are laid out at home or in a mortuary, then there must be others who only come to after they have been buried. These poor souls are as unlucky as the former are lucky. They have little or no chance of escape, and the horror they must experience within the cramped confines of their pitch dark, virtually airless coffins is almost beyond imagination. God save us all from such a ghastly fate!

Yet living burials have always taken place, and in ancient times they were quite widely used as a punishment, notably for female members of religious sects or orders who impiously lost their virginity. In ancient Rome, for example, the sacred flame of Vesta, the goddess of the hearth and home, was kept alight in her temple by six specially trained attendants, the Vestales or Vestal Virgins. To ensure their sexual purity, girls as young as six were taken into the order and they had to remain virgins for the next thirty years, after which they could retire and marry if they wished. If at any time before that a Vestalis insulted the goddess by giving herself to a man, she was taken to an open space named the Campus

Sceleratus, which stood outside Rome, stripped of her sacred robes, and immured in an underground chamber or pit, along with a lighted candle, some bread and a little water mixed with milk, and left to die. Her seducer was punished equally unpleasantly by being whipped to death. Hence it comes as little surprise to note that during the 1,000-year period when the sacred flame of Vesta was kept burning by the Vestales, only eighteen ever violated their holy vow to the goddess and were punished by being buried alive.

This cruel pagan practice was adopted by Christians, who used it to punish any nun, the sacred bride of Christ, who cuckolded her blessed Saviour by fornicating with a man. However, the offending nun was not buried alive in a pit, but was instead immured in a recess hollowed out from one of her convent's thick walls, although like her pagan predecessor, she was shut in with a lighted candle, a glass of water and some bread, the opening then being closed by stones cemented into place. And there she was left to die a lonely and lingering death, of hunger and thirst. Such was also the unhappy fate of any nun caught trying to flee her convent and return to the outside world.

When Sir Walter Scott heard that a female skeleton had been discovered walled up at the Abbey of Coldingham, Yorkshire, he was sufficiently intrigued by the awful find to include the possibility of such entombment in his poem *Marmion*. Thus when Constance de Beverley, who has become a nun at Lindisfarne, is captured along with a male accomplice as she tries to escape, they are both put on trial. And behind their judges, the heads of three abbeys, stand what might be Constance's and her companion's last resting place.

> For there were seen in that dark wall,
> Two niches, narrow, deep and tall; –
> Who enters at such grisly door,
> Shall ne'er, I ween, find exit more.

In each a slender meal was laid,
Of roots, of water, and of bread.

Constance, being a spunky girl, does not quail before them. Rather, she warns the judges that when Marmion, who loves her, learns what they have done, he will kill them and pull down their abbeys. And her spirited speech contains these marvellous lines:

Now, men of death, work forth your will,
For I can suffer, and be still;
And come he slow, or come he fast,
It is but Death who comes at last.

The three judges, perhaps not surprisingly, are sufficiently persuaded by her grim portrayal of their likely futures, that they generously decide she and her helper are innocent and can go home. And so the two wall niches remain unoccupied.

Sometimes people are entombed alive through the simple malice of others. Such a terrifying end befell one of the emperors of the Eastern Roman Empire. His story is worth repeating not only because it is true, but because it warns how lust and ambition can turn even women into unfeeling monsters.

The unfortunate emperor was Zeno, who ruled at Constantinople from AD 474 until his heartless murder seventeen years later. He was an Isaurian chieftain by birth, whose tribal name was Tarasicodissa, and who adopted a Greek name (that of the founder of Stoic philosophy) when he married Ariadne, the daughter of Emperor Leo I, in 467. Leo died early in 474, and the couple's seven-year-old son, named after his grandfather, inherited the empire. As he was too young to rule, his duties were carried out by Zeno, who was made co-ruler by little Leo later that year. And when Leo II died not long afterwards, Zeno grabbed the reigns of power and proclaimed himself emperor.

Zeno had to contend with many problems, both internal and

external and was actually deposed for twenty months, from 475 to 477, by his brother-in-law Basilicus, at the instigation of Vernia, the Dowager Empress. He regained the empire, however, and went on to rule it until 491.

But if Zeno was a man of considerable toughness, shrewdness, and energy, he had two weaknesses, and these were exploited by the woman closest to him, his own wife, who used them to bring about his downfall. First, he was an epileptic, which was then a terrifying disease, as there were no drugs available to control its associated fits or seizures. He also had a serious drink problem and his heavy drinking tended to prompt an epileptic fit. The two together would have him falling helplessly down, writhing madly on the floor, foaming at the mouth, vomiting on and urinating in his purple robe, and generally presenting anything but an edifying sight. By 491, he was also an old man of sixty-five. Hence it was hardly surprising that Ariadne, who by then had a handsome toy-boy with ambitions to be Emperor, decided to replace her sick, elderly and debauched husband with her lover. Their marriage had, in any case, been a politically expedient union, not a love match.

Ariadne's opportunity came on the evening of Tuesday, 9 April 491, when Zeno gave a feast at his palace, which turned into yet another debauch. As expected, his carousing eventually brought on an epileptic fit, but one so violent that, when the spasm was over, he lay as if he was dead. Scarcely able to believe her luck, the Empress hurriedly bade his servants to remove him from the hall, carry him to his bedroom and undress him, and lay him on a bench. They were then instructed to go to bed and report to her at daybreak. Her moment had come.

At sunrise, she took the servants with her to Zeno's bedroom. The Emperor was found where he had been left, showing no apparent signs of life. Sniffing back a tear and declaring him to be dead, Ariadne ordered a shroud to be thrown over him, and then told the servants to pick him up and follow her to the sepulchre of the emperors. The hapless Zeno was placed inside and it was shut with a heavy stone slab. Ariadne then posted guards loyal to her around it, with instructions, on pain of death, to keep anyone away and to ignore any sounds that might come from it. Some hours later groans and lamentable cries did emerge from the sepulchre as Zeno finally returned to his senses, and he first ordered then implored those outside to release him from his stone prison, shouting that he was not dead. He was ignored, because those listening did not dare to do otherwise.

Some days later, when Ariadne thought her husband must really be dead, she had the sepulchre opened to make quite sure. His corpse was found inside, his body contorted from his efforts to escape, and with bloody strips visible on his bare arms, where he had ripped away the flesh with his teeth in a desperate attempt to assuage his hunger and his raging thirst. For in his last moments, the Emperor of the East had been forced to cannibalize himself.

Zeno's terrifying end was of course intentional, not accidental, but it is similar to what has happened on numerous occasions to others by unfortunate chance. Someone collapses and is thought to be dead; he (or she) is mistakenly buried alive, wakes in the darkness and silence of the tomb or grave sometime later, struggles to escape and screams for assistance. And when no help is forthcoming, he may be driven to eat his own flesh.

Those who are prematurely entombed uncoffined in vaults and sepulchres have a better chance of surviving the experience, if only because they have more room and more air. Their screams and cries are also more likely to be heard by those outside. Yet even when help arrives quickly, the experience is so terrifying that they may die anyway.

This was the fate of the tenth-century Arabian poet Hamadani, whose poetry was so beautiful that his contemporaries gave him the title Bedi-Alzeman or 'The Mavel of His Century'. Hamadani was struck down by apoplexy in 1007, which left him apparently dead. He was buried, like all followers of Islam, within twenty-four hours. His tomb was a stone vault, in which he eventually recovered consciousness. His frantic cries were heard, and his rescuers opened the tomb as fast as they were able. Yet although Hamadani was still alive when he was brought out, he died soon afterwards, a victim of shock and of his efforts to free himself.

Another marvel of his century, John Scot Duns, was a medieval sage whose philosophical works and religious commentaries earned him the title Doctor Subtilis. Duns suffered a brain haemorrhage at Cologne on Friday, 8 November 1308, and he was adjudged to be dead by the doctors who examined him. He was buried by his grieving friends and admirers, and that would have been the end of the matter had not his tomb afterwards been opened, presumably for the burial of someone else. To the horror of those present, his body was found to have turned over to one side, which immediately revealed he had come back to life. Further evidence was provided by his broken fingernails. But worse, the teeth marks on his hands and the flesh ripped from them, revealed that he had also tried to eat himself. He also had a gaping wound on his head, beneath which his skull was fractured. This suggested that the terrified academic, realizing the hopelessness of his situation, had killed himself by smashing his head against the stone side of his last resting place. His ghastly end led his friends to place a Latin inscription over his tomb, which in translation reads:

> Mark this man's demise, traveller.
> For here lies John Scot, once interr'd
> But twice dead; we are now shrewder
> And yet alive, who had then so erred.

John Scot Duns's desperate suicide within his tomb is not unique. A similar incident was reported in the *Norfolk Chronicle* of 9 January 1819, almost exactly 500 years later, and the man who so bizarrely killed himself was Baron Horstein, a courtier to

Maximilian Joseph, King of Bavaria. After apparently dying suddenly the Baron was given a magnificent state funeral and was then interred in his family's mausoleum. However, two days later the mausoleum was entered by workmen, who were horrified to find the body of the Baron lying behind its metal door, covered in blood. The court favourite had recovered from the trance into which he had fallen, and had then managed to force open the lid of his coffin. But he had evidently been unable to attract anyone's attention which, it seemed, had caused him to dash his 'brains out against the wall'. The account ends, perhaps not suprisingly, by stating: 'The Royal Family, and indeed the whole city, are plunged into grief at the horrid catastrophe.'

That self-cannibalism is not rare in such grim circumstances is revealed by the celebrated Italian anatomist Girolami Fabrizi of Aquapendente, who counted William Harvey, the disoverer of the circulation of the blood, among his pupils at Padua, where he held a professorship. In his *Opera Chirugica*, published in 1617, Fabrizi (who is better known by his Latinized name of Fabricius) makes reference to a letter he received from Dr John James Grafft, a physician of Neufchastel, in which Grafft recounts a case of the premature interment and subsequent revival of a young female, who later apparently ate several of her fingers.

He in a particular Manner makes mention of a young Lady of Auxbourg, who falling into a Syncope, in consequence of a Suffocation of the Matrix, was buried in a deep Vault, without being covered with Earth, because her Friends thought it sufficient to have the Vault carefully shut up. Some years after, however, one of the same Family happening to die, the Vault was opened, and the Body of the young Lady found on the Stairs at its Entry, without any Fingers on the Right Hand.

Furthermore, the *Undertakers' Journal and Funeral Directors' Review* of July 1889 not only declares in an article devoted to premature interments that 'it has been proved beyond all contradiction that there are more burials alive than is generally supposed', but goes on to mention a dreadful case of self-cannibalism very similar to the above, which was said to have happened in America thirty-five years earlier, in 1854. The details of the case were obtained, it was claimed, from the New York undertaker who arranged the funeral. Following the sudden death of his daughter, a Court Street baker had her coffin placed temporarily in a vault in order to give her elder siser, who lived in distant St Louis, time to get to New York and take a last look at her before she was buried. This was possible because the death occurred in winter, which prevented decomposition from happening. But alas, the fond farwell turned into a nightmare. 'The sister came, the vault was opened, the lid of the coffin taken off, when to the unutterable horror of the friends assembled, they found the grave clothes in shreds, and the fingers of both hands eaten off. The girl had been buried alive.'

However, while I am inclined to accept the veracity of Grafft's account, I reather suspect that the story of the baker's daughter may simply be an updated, and geographically shifted, version of the same happening, with the added exaggeration that the fingers of both the girl's hands were eaten rather than those of the right one alone. For as I pointed out in my book *Supernatural Disappearances*, strange incidents, whether real or imaginary, have a remarkable habit of being mysteriously moved to a distant setting (often from Europe to America and vice versa) and acquiring a later date, with some of their details changing in the process.

However, there is evidence which we cannot ignore. An account in *Eddowes's Journal* dated 24 August 1844, tells of the rescue some days earlier of a child as he was being buried alive at a cemetery in Arles, France. While the sexton was busy filling in the grave, the boy suddenly woke from his trance or lethargy and cried out. Hearing the yell, the startled sexton hurriedly dug up and removed the coffin from the ground, then ran with it to the house of the boy's mother. When its lid was unscrewed, the child was found alive and was brought to a full recovery. But although this particular incident had a happy ending, it was followed by these terrifying lines: 'Not long ago, in making a grave in the same cemetery, a coffin was broken into, and it was found that the occupant had revived after burial, and had gnawed the flesh of both wrists before life was finally extinguished.'

Moreover Dr Peron-Autret, in his book *Buried Alive*, published in 1979, describes how he and his colleague Dr Louis-Claude Vincent interviewed sixty grave-diggers working in cemeteries in Paris and elsewhere in France, all of whom had been in their employment for many years, to discover if any had ever come across corpses which showed signs that they had been buried alive. To the pair's astonishment, every one of them answered that they had. Dr Peron-Autret writes:

The most frequently observed phenomenon was a skeleton with all the bones intact save those of hand and arm, which had been gnawed, as if by rats – except, as they pointed out, how could a rat get inside a sealed coffin, and why should it only ever attack hands and arms? None of the coffins had shown any signs of having been broken into, and no bones other than human were ever discovered. What most of the coffins had shown signs of, however, were internal marks as of frenzied scraping and tearing by fingernails. One man even went so far as to speak of fingernails which had become 'encrusted in the wood'.

When Dr Peron-Autret inquired why they did not report their gruesome finds to the press, most of the grave-diggers claimed that they preferred to blank out what they had seen, not even discussing it with each other. Moreover, they feared that once it was known that such things happened people would start having their loved ones cremated, which would put them out of work!

But while those who revive in their coffins may eat parts of their hands or arms, or perhaps bite chunks from them in their state of terror, it is more usual to find physical damage caused by frantic efforts to escape. The following is an example of such self-injury.

During the Second World War a German bomb accidentally struck a cemetery in south-east London, whose name shall be left unrecorded in order to spare the descendants of those buried there the horror of knowing that they may have been interred alive. The explosion blasted out a crater and of course blew open many graves, splintering coffins and exposing partially decayed bodies as well as bare bones. The grave-diggers who worked to rebury the bodies were astonished to notice that some of them exhibited distinct signs of having returned to life within the grave. Not only was skin found to be abraded from the hands and knees, but the fingernails were split and broken and had fabric strands or wood splinters beneath them, and some bodies even had broken fingers and occasionally toes. These awful discoveries were kept secret from the public, but one of the older grave-diggers later told William Repton, a local policeman, about them, whose daughter Wendy was my informant. She said that the disclosure had shocked her father so much that it prompted him to make her and her mother promise to have him cremated when he died. Yet although his reaction was, and is, entirely under-standable, the fact remains that while cremation will prevent premature burial, it may result in an equally horrible death – by being burned alive.

Such self-inflicted injuries were also a feature of a case reported in the *Annual Register* and *The Gentleman's Magazine* in 1776. In July of that year, at Fulham, a coachman who had gone to stable his horses was found lying senseless in the straw, having apparently collapsed and died. A funeral service was conducted in a local church and the man was afterwards buried in the churchyard. However, one of the congregation suddenly announced that during the service he had heard 'a rumbling and a struggling in the coffin', which suggested to him that the coachman was not dead. His testimony was sufficient to persuade the coachman's friends to have his coffin dug up. 'On opening it, there appeared evident proofs, that the unhappy man, though absolutely dead, had come to himself, as his body was very much bruised in several places, some of which were still bleeding; and there appeared besides a quantity of blood in the coffin.'

And in the early years of the nineteenth century, the body of a prematurely buried Welsh seaman named Stephen Evans displayed comparable injuries on being exhumed. Evans, a deckhand aboard the *Harriot*, which at the time was anchored at Custom House Quay in Milford, had one morning gone ashore and got drunk on neat alcohol at a public house. Returning unsteadily to the vessel, he fell into such a deep sleep in his hammock that it was thought by his crew mates that he had died. A coffin was sent for and the apparently dead man was nailed up in it; both were then stored for a couple of days in the ship's hold. Finally at one o'clock on the afternoon of Thursday, 21 June 1821, Stephen Evans was buried in Selskar churchyard, in Wexford.

The following day, about twenty-four hours later, two small boys went into Selskar churchyard to collect birds' eggs. While one climbed up into a tree to reach a nest, the other watched his ascent from the top of the newly filled-in grave. Suddenly, the latter heard what he described as 'a strange noise' coming from the grave, which sent both lads running in terror from the churchyard, shouting out what had happened. Aghast at the news, people hurried to the churchyard, where they took turns in shovelling away the earth from Stephen Evans's coffin. But none was prepared for the awful sight that greeted them when the coffin was finally opened, for it was evident that the sailor had returned to life. The *Wexford Herald* reported:

The struggles of the unhappy victim appeared to have been violent! The nose was somewhat flattened by striking against the lid of the coffin, the hands and knees were contracted as much as the situation would permit, and a slight excoriation of the skin was perceptible on the upper part of the knees. The body was examined by several medical gentlemen present, who pronounced that life had totally left it.

Over half a century later some discussion of burial alive was occasioned in *The Lancet*, when David Williams, the vicar of Llanelly, in Wales, wrote in May 1884 to say that when a brick tomb in his churchyard was opened to inter another person, it was discovered that 'the lid of the coffin had been forced upwards against the stone slabs, leaving an opening in the coffin of about eight inches, the right arm and right leg of the woman's body hanging over the left side of the coffin, and her face lying sideways, or nearly downwards, the right knee being placed against the north side of the grave, outside the coffin'. The elderly woman, the vicar explained, had been buried eleven years earlier, and he asked *The Lancet*'s readers if they thought it possible that she had mistakenly been buried alive.

It was pointed out by correspondents that if the lid of the coffin had been properly screwed down, the woman could not possibly have forced it open if she had revived, nor could any spontaneous movements, brought about by muscle contractions during rigor mortis, have caused her to turn over and thrust an arm and a leg out of the coffin, for such movements would certainly have taken place during the five days that went by before she was buried, if she had died when she apparently did.

Although the vicar interviewed the carpenter, who said that he did screw down the coffin lid, as one might expect, he apparently did not examine the tomb's interior for any sign of screws, nor did he report any splitting of the coffin's woodwork, which must have occurred if a build-up of putrefying gases within it had blown the lid off. Such post-mortem explosions do occur, as readers of my book *Doubles* will know, for in it I recorded the bizarre bursting of Queen Elizabeth I's body and coffin only three days after her death. The toxicity and inflammability of these gases are considered in a later chapter.

So if the coffin lid was actually not secured, then the woman may well have returned to life in the coffin and half climbed out of it, but if the lid was screwed down then its opening and her movements must, I believe, remain an enigma.

A correspondent from Bayswater, whose letter was published in *The Lancet* on 10 June under the initials H.S., did take the opportunity of describing two bodies he had seen in the crypt of Bordeaux Cathedral, which showed signs that they had been buried prematurely. He wrote:

In the case of one of these bodies, which was found lying on its side, the legs were drawn up nearly to a level with the abdomen, and the arms were in such a position as to convey the impression that both they and the legs had been used in a desperate but futile attempt to push out the side of the coffin, whilst the look of horror remaining on the face was simply indescribable. In the other case, the body was found lying on its face, the arms extended above the head as if attempting to push out the top of the coffin.

Another dreadful instance of premature burial happened at the village of Douglas, near Cork, Ireland, in May 1894. The unfortunate victim was an elderly labourer, who had apparently died suddenly. On the day of his burial he was carried to the churchyard in his coffin and, after a brief service, lowered into the grave. A few of the man's friends and some family members were there to bid him goodbye, and one or two of them threw clods of earth on to the lid of the coffin. The thump these made when they landed apparently reanimated the 'corpse', for almost immediately afterwards the sound of movement was heard from within the coffin, which alerted those at the graveside that he was not dead. The coffin was hurriedly pulled out of the grave and opened, but unhappily the recovered labourer did not survive the terrifying experience.

He was found at his last gasp, face downwards in the coffin, having turned right over in a frantic but futile bid to burst it open; and his features, contorted and almost black, bore unmistakable signs of the fearful agony of his real end. It was conjectured that the unfortunate man had been in a state of trance.

A premature burial in Ireland that had a much happier ending occurred at Cork on 7 June 1815, according to the *Lady's Magazine*, and involved a soldier of the 93rd Regiment, which was quartered at the barracks there. Following his apparent death, he was laid out for two days and then taken, in his coffin, by his comrades-in-arms to St Nicholas's churchyard for burial. As they placed the coffin into the grave, a sound of struggling came from within it, which quickly had the soldiers peering through the cracks in the crudely made receptacle, whereupon they 'found the man whom they were burying, endeavouring with his hands and knees to force up the lid. To their astonishment they found their comrade still alive, and conveyed him home in the open coffin'.

It was 'a strange groaning in the ground' that alerted passers-by to the fact that Lawrence Cawthorn, a butcher of St Nicholas Shambles, in London, had been too hastily buried. His premature interment, however, was not accidental but the result of an over-dose of opium given to him by his wife, who had hoped thereby to get her hands on his money. When the drugged Lawrence had lain sleeping and barely breathing for a night and a day, Mrs Cawthorn announced that he had died. She then had him buried, despite knowing that he was really still alive. This grievous act of female criminality happened in 1661, and it was recorded, although hopefully not as a recommended way of dealing with husbands with savings, in the *Ladies' Dictionary: Being an Entertainment for the Fair Sex*, published in 1694.

Unfortunately for Mrs Cawthorn, her husband was buried on a Saturday, which meant that the churchyard where he lay was visited the following morning by numerous people on their way to church. Several heard the odd noise mentioned above, which became gradually louder, 'tho' a kind of hollow sound', and which prompted them to bring it to the attention of the churchwardens. They did not act immediately, but waited until the next day, by which time they had concluded that Lawrence Cawthorn might have been buried alive and that they should therefore take steps to find out if he had. Their delay, however, was the death of poor Lawrence, for the *Ladies' Dictionary* reveals: 'This new Grave was opened, and the Body found warm, tho' dead with the stifling Vapours and violent Beatings against the Sides of the Coffin; upon News of which the barbarous old Woman fled, and we do not hear she was ever found again.'

Early in the following century a Mrs Blunden of Basingstoke suffered a similar fate, although she brought her untimely inter-ment on herself, for she mistakenly ingested too large a quantity of laudanum or opium solution, which threw her into a lethargy so profound that it was mistaken for death. Her revival was also revealed by noises coming from her grave, but the spark of life had quite departed by the time her coffin was opened. Further proof of her living state was shown by the water vapour, emitted with her breath, that had condensed on the underside of the coffin's lid.

It was once a common belief that if a murderer touched his or her victim's corpse, the latter would start to bleed afresh from its wounds, thereby identifying the culprit of the crime. Such 'trial by corpse' was carried out as late as the seventeenth century, and the fact that the corpse did on occasions actually bleed or even move suggests that the person was not really dead but was instead lying in a trance. For, if he (or she) was aware of what was going on around him, then the emotions engendered by the touch of his murderer may have accelerated his heartbeat sufficiently to prompt fresh eruptions of blood.

In 1629, a murder took place in a Hertfordshire village which resulted in those accused of the crime being subjected to this test and which produced a result so staggering that the case deserves inclusion here. The remarkable affair was 'fair written with his own hands' by Serjeant-at-law (later Sir) John Maynard, who attended the High Court trial of the four people involved.

A woman named Joan Norkot was found dead in bed one morning with her throat cut, and with a blood-stained knife sticking in the floor several feet from the bed. Her baby was asleep beside her, while in the adjoining room, which gave access to hers, were her mother-in-law Mary Norkot, her husband's sister Agnes and Agnes's spouse John Okeman. Joan's husband, Arthur Norkot, was absent from the house that night on unspecified business. Because the three relatives claimed that no third party could possibly have done the deed, it was initially concluded by the coroner's jury that Joan Norkot had taken her own life. She was accordingly buried soon afterwards in unconsecrated ground.

Although the village is not named by Maynard, I have discovered that a John Ockeman married Ann Norket on Thursday, 1 November 1615, at Great Berkhampstead, in eastern Herfordshire. Indeed, the name Norkot or Norket seems to be common to the area. A Mary Norket, for example, who may be Arthur's and Agnes's (or Ann's) mother, christened another son, Edward Norket, at nearby Tring, on 5 October 1614. This suggests that Great Berkhampstead is likely to have been the village.

In the following days and weeks, village and neighbourhood opinion decided that Joan had really been murdered and that those responsible were her relatives; no motive was suggested, but it was common knowledge that the relationship between Joan and her husband Arthur had been volatile. The idea that a murder had been committed followed from the discovery that Joan's neck had also been broken; she obviously could not have both cut her throat and broken her neck, for by doing one she would effectively have prevented herself from doing the other.

The coroner's jury therefore requested that Joan Norkot's body be exhumed, and that Mary Norkot, the Okemans and Arthur Norkot be made to touch it, in order to undergo 'trial by corpse'. And so, thirty days after she had been buried, Joan's cadaver was dug up and laid on the grass beside the grave, where, in the presence of a throng of witnesses, the ancient test was conducted. What happened next was amazing, to say the least.

The appellers did touch the dead body, whereupon the brow of the dead, which was of a livid carrion colour began to have a dew of gentle sweat [which] ran down in drops on the face, and the brow turned and changed to a lively and fresh colour, and the dead opened one of her eyes and shut it again, and this opening of the eye was done three several times. She likewise thrust out the ring or marriage finger three times and pulled it in again, and the finger dropt blood from it on the grass.

While these ghastly happenings terrifed Joan's in-laws and caused them to fail the 'trial by corpse' test, they were none the less acquitted by the jury at Hertford assizes. However, this was such a contentious verdict, and one that so obviously went against the available evidence, that on the advice of the judge an appeal was lodged against it, in the name of Joan Norkot's child. The appeal was eventually heard in the High Court, where to everyone's satisfaction the verdict was overturned and Arthur Norkot, Mary Norkot and Agnes Okeman were convicted of Joan's murder, although John Okeman was acquitted. Shortly afterwards Arthur Norkot and his mother were hanged. Agnes Okeman, however, was 'spared execution, being with child'.

If we compare the above description of Joan Norkot's corpse – its sweating, coloration and movements – with those of people mentioned earlier who were either about to be buried alive or who had actually been consigned to the grave, we cannot help but notice the similarities between them. This suggests that not only was Joan Norkot alive when she was discovered in bed with her throat cut and her neck broken, but she was still alive when she was buried, and remained alive underground in a comatose state for thirty days. Indeed, her survival is a compelling example of the powers of endurance of the human body.

There were a number of factors which doubtlessly helped her grim subterranean continuance for so long. First, her coffin was almost certainly constructed from rough-hewn boards; the spaces between these would have allowed the free passage of air. Secondly, because burials were shallow in the early 1600s, her coffin would probably only have had loose soil to the depth of 2 or 3 feet shovelled in above it. This too would have enabled an exchange of gases. Thirdly, her oxygen needs would have been reduced by her comatose state, as would her energy needs. And fourthly, rainwater percolating down through the shallow soil into the coffin would have been enough to satisfy her thirst in those moments when she revived sufficiently to open her mouth and swallow.

Any doubts that Joan Norkot could possibly survive for a month without food and with little water, may be dispelled by the following modern case, with which her story shares some parallels.

In October 1997, a 26-year-old Bath University student named Catherine Roberts suffered a brain haemorrhage, which left her, despite undergoing an emergency operation, in a seemingly irreversible coma. She was put on a life-support machine, given fluids intravenously, and fed through a tube inserted via her nose into her stomach.

Her medical team held out so little hope for her survival, however, that when her nasal feeding tube fell out one day, they decided not to replace it. Yet astonishingly, Catherine continued living, without food, for two months, until her doctors, in order to speed up what they firmly believed was her inevitable end, stopped giving her fluids. Her parents were informed that her breathing tube would be withdrawn in one week. This news prompted them to arrange Catherine's funeral and to reserve a grave site for her.

But the day before her oxygen supply was due to be turned off, Catherine's mother Wendy noticed a slight change in her, which suggested that she may have regained some degree of consciousness. So she said, 'If you can hear me Catherine, blink.' And to her delight and astonishment, Catherine blinked. She then asked her daughter to poke out her tongue if she could understand her, and again she complied. Indeed, Catherine Roberts had not only survived without food for two months and without water for several days, but had emerged from what was feared to be a persistent vegetative state. She has since made slow but steady progress, and while badly handicapped, is now studying for an Open Univesity degree.

Another woman who was mistakenly buried but who managed to survive the awful experience, only to die later from a secondary cause, was a 52-year-old from Segovia, in north-central Spain, whom I shall call Inez Martinez.

One morning in January 1977, Senora Martinez was knocked off her moped and apparently killed instantly. She was buried with traditional haste that afternoon, because it is usual in hot countries, when refrigeration is not available and where putrefaction proceeds rapidly, for bodies to be temporarily consigned to the ground, while arrangements are made for their funeral.

Six days later the coffin was exhumed and taken to the local church, where it was placed on a bier in the nave. The funeral service then began, and some liquid was seen oozing from one corner of the coffin. This caused no alarm as it was thought to be part of the normal secretions engendered by putrefaction. However not long afterwards, during moments of silence in the service, a scraping noise was heard coming from within the coffin. The service was stopped, and the shocked yet scarcely-believing mourners hurriedly unscrewed the coffin's lid to find out if Inez Martinez was still alive or if something else was responsible for the sound.

When the lid was finally removed, the sight and odours that greeted those gathered around the coffin were almost too revolting to bear. Inez was indeed still among the living, if only just. Her pale, ghastly face was covered in sweat, her fingernails were broken and her fingertips were bloody from clawing frantically against the wooden interior, while the skin and flesh had been scraped from her elbows to such an extent that the tendons lay exposed like white cords around them. The fluid dripping from the coffin was not a product of putrefaction, but voided urine. Inez Martinez had survived underground for an incredible six days, the victim of shocking medical incompetence and haste, for she had been incorrectly certified as dead at the accident site. She was rushed to hospital and placed in intensive care, yet despite every effort to bring her back from the brink, she suffered a cerebral embolism one month later, followed by respiratory paralysis, which irrevocably killed her. Her second funeral service was doubly solemn; it also reached its end without interruption from its subject.

This dreadful case was important in bringing home to the Spanish authorities that too rapid burial leads, on occasion, to such tragedies. Indeed, Dr Peron-Autret says that forty-seven Spaniards were rescued from their coffins in the two-year period between 1976 and 1978, either because like Inez Martinez they had managed to alert those attending their funeral services that they were still alive, or because they had produced a suspicious noise from their graves, as Stephen Evans did. More chillingly, he believes that many more living burials go undetected.

In Chapter 2, I mentioned several instances of people who, while in a trance or a cataleptic state, narrowly escaped being buried alive. Their trauma was made worse by the fact that they knew what was about to happen to them. We can therefore only guess at the horror felt by those who are prematurely interred, especially as few such unfortunates are ever rescued from their underground prison. One who was, however, was a 25-year-old Scot from Edinburgh. According to an edition of *The Undertakers' Journal* published in 1904, he was buried 'some years' earlier after having apparently died following a short illness, but was quickly dug up again and saved. This is what he wrote of the experience:

It was the black loneliness of the situation, and the thought that I would come out of the trance state before death ensued, that caused me most concern, and I wondered if there was any way by which I could quickly destroy myself when nature asserted itself. As I lay there, six feet below the surface, I wondered who my neighbour was on the right, and who on the left, and if they, too, had been buried alive. Suddenly I felt a muscle twitch. 'It's coming now,' I thought; 'a moment more and I shall be struggling for breath.' I gave a little gasp, but the air seemed laden with lead, and trying to breathe was like drawing foetid water into my lungs. I had resolved to die with my hands folded on my breast, so that if my body was ever exhumed my relatives would not suspect the awful truth, but I could not lie still.

The struggle began, and I fought in my narrow prison-house as a man only fights for life. Horrible as it was, I seemed to hear my wife's voice ringing in my ears. It was a cry of agony, and I tried to answer it, but could not. All at once a

succession of thunder peals shook my prison-house, caused
by the heavy blows of axes breaking open the box containing
my coffin. A moment later I was lying on the grass in my wife's
arms. After my interment she conceived the notion that I had
been buried alive, and, to calm her fears, the grave was
opened. I went into it a young man, and came out old, after
an incarceration of only three hours.

This young man was happily saved by his wife's seemingly irra-
tional belief that he was still alive, but would she be able to effect
such a rapid exhumation today? The answer is no, she would not.
A modern wife would instead be offered counselling to come to
terms with her grief, for it would automatically be assumed that
she was deluded and that her husband was as dead as the prover-
bial dodo. And anyhow, exhumation needs official permission;
very good reasons are required before it is granted, and a belief
that the buried person is still alive is not one of them. Moreover,
as an exhumation application takes several days or even weeks to
process, there is little hope that its execution would lead to the
successful rescue of someone prematurely buried. He (or she)
would probably have expired long before the grave-digger's spade
finally uncovered his coffin's lid.

The above examples of those lucky enough to have been
released alive from their graves may help us to evaluate the raising of Lazarus, perhaps Christ's most celebrated miracle, which is
described in St John's Gospel. 'Now a certain man was sick,
named Lazarus, of Bethany, the town of Mary and her sister
Martha.' So begins the eleventh chapter of St John. Lazarus is in
fact the brother of Mary and Martha, all three of whom are
known and loved by Jesus. Jesus was then about 20 miles away, at
Bethabara, beyond the Jordan, and Mary and Martha anxiously
sent word to him there of their brother's illness.

But Jesus, rather surprisingly, did not immediately leave for
Bethany to heal Lazarus by touch, nor did he direct healing

words of power across the miles to effect the same result. Instead he remained in Bethabara for another two days, commenting, perhaps significantly, that 'This sickness is not unto death' and then saying: 'Our friend Lazarus sleepeth; but I go, that I may wake him out of sleep.' These are admittedly psychic impressions, but if true, they suggest that while the sickness had not killed Lazarus, it had put him into a trance or a coma.

But later, 'Jesus said unto them plainly, Lazarus is dead.' Following this surprise announcement he departed for Bethany accompanied by some of his disciples. Yet when he finally arrrived at Bethany, it transpired that Lazarus had not only died but had been interred in a tomb for four days. His sisters were grieving his loss, and Martha was somewhat angry with Jesus for not coming to heal him. Yet she added, 'But I know, that even now, whatsoever thou wilt ask of God, God will give it thee.' To which Jesus replied: 'Thy brother shall rise again.'

Going to the cave in which Lazarus lay, Jesus commanded his disciples to roll away the stone from its entrance. Martha objected to this, pointing out 'Lord, by this time he stinketh: for he has been dead four days.' To which Jesus replied, 'Said I not unto thee, that, if thou wouldst believe, thou shouldest see the glory of God?'

Then, and perhaps significantly, after thanking God for always hearing him, Jesus 'cried with a loud voice, "Lazarus, come forth." And he that was dead came forth, bound hand and foot with grave-clothes: and his face was bound about with a napkin. Jesus said unto them, "Loose him, and let him go." '

The fact that Lazarus did not putrefy after four days surely indicates that he was not really dead, but was instead lying in a trance or a similar comatose state. Indeed, Jesus's initial comment that Lazarus was not dead but sleeping suggests as much, and may even mean that Lazarus was prone to such attacks of insensibility and that Jesus knew this. Likewise his crying to him 'with a loud voice' suggests that Lazarus was being shocked into wakefulness, for as we have seen, the shouting of someone's name or another loud sound can rouse him or her from a trance or catalepsy.

Taken together, these facts suggest that Jesus did not raise Lazarus from real death, but rather from apparent death. The Jews of that time (AD 33), as today, buried their dead within twenty-four hours, and such speed means that if life has not entirely left a body, the person may regain consciousness in the grave. Moslems also follow the same rapid interment procedures. This implies that far more Jews and Moslems may be buried alive than Christians, especially as they also frown on autopsies.

A similar but even earlier miracle of resuscitation was performed by the Greek philosopher and wonder-worker Empedocles, who in the third year of the eighty-fourth Olympiad (i.e. 442–41 BC) brought back to life a woman named Ponthia, who was about to be interred. Like her saviour, she was a citizen of the Greek colonial town of Agrigentum (or Acragas), in Sicily. And among Christian saints, St Martin is credited with resurrecting one of his female disciples, who had, perhaps significantly, died suddenly after falling ill with fever, and later a slave who had hanged himself. In both cases he is said to have lain upon the corpse and prayed for its revival, which suggests that his own warmth played some part in reviving the person concerned.

Anxiety about being buried alive, which is generally caused by people being buried too quickly or their deaths not being properly certified (although doctors are far from infallible in this regard), grew during the eighteenth century. It was encouraged by the increasing number of cases coming to light and by the publicity they received, as well as by the warnings of physicians like Jacobus Winslow in France and, in the early part of the nineteenth century, Joseph Taylor and the Revd Walter Whiter in England.

But how frequently does premature interment happen? Certainly the likelihood was greater in the past, when there was no law obliging a doctor to examine a supposedly dead person before he signed his or her death certificate. Indeed Colonel Edward P. Vollum, a doctor with the United States Army and the co-author, with William Tebb, of *Premature Burial*, writing in the April 1904 issue of *The Undertakers' Journal*, made the following chilling disclosure:

> The estimates of such disasters are based upon the discoveries made when the dead are removed from cemeteries, as is done in some great cities every five years. A portion of the skeletons are always found turned to one side or on the face, twisted, or with the hands up to the head. These are counted as living burials.

He goes on to add that 'a personal inquiry in Europe and in the United States for several years past has convinced me that they are alarmingly frequent'. His findings led him to recommend that in future all American soldiers who fell in battle and who were not embalmed should be buried with a phial of chloroform in their hand. This would enable them to kill themselves painlessly if they reawakened in their coffins. Needless to say, his sensible advice was ignored.

Colonel Vollum quotes two French authorities, the first of whom, Dr Lionce Lenormand, concluded that one in every thousand people interred annually is buried alive, while the second, M. le Guen, opted for the slightly higher figure of two per thousand. A fellow American, however, Carl Sextus of New York, who had collected some 1,500 cases of premature burial over a period of eigheen years, believed that the number of live interments was ten times higher than M. le Guen's estimate, averaging 2 per cent per annum.

Four years later, Dr John Dixwell of Harvard University, who had himself once been certified as dead and narrowly escaped burial alive, told an examining committee of the Massachusetts Legislature, which was examining a bill to require local boards of health to certify all deaths properly, that his research indicated, like that of M. le Guen, that two persons out of every thousand were buried alive.

An English doctor named J.C. Ouseley, on the other hand, had earlier claimed that an average of 2,700 people were buried alive in England and Wales every year. Quite how he arrived at this figure is by no means clear, but if we take the year 1895 as an example, when there were 568,997 recorded deaths, virtually all of whom were buried, this would mean that the number of living burials averages 4.7 per thousand (or 0.47 per cent), which is over twice as high as that suggested by M. le Guen and Dr J Dixwell, although considerably less than the 2 per cent proposed by Carl Sextus.

But even that 2 per cent is an underestimate where burials during wartime are concerned, as mistakes are far more likely to happen in the confusion of battle, especially when there are large numbers of injured and comatose men to be examined, and when the medical personnel are insufficiently trained to distinguish the apparently dead from the truly dead, which, as we have seen, is no easy matter even in peace-time.

In 1950, while carrying out checks on the water supplies needed to maintain American war-dead cemeteries in France and elsewhere in Europe, Dr Louis-Claude Vincent happened to discover that those buried in them (totalling 150,000 corpses) were being systematically exhumed, and that the skeletons in the plain white coffins were being secretly examined, cleaned and wired up. They were then rehoused in new mahogany coffins, each of which was placed entire in an oak box and afterwards covered in lead, before being returned to its grave. This enormous and very expensive operation was being carried out by the United States Government in order to learn, so Dr Vincent ascertained, how many of the troops had been mistakenly buried alive.

When the work was completed, the results showed that 4 per

cent of those buried, or 6,000 individuals altogether, had been interred while they were still living. These soldiers, sailors and airmen had, in other words, suffered twice, having first been shot or blown up for their country, and then, after they had spontaneously revived, found themselves ghoulishly imprisoned in a narrow pine coffin, where they died unheard and unheeded. No other statistic of the Second World War is more shocking than this.

Another thorough investigation of the same kind took place at the end of the Vietnam War, prior to the return of American dead to the United States. Nothing had changed in the intervening thirty years, as 4 per cent of the buried heroes, or 2,000 individuals in total, were revealed to have been buried alive. It was enough to make American mothers weep, if they had ever found out what had happened to their sons. But by exhuming their coffins and destroying the frightful evidence within, the United States Government made sure that no mother would ever learn that anything untoward had happened, let alone that their boys had paid such a terrible and unnecessary price.

We cannot of course know exactly how many people are buried alive in Great Britain each year. But by using some of the above percentages we can perhaps get a rough idea. Certainly the treatment of the dead in some respects has greatly improved. They are no longer buried so hastily, and each death must be certified by a qualified doctor. But against this must be set the fact that while deaths from infectious diseases have fallen dramatically since the discovery of penicillin and other antibiotics in the 1930s, those due to heart attacks and cerebral strokes have equally dramatically increased. And these produce collapses that can easily be confused with death.

But let us make some estimates. In 1996, for example, 179,706 people were buried in Great Britain. If one per thousand (or 0.1 per cent) was a living burial, 179 people would have been prematurely consigned to the grave. Two per thousand would give double that number, or 358. And if Ouseley's extrapolated 4.7 per thousand is taken, the number rises to 841. If 1 per cent of the burials were mistakes, then the number of those interred before their time shoots up to 1,797, and if 2 per cent was the actual average, then a shocking 3,594 people did not die in their beds, but in their coffins.

I will end this chapter by recording an unusual and puzzling experience that happened to Mrs Brenda Collins of Poole, in Dorset, and which she related to me. She was once a church-cleaner, and on Easter Saturday 1978, a lovely sunny day, she was at the church, accompanied by her then husband and their two children, sweeping and dusting in readiness for the following day's services. But suddenly she felt the air become icy cold and at that moment she noticed an old man walking around the church, peering about him as if he had lost something. This is what she said he looked like:

The man's clothes were Victorian. He was short and stout, and had sideboards. His suit was dark brown, with a pale stripe in it, and he had a pocket watch on a chain. I remember this quite clearly as my grandfather wore one. He looked quite normal, walking all around the altar and through the choir stalls, then out through the door to the back rooms of the church. I asked the lady who was arranging the flowers who he was, but she said, 'There's no one here.'

'Yes, there is,' I insisted. 'He's over there.'

Despite the flower lady's apparent inability to see the man, he reappeared shortly afterwards and walked across to Brenda and her ex-husband and children. He reached out and touched one of Brenda's hands. His skin, she noticed, was colder than ice.

His fingers were bleeding and very dirty, with dirt under all his finger nails. His brown shoes were worn through at the toes . . . . My ex asked him where he had come from. He replied, 'You could say I have kicked and clawed my way out of my grave.' Then he turned and walked away. I followed him outside but he had disappeared. The church went warm again.

Brenda says that the present church has no graveyard, and adds that although she continued working there for another five years, she never saw the man again. She has no idea who he was, but suspects, and I am inclined to agree with her, that he may have been the wraith of a man who was once buried alive.

6 Remarkable Releases

                                And then,
Then I saw something more – Queen Mary's vault,
And – it was open!...
                                Then, I heard a voice,
A strange deep broken voice, whispering love
In soft French words, that clasped and clung like hands;
And then – two shadows passed against the West.

                From 'The Burial of a Queen' by Alfred Noyes

In his *Voyage through Italy*, Francois Maximilian Misson sagely remarks that 'the number of Persons who have been inter'd as dead, when they were really alive, is very great in comparison to those who have been happily rescued from the Grave'. As we have seen, this is all too true.

In this chapter I shall look at some amazing resurrections that happened either by pure chance, through love or from greed (hardly surprisingly, the last are the most numerous), and which are all classic cases.

Pure chance, coupled with greed, is invoked by William Shakespeare to account for the rescue of Thaisa, the wife of Pericles, from her improvised coffin in his play, *Pericles, Prince of Tyre*. While the royal couple are on board a ship in the Mediterranean, a storm breaks out and prompts the pregnant Thaisa to give birth, following which she apparently dies. A sailor tells Pericles, 'Sir, we have a chest beneath the hatches, caulk'd and bitumed ready.' As the storm worsens, threatening shipwreck, Pericles has his dead wife put in it and thrown overboad. Later, the chest is found washed ashore on the coast of Asia Minor by two servants of Cerimon, a merchant at Ephesus. They carrry it to him. Feeling its tempting weight, Cerimon remarks:

> Wrench it open straight;
> If the sea's stomach be o'ercharg'd with gold,
> 'Tis a good constraint of fortune it belches upon us.

But within they find the beautiful Thaisa, accompanied by some jewels and a letter from Pericles, requesting that the finder bury his wife and keep the jewels as payment. Cerimon, however, knowing how easily errors can be made when determing death, is by no means certain that Thaisa is really dead. He exclaims:

> For look, how fresh she looks. They were too rough
> That threw her in the sea. Make fire within;
> Fetch hither all the boxes in my closet.
> Death may usurp on nature many hours,
> And yet the fire of life kindle again
> The overpress'd spirits. I heard
> Of an Eyptian, that had nine hours lien dead,
> Who was by good appliances recovered.

A fire is lit beside Thaisa, and to further stimulate her, music is played on a viol. It is not long before the signs of life return. Cerimon is delighted.

> This queen will live; nature awakes, a warmth
> Breaths out of her; she has not been entranc'd
> Above five hours. See! how she 'gins to blow
> Into life's flower again.

In due course Thaisa is reunited not only with Pericles, but even more remarkably with the daughter to whom she gave birth, who fortunately survived her watery entry into the world.

An even earlier account of a young woman's revival from apparent death is told by Giovanni Boccaccio in *The Decameron*. The woman is Madonna Catalina, the wife of Niccoluccino Caccianimico of Bologna in Lombardy, who goes to stay at a house 3 miles outside the city, where she intends to give birth to the child she is carrying. While there she either catches or develops a virulent sickness, and is soon pronounced dead by her doctors. 'And they, without more ado, laid her in a tomb in a neighbouring church, and after long lamentation closed it upon her.'

But Madonna Catalina has a youthful admirer named Gentile Carisendi, a nobleman, who dearly loves her. When he hears of her death, he travels broken-hearted to the church by night, accompanied by a servant, in order both to gaze once more upon her beautiful face and to take the kiss he was always denied while she lived. On opening the tomb,

Obeying some impulse, he laid his hand on her bosom, and keeping it there some time, felt, as he thought, her heart faintly beating. Whereupon, banishing all fear, and examining the body with closer attention, he discovered that life was not extinct, though he judged it but scant and flickering: and so, aided by his servant, he bore her, as gently as he might, out of the tomb; and set her before him upon his horse, and brought her privily to his house at Bologna, where dwelt his wise and worthy mother, who, being apprised by him of the circumstances, took pity on the lady, and had a huge fire kindled, and a bath made ready, whereby she restored her to life.

Soon afterwards Madonna Catalina gives birth to a son, and she remains at Gentile's house for three months, chaperoned by his mother, until she is strong enough to return to her husband. For unlike the ending of a modern romance, there is to be no running off with the handsome Gentile, as the preservation of her honour and her good name, and that of her husband, is far more important to her.

Many of the tales in *The Decameron* were based on actual events, which may mean that a pregnant woman who lived in fourteenth-century Bologna *was* prematurely buried, to be happily rescued from her tomb by the man who loved her. Moreover, it is delightful to know that a resuscitation very like it certainly happened in Paris some 400 years later.

According to the story, two merchants who lived in the Rue St Honoré and were good friends and of equal fortune each had a child of marriageable age, one a son and the other a daughter. The young people, moreover, were in love, and they naturally hoped that they would soon be allowed to marry. They were destined to be disappointed, however, as the father of the girl received an offer of marriage from a very wealthy man, and to her distress, accepted it. The pair were married, but the daughter became so distraught that she took sick and eventually died.

Her childhood sweetheart, who had himself suffered agonies as a result of her forced marriage, did not break down in despair, but instead felt somewhat hopeful, as he remembered that she had once fallen into a lethargy which had been mistaken for death. Therefore on the night of her burial he went to the churchyard with a grave-digger whom he had bribed, and had her dug up. After removing her from the coffin, he took her home and earnestly set about trying to revive her. He was successful, and the resuscitated woman was amazed and delighted to see her lover. When she heard how he had saved her from burial alive, she was quickly persuaded to remain with him and to forget the husband she despised. But as they could not remain safely in Paris, they fled to England, where they bought a small country estate, upon which they lived happily together for the remainder of their lives.

Boccaccio's heroine Madonna Catalina was not the only pregnant woman to be mistakenly buried alive and later give birth. And whereas Madonna Catalina was exhumed before her child was born, there is a well-authenticated English case of a pregnant woman who actually gave birth inside her coffin, although quite how she managed this feat is not specified.

According to *Observations in Midwifery*, by Percivall Willughby, an eminent Derbyshire obstetrician and intimate friend of William Harvey, Emme, the heavily pregnant wife of Thomas Toplace of Ashbourne, Derbyshire, went into labour, but after five days had still not managed to give birth. The following day, Saturday, 20 April 1650, a local doctor of divinity named Kettleby, who pretended a knowledge of medicine, gave her a potion to hurry the proceedings along, but this had the opposite effect and apparently killed her. What happened next was suspicious, to say the least. 'Her Husband, with his mother, and the midwife, with some other women, made haste to bury her, having, among other things, filled her mouth with hurds.' 'Hurds' (or 'hards') are pieces of coarse cloth, made of flax or hemp, and they were seemingly placed in Emme Toplace's mouth to prevent her crying out. That she wasn't actually dead is certainly suggested by what followed. 'As shee was carried to the grave, some thought, that they heard a rumbling in the coffin. A noise was heard like the breaking of a bladder, after which followed a noisome smell. She had an ill conditioned man to her husband, that frequently gave her evill words, and, oft, blows with them.'

Despite the noises, her husband and mother-in-law insisted the burial went ahead. And so, at nine o'clock that evening, Emme was lowered into her grave. But some of the other women of the village were troubled by what had taken place, and loitered near the churchyard after Thomas Toplace, his mother and their friends had returned home. 'Among this company there was one Anne Chadwick, by name, that returned to the grave; and, laying her eare to the ground, shee heard a sighing, as might be of one dying in that grave. A souldier, being with her, heard the same, and hee affirmed, besides the sighing, that hee heard the crying of a child.'

Anne Chadwick (or Chadweeke) and the soldier went straight to Mr Pegg, a justice of the peace, and told him, along with the church minister and others, what had happened, Anne insisting that Emme Toplace was still alive. On hearing their accounts, Mr Pegg decided to have the grave opened immediately to ascertain the truth.

Thus Emme Toplace's coffin was unearthed a mere two hours after it was buried. Not only was it found to be 'somewhat opened' but the boards it was made of were 'hot' to the touch. Even more revealingly, the body within showed distinct signs of having afterwards come to life. The poor woman, for example, had pulled the hurds from her mouth and some lay on her chest, while others were clasped in her hand. But most shocking of all, it was discovered that the now-dead Emme had given birth. 'Another woman put down her hand, and found a child delivered in the coffin, and descended as low as her knees, or *lower, with one hand in the mouth, and the other extended by the side*, and the after-burden was also come from her.'

This dreadful incident, which was attested by witnesses, convinced Percivall Willughby that no woman who appeared to die in childbirth should be buried too quickly. He therefore advised: 'For this woman's sake, I would not have women to bee suddenly buried, dying in child-bed, before signes of putrefaction do manifestly appeare. Especially, if that they have taken any medicine to ease pain, and cause sleep.'

Even more bizarrely, Percivall Willughby quotes the case decribed by William Harvey of a *dead* woman giving birth to the child she was carrying: 'A certain woman here among us (I speak it knowingly) was (being dead over night) left alone in her chamber. But, the next morning, an infant was there found between her legs, which had, by his own force, wrought his release.'

Another birth to a woman who had been placed in a coffin but not yet buried, is recorded in the *Annual Register* of 12 August 1760. The woman in question was the wife of Edward Knight, of Warwick. She had apparently died a few days earlier at 5 a.m., while in labour, despite having the assistance of a midwife. This is perhaps not surprising, for as William Harvey once observed, midwives were more often a hindrance than a help, because 'being impatient of a competent expectation by their desire to hasten and promote the Birth, they do rather retard and pervert it, and make it an unnatural and difficult delivery . . . and bring (the women) in danger of their lives'. The *Annual Register* records the strange aftermath to Anne Knight's death.

> About five in the afternoon the dead woman was put into a coffin, with a shroud over her. The next morning the nurse going into the room where the corpse lay, she fancied she saw something move the shroud up and down in the coffin, and she ran away much frightened to acquaint the people of the house below, who immediately went upstairs with her to examine what it could be; when turning down the shroud, to their astonishment they saw a live child grovelling in the saw dust, which had delivered itself from the corpse as it lay in the coffin.

Unfortunately, this delivery did not have a happy ending either, as the new-born baby, despite being taken up, warmed and treated with all possible care, 'died before they could dress it'. And poor Anne Knight, if she was still alive at the baby's birth, was dead when her hapless infant was found.

One of the most incredible post-mortem births happened in France during the sixteenth century. In April 1537, at Rouen, the pregnant wife of a Huguenot nobleman named de Civille was about to give birth. Her husband, however, was obliged to be away from home on business, and in his absence she took sick and soon afterwards died. She was immediately buried, along with her unborn baby. However, Seigneur de Civille returned home the next day and, on learning of his wife's death, he ordered her body to be exhumed. When it was brought up from the ground, he had her abdomen opened, from which the still living child, a son, was taken out. And thus did François de Civille enter the world!

François de Civille's story is all the more remarkable for the fact that he was twice afterwards thought to be dead and was buried, yet he was happily returned to life. Indeed, when in later years de Civille became a deputy in Normandy, and was called upon to add his name to the results of the national assemblies, he proudly wrote after it: 'Three times dead, three times buried, and three times, by the grace of God, resuscitated'.

The Huguenots, who were Protestants, suffered greatly from Catholic state persecution during the sixteenth century, which began during the long reign of François I (1515–47), a contemporary of England's Henry VIII, and which reached its bloody climax during that of his fanatical grandson, Charles IX, who became king in 1560. In October 1562, Charles besieged Rouen, which was a Huguenot stronghold, one of whose defenders was François de Civille, then the captain of a detachment of one hundred soldiers.

At eleven o'clock on Thursday, 15 October, while attempting to repel an assault on the St Hilaire gate, Captain de Civille was shot in the right cheek and the nape of the neck by an arquebuser. He fell from the rampart into the ditch within, where he lay apparently dead. The body of another man was soon thrown on top of him and they were covered in earth. De Civille remained undisturbed until 6:30 that evening, when his valet Barre, worried about his master, tried to find him. He came to the spot and, with the assistance of an officer, removed both bodies from the ditch. Yet de Civille was so disfigured by blood, the swelling accompanying his wound, mud and his pallor, that neither man recognized him, and he was returned to the ditch along with the other man, and hurriedly covered with more earth.

However, as they walked away, the officer noticed that a hand was protruding from the earth, and he went back to tread it down. Then his eye was caught by the moonlight glinting on a ring. He bent and pulled it from the finger, and passed it to the valet, saying that his efforts were not entirely without reward. To his astonishment, Barre recognized the ring's triangular diamond setting as belonging to his master. He hurriedly removed the body again from the ditch, and when the face had been carefully cleaned and examined by lamplight, he saw that the features were those of de Civille. On kissing him, he was overjoyed to notice some semblance of life's warmth within the body.

He therefore carried him to the army surgeons, but they refused to waste time on what they regarded as a corpse, so he took him to the Captain's own lodgings, and placed him upon his bed. There the wounded man remained, completely immobile, for five days and nights. However, his coldness was soon replaced by a raging fever, which indicated without doubt that he was still alive. The valet sent word to his master's relatives, who came to see him and afterwards summoned two doctors to treat him. The doctors cleaned and dressed de Civille's awful wound and then managed to get him to swallow a little soup. My source *Curiosités biographiques* notes:

> The next day, when they lifted the dressing, a great quantity of pus left the wound, and the swelling of the head and of the neck was much diminished. The patient started to show some signs of life. He similarly uttered some words, and complained of pain in his arms; but he did not at first know anyone. He was in deep shock, like a man wakened from a deep sleep.

De Civille's condition slowly improved in the following days, although his fever continued. But on 26 October Rouen was successfully attacked and taken by Charles's Catholic troops. Massacre and pillage followed, which worsened the sick man's fever, and his house was entered and ransacked by four enemy soldiers, who slept there themselves, although they treated de Civille kindly. However, these men were soon ordered to vacate it, as it was required by a royal officer. This man's valet threw the hapless de Civille on to a straw mattress in the small back room, but worse was to follow. Soon afterwards some enemies of de Civille's younger brother came to the house looking for him with the intention of killing him. When they found that their information was wrong, they angrily picked up de Civille and tossed him out of the window. Luckily, his fall was broken by the stable dung heap beneath the window, and he lay there for three days and three nights, clad only in a nightshirt and a nightcap, helplessly exposed to the elements.

When a Catholic relative of de Civille's named M. de Croisset finally came to the house to enquire after him, the old charwoman he spoke to told him that his nephew's corpse was at the back of the house, lying on the dung heap. Yet he found to his delight that de Civille was still alive, if only barely. The sick man indicated by signs that he was very thirsty, and was immediately given some beer and afterwards some morsels of bread. The cold nights had reduced de Civille's fever, so de Croisset decided it was safe to move him to the family château at Canteleu, 3 miles down the Seine. He remained there for several months, having earlier also contracted a bad cold, to add to his woes.

But finally, he was taken into the care of two brothers, both skilled healers, who lived in the neighbouring county of Caux. He stayed with them for six weeks, until at last, in August 1563, he was restored to a semblance of health. He was, however, left a little deaf, and the use of his right little finger was lost, its tendon having been severed by the shot that wounded his face and neck. Later, his facial wound was occasionally to reopen, forming painful suppurations which also brought him close to death. He was none the less able to rejoin the Huguenot army, and he fought in several other engagements until he was obliged to flee France to escape the wrath of Henri III, who began tracking down and executing the opponents of royalty. And so, in 1585, François de Civille, the man who had been buried alive three times, came to England, where the following year he was placed in the hands of two famous doctors, who completely cured him.

François de Civille's diamond ring was the means by which he was found and restored to life. There are other cases where rings were the targets of robbers who thought they were stealing from corpses, and who were terrified out of their senses when the 'dead' woke and took hold of them! A couple of thieves, in fact, died of shock, which perhaps shows that there is some justice in the world.

The first case, which is described by Simon Goulart the Elder in *Histoires admirable et memorable de notre temps* (1606), happened at Cologne in 1571 during an epidemic of the plague. Reichmuth Adolch, the wife of a magistrate, was infected and apparently died. She was buried, wearing a favourite and valuable ring, in a nearby churchyard. That night, however, the grave-digger (or, as later writers say, the sexton), who knew of the wealth that encircled her finger, dug up her coffin, opened it, and began twisting off the ring.

In doing so he roused Frau Adolch from the trance into which she had fallen, and she clasped hold of his hand and began pulling herself up, clad in her shroud. Hardly surprisingly, this so frightened the grave-digger that he ran off screaming, leaving the revived woman to struggle out of her coffin and grave as best she could. She took up the grave-digger's lantern and, showing great presence of mind, lighted her way home through the streets with it. But when she knocked on her own front door and announced who she was, the servant was so frightened by the sound of her voice, which he assumed was that of her ghost that he ran in terror to his master, who berated him for his childishness.

However, further knocks from Reichmuth brought Herr Adolch himself to the door. Delighted and amazed by her return from the dead, he helped her in, warmed her at the fire, and gave her something nourishing to eat and drink. Indeed, Simon Goulart goes on to say that she not only 'recovered her Health, but also brought into the World three sons who in the Process of Time were advanced to Livings in the Church: but having for several Years after this deliverance liv'd honourably with her Husband, she at last died a natural Death.'

Her revival was so wonderful that at her death she was interred in the church of the Holy Apostles at Cologne, 'under a lofty and magnificent Monument of Stone'. And to further perpetuate her memory, a painting of her restoration by the thief was commissioned and attached to the monument. A likeness of the painting was printed and circulated by John Bussenmacher in 1604, but copies are now very rare.

The next case has certain parallels with that of François de Civille. It concerns the mother of the Baron of Panat, also a Huguenot nobleman. When she was nine months pregnant with him, she swallowed and choked on a bone in some mince she was eating, which apparently killed her. Her ladyship was buried with some valuable rings on her fingers, and that same night, two of her servants, both greedy for gain, exhumed her, intending to steal them. One of the men, angry at her mistreatment of him when she was alive, took the opportunity to give her face and neck several hard slaps. These fortuitously cleared her throat of the obstruction and got her breathing again, and she sat up. The men understandably ran off in terror. She shortly afterwards gave birth to the Baron, of whom it was joculary said, 'He was quicker dead than born.'

Another remarkable recovery, whose authenticity is well established, happened to the aunt of Father Jean Leclerc, a reformed theologian from Geneva, who in 1684 was appointed Professor of Theology at Amsterdam. The French traveller and social observer François Maximilian Misson heard of the incident while he was tutor to Charles Butler, whom he accompanied on his Grand Tour, and included it in the work based on these travels, *Voyage through Italy*. According to him, Father Leclerc was . . .

a Man universally esteemed for Probity and Candour: This Gentleman will inform any Person, who has a Mind to apply to him, that the Sister of his Father's first wife being interred with a Ring on her Finger in the publick Church-yard of Orleans, next night a Domestick, induced by the Hopes of Gain, uncovered and opened the Coffin, but finding that he could not pull the Ring off the Finger, began to cut the latter; the violent Agitation produced in the Nerves by the Wound, rouzed the Woman, whose hideous Shrieks, extorted by the Pain, not only struck Terror into the sacrilegious Robber, but also put him to Flight without his intended Booty.

Like Reichmuth Adolch, the woman then managed to disentangle herself from her shroud, climbed from her grave and walked home through the dark streets. She lived with her husband another ten years, adds Misson, 'during which Time she furnished him with an Heir and Representative of his Family'.

A very similar case, also reported by François Misson, happened in the French town of Poictiers 'some years' before the publication of the first edition of his book (1691). The lady in question was Madame Mervache, the wife of a goldsmith, who was struck down by apoplexy. She had previously expressed a wish to be buried wearing some valuable rings, and this was done.

The following night a poor neighbour, who knew of her request, dug her up and attempted to pull the rings from her fingers. This proved more difficult than he had expected, and the violence he was obliged to use brought the comatose Madame Mervache suddenly back to life. She immediately and loudly 'complained of the injury done to her'. The frightened robber ran off, and like the others, she returned home under her own steam. Misson concludes by saying that Madame Mervache lived many years afterwards and 'also bore several children, some of whom at present follow the Business of their Father at Poictiers'.

The next case, which was said to have happened in England, is very similar to that of Jean Leclerc's aunt, although one or two differences heighten the drama. A brief account appeared in *The New Wonderful and Marvellous Chronicle* of 1794.

A shoemaker's wife in the parish of Cripplegate, being thought dead, was, aggreeable to her desire, buried in her wedding cloths; her ring being on her finger, induced the sexton to open her grave in the night, in order to steal it, when, finding it not easy to come off, he took his knife, to cut the finger from the hand; which operation recalled the woman to her senses, and she rose from her coffin. The affrighted villain took to his heels, and she, taking his lantern, walked home, knocked up her husband, and lived several years after. Her monument is yet standing in Cripplegate-Church.

The church of St Giles, which is now enclosed by the Barbican development, is 'Cripplegate-Church', although there is no monument inside that can be positively identified as the one mentioned above. I went to the church to look for it on two occasions and even discussed its possible whereabouts with Mr Frank Major, who gives weekly talks on the history of the church and who probably knows more about the building than anyone. But he had never heard of such a wild tale connected with it.

However, there was once a wall tablet there dedicated to a young lady named Constance Whitney. It was destroyed, along with so many of the other wall tablets, during an incendiary bomb attack of the last war, but was fortunately photographed before that happened and a copy is on display in the church. It shows that the monument bore a carved relief depicting Constance half-risen from an open coffin. This could easily be mistaken for a resurrection of the above sort, although it almost certainly represents her rising on Judgement Day. And the inscription makes no mention of a revival by robbery, but refers only to the young lady's family origins and to her qualities of character. She had, it records, 'a delightful sharpness of wit, and offenceless modestie of conversation, and a singular respect and piety to her parents'. Oddly, no date for her birth or for her death is given, although I have since determined that she came into the world in 1610 and left it seventeen short years later, in 1627. But she was not a shoemaker's wife; indeed, she was not married. She was in fact an aristocrat, being the daughter of Sir Robert Whitney and his wife Anne. Hence unless some evidence to the contrary appears, it seems likely that Constance Whitney is not the woman referred to in *The New Wonderful and Marvellous Chronicle*.

Interestingly, if not entirely surprisingly, similar bizarre happenings have been reported from both the United States and Canada. For example, one evening in New York, in about 1849, a flour merchant from Division Street went to a ball with his wife. She was beautifully dressed in a fine gown and wore expensive jewellery, and he was very proud of her. While they were dancing, she suddenly collapsed and apparently died. The flour merchant was heartbroken and decided to bury his wife just as she was, looking her loveliest. He therefore insisted that she was not to be defiled by an autopsy.

On the day of the funeral the weather was very wet and to avoid the mourners getting drenched, the husband had the event postponed and the woman's coffin temporarily placed in a holding vault. The undertaker took advantage of the delay to open the coffin that night, intending to strip its occupant of her jewellery. Yet when he tried to wrench a diamond ring from her finger, he tore the woman's skin, and she suddenly regained consciousness and opened her eyes and groaned. The thief fled in terror, leaving the woman to climb from her coffin and in some unexplained manner make her way back home. She afterwards fully recovered from her ordeal, and went on to have several children, 'two at least of whom are alive today,' said the undertaker who related the incident in 1889, 'and made her husband happy, and I myself, during the absence of her husband, who, as I have said, was a flour merchant, paid money into her hands for goods received'.

The last case of this type was said to have happened at Lunenburg, a fishing village on the east coast of Nova Scotia, Canada, and is described by folklorist Helen Creighton in her book *Bluenose Ghosts* (1954). Athough no date is mentioned, the general tenor of the account places the event at either the end of the nineteenth century or the beginning of the twentieth.

The woman in question was buried wearing a diamond ring, which was seen by three unscrupulous young men before her coffin was closed. That night they went with spades to the churchyard and dug her up. However, as they tried to remove the ring from her finger, the woman recovered from her trance, sat up and spoke to her robbers, one of whom collapsed on the spot and died of shock. The other two fled in terror, although one lived for only a short while. The woman managed to walk home, but when she arrived at her house, her family would not at first believe she had returned from the grave. And while she lived for several years afterwards, it is said that she never smiled or spoke again.

Hoping to find out more about this incident, I wrote to Clary Croft, who catalogued Dr Creighton's papers after her death and who is the most knowledgeable living Nova Scotian folklorist, to ask if he knew whether the account was true or not, and if it was, when it happened and what was the woman's name. He replied, 'To my knowledge, and through my recollections of conversations with Helen, I do not know of any factual basis for that individual story; there have certainly been many factual instances of these kinds of things happening, but they have less of the supernatural surrounding them.' And he added:

It is interesting, however, that similar tales should be found in Germany, because the area in which this one takes place in Nova Scotia is an area known locally as the 'Dutch shore' – 'Dutch' being a derivative of the 'Deutsch' spoken by the early settlers who arrived from the German speaking states in 1752 to settle in Lunenburg County.

This suggests that German immigrants from the Cologne region, who knew about Reichmuth Adolch, may have introduced the story to Lunenburg, where it became part of local folklore in a new guise. Or the event may actually have happened there, with some of the details being forgotten over the years. I should therefore be grateful to hear from any Nova Scotians who can shed further light on the matter.

7 Cremation Alive

The Northern Lights have seen queer sights,
But the queerest they ever did see
Was that night on the marge of Lake Lebarge
I cremated Sam McGee.

From 'The Cremation of Sam McGee' by Robert Service

Cremation was widely used in the pagan world for disposing of the dead, and although it was largely superseded by burial for many centuries in Christian Europe, it has undergone a remarkable resurgence during the past hundred years, thanks in part to updated methods of incineration. Today, for example, over 70 per cent of those dying in Great Britain are cremated, and this proportion grows each year.

According to early literary sources like Homer's *Iliad* and *Odyssey*, cremation was the preferred means of corpse disposal among the Greeks at the time of the Trojan War (1194–84 BC). And Plato, writing in *The Republic*, describes how Er, the son of Armenius, a Greek colonist from Pamphylia, in Asia Minor, was apparently killed in battle and then left for ten days among the other corpses. However, when his undecomposed body was finally taken up and placed on a pyre to be cremated, he returned to life before it was lit. His lucky escape from immolation is one of the earliest known.

Both the Greeks and the Romans believed that cremation aided the release of the soul from its material shell, but they also practised burial, particularly in later times. Indeed, they held that if a body was neither buried nor cremated, its soul was denied entrance to Elysium for one thousand years. Hence proper disposal of the dead was an essential rite.

Similarly, both peoples were aware that the signs of death are by no means infallible, which is why various precautions were taken to ensure that no one was mistakenly cremated or buried alive. The corpse, for example, was first washed with warm water, so that if some spark of life remained the rubbing and the warmth might bring about its resuscitation. Then, when it had been perfumed and wrapped in white robes, a group of women known as *praeficae* would stand or sit around it, singing and making loud lamentations, sometimes even howling, in the hope that the noise would rouse the person if he or she was not really dead. This was known as the *conclamatio* (from which our English word 'clamour' derives) and it was traditionally continued at intervals for eight days. The body was not usually taken to the funeral pyre or grave until the ninth day, although the wait was not always that long.

But as we have seen in the case of Er, a delay of nine days is not always long enough to prevent tragic accidents, even when accompanied by washing and the *conclamatio*. Three Romans who returned to life on their funeral pyres are reported by Pliny the Elder in his *Natural History*, although none of them could be saved.

The first of these was Caelius Tubero, the second Acilius Aviola, and the third Lucius Lamias. Pliny notes that Acilius Aviola, like Caelius Tubero, was certified dead by his doctors, and had gone through the standard funeral preparations described above. He did not revive until after the pyre had been lit and the flames had actually begun to burn him, by which time most of the mourners had left the scene. Only one man, his old schoolmaster, remained, but despite his frantic efforts, he was unable to stop his screaming former pupil from burning to death.

The most eminent of the three was Lucius Lamias, a Praetor or Chief Magistrate, who like both Acilius Aviola and Caelius Tubero, only woke from his trance when his funeral pyre was well alight, which prevented the mourners from rescuing him before it was too late. Rescue was made very difficult by the fact that the funeral pyre of an important Roman was several feet high and wide, and was built with soft woods like pine and fir, which contain a lot of resin, whose flammability was enhanced by the addition of oil, fat, frankincense, and similar combustible substances. Hence the pyre quickly became a roaring, blazing mound that was far too hot to approach.

Burning alive was also used as a punishment in ancient Rome. Known as *crematio*, it was inflicted on those who maliciously started fires, particularly if the blaze resulted in loss of life, and on traitors, some army deserters, and anyone who counterfeited coins. A nasty variant of burning alive was employed by the Jews, who punished blasphemers by burying them up to their knees in the ground and then pouring molten lead down their throats.

Cremation on wood pyres is still carried out among the Hindus of India, and from time to time those who are about to be burned startle mourners by waking up either beside or on their pyres. Such an unexpected arousal happened to a 100-year-old woman as recently as January 1989.

The numerous children, grandchildren and other relatives of Kalenben Balabhai were determined to give her a fond farewell. Two days after her death, she was tenderly carried from her home in the village of Malanka to the nearby *smashan* or cremation ground, where a *chita* or pyre had been carefully constructed from dry logs. She was laid on top of it, clad in a white satin robe sprinkled with flower petals, and her relatives watched as her eldest surviving son prepared to light the *chita*.

But to everyone's astonishment, just as he bent to ignite the *chita*, there was a sudden movement from on top of it, and Kalenben Balabhai, throwing out an arm from her white robe and blinking in the sunlight, sat up. Then she glared at the shocked faces around her and demanded, with a beguiling impatience, what on earth they thought they were doing and would they please take her home.

The next case also happened in India, although earlier in the century. The lucky escape is in fact just one episode in an astonishing saga that reads like a work of fiction, and which also features an aristocratic disappearance, a threatened disinheritance, and ultimately the restoration of title and property. It thus deserves to be reported in full.

Kumar Ramendra Narayan Roy was the second son of Raja Rajendra Narayan Roy Chowdhuri of Bhowral, the owner of the magnificent 100-square-mile Bhowral Raj estate, situated in the districts of Dacca and Mymensingh in Eastern Bengal, now Bangladesh. In May 1909, he was twenty-five years of age and was happily married to Srimati Biblabati Devi, aged twenty.

Early that month, the young couple went with some friends to Darjeeling, in the foothills of the Himalayas, for a short holiday. But unfortunately not long after the group arrived at the town, Kumar Ramendra fell violently ill, lost consciousness and was thought to have died. His wife decided to have him cremated at the local *smashan*, and thus, on the night of Saturday, 8 May 1909, his body was carried there, a *chita* having already been built for it.

But before the pyre could be lit, there was a torrential downpour of rain, which drenched the area and sent everybody running for shelter. The supposedly dead Kumar Ramendra was of course left lying where he was, but when the rain finally abated and the mourners returned to the site, they were astonished to find that his body was no longer there.

The heavy rain had revived Kumar Ramendra and restored him to consciousness, but without any memory of who he was or where he was. He had got up and stumbled away from the dreadful pyre, to lose himself in the darkness of the night. Two or three days later, still lost and confused, he chanced to meet a group of naked forest-dwelling Hindu mendicants known as the Naga Sannyasis, who gave him food and took care of him, and who adopted him into their band. Astonishingly, this son of a wealthy aristocrat remained with them, seeking enlightenment and begging for food and alms, for twelve long years.

But then, in 1921, the Naga Sannyasis wandered as far south as Dacca (now Dhaka), where by an amazing coincidence, Ramendra was recognized by someone who had formerly been his friend. This startling discovery led him to recover his memory, and he suddenly knew, to his surprise, who he really was. The puzzling emptiness of his life was filled, and he, the naked, homeless beggar, was really a prince! It was the stuff of a fairy tale, and it was true.

None the less, his return was not immediately accepted by his family, and indeed Biblabati Devi refused to believe that he was her long-lost husband. She even went so far as to claim, according to *The Times*, that the real Kumar Ramendra 'had died in her presence at about midnight on 8 May 1909, following an acute attack of biliary colic, and that his body was cremated the following morning'. And she swore that the beggar was not only an impostor, but was not even a Bengali.

Unfortunately Raja Rajendra himself, Kumar Ramendra's father, was dead by this time, and Ramendra's siblings were unsure of his identity. Biblabati Devi's virulent opposition to his claim is perhaps understandable, for she had acquired some valuable properties following his death, which would revert to him if he could prove who he was. A long series of legal battles followed, until, in 1946, the High Court of India ruled in Ramendra's favour. In the considered judgement of Lord Thankerton, Lord du Parcq, and Sir Madhavan Nair, who heard the testimony of hundreds of witnesses, he was the second Kumar of Bhowral, and he was therefore restored to his rightful position in society and to his property!

Outdoor cremation does not of course take place nowadays

in Great Britain, which limits the number of observed returns to life, as does the fact that those cremated are hidden inside coffins. But on the positive side, cremation can only take place after a corpse has been examined and certified dead by two independent doctors, which certainly reduces the chance of a mistaken diagnosis being made. This in turn probably indicates that a far smaller percentage of people are cremated alive than buried alive.

As I have already pointed out, cremation was widely practised in Europe by its early pagan peoples, although it was gradually superseded by burial as Christianity spread throughout the Continent. It was an article of faith among Christians that the dead would be resurrected on Judgement Day, and this would not be possible if they were cremated. Hence burning was reserved in the Christian world for witches, heretics, regicides, and, interestingly enough, female traitors (men were beheaded), and in the next world for those who went to Hell.

But during the early nineteenth century, when urban populations grew rapidly, lack of adequate burial space became a serious problem. The parish churchyards were obliged to cope with an excess of corpses. The shallow burials that resulted led to the air around churchyards becoming polluted with the stench of decaying bodies, particularly in summer, and on occasions gravediggers were fatally overcome by the noxious fumes. And because the clergy were reluctant to forgo their burial fees, which were an important part of their income, all sorts of shady activities were connived at or encouraged, in order to keep some space for fresh interments. Peter Jupp describes the terrible things that sometimes went on in his book *From Dust to Ashes*:

In the cheapest burial grounds, disinterment, burning or removal down sewers, into the foundations of new roads or bridges were devices used by unscrupulous workmen and managers. In those days, clergymen often buried paupers en masse on Sunday afternoons, whence the popular quip about clergy only working on Sundays.

He mentions how, in the 1840s, improvised cremation played a part in the continued use of London's Spa Fields graveyard, where an incredible 80,000 corpses were packed into a space meant for 1,000. This was partly made possible by the fact that 'fresh corpses were dug up at night and burned in a workman's hut'. This gruesome nocturnal activity was only exposed and stopped when the hut in question caught fire and grandly illuminated the piles of cadavers waiting to be incinerated.

It was during this period that the activities of 'resurrection men' or body-snatchers reached their peak. These disreputable individuals supplied fresh corpses to surgeons, who required them either for their students to practise on or for their own use when giving anatomical demonstrations. Some resurrectionists were simply middle-men, carrying stolen cadavers from graveyards to the dissection halls, but most dug them up as well. It was an unsavoury occupation, but the market was expanding and the customers paid very well. And curiously, stealing a corpse was not illegal, as the dead were not considered to belong to anyone. The same was not true, however, of the shroud in which the body was wrapped and the coffin in which it was buried, which meant that body-snatchers were very careful to remove only the body from the graveyard. The following advertisement, taken from Charles Bell's famous anatomical textbook (1816 edition), gives some idea of the demand for bodies:

A Room is likewise opened for DISSECTIONS, from Nine in the Morning till Two in the Afternoon, from the 10th Day of *October* till the 20th Day of *April*, where regular and full Demonstrations of the Parts dissected are given; where the application of Anatomy to Surgery is explained; the Methods of *operating* shown on the dead Body; and where also the various Arts of *Injecting and making Preparations* are taught.

A few body-snatchers, like Edinburgh's notorious Burke and Hare, actually found that murdering people was the easiest way to obtain corpses for their medical clients.

Fortunately, the Anatomy Act of 1832 put a stop to body-snatching and made it legal and acceptable for people to donate their bodies for dissection, although the problem of overcrowded churchyards was not dealt with until after the serious cholera outbreak of 1848, which many doctors thought was caused (like that of 1831–2) by the foul miasma emanating from them. The public outcry prompted Lord John Russell's Whig government to pass the Metropolitan Interments Act of 1850, which prohibited further burial in London's churchyards, and curtailed the use of those in towns and cities elsewhere. Indeed, according to Jupp, some 4,000 churchyards were closed for burial between 1852 and 1862.

Hence it is no coincidence that 1850 also saw the founding of a cremation society, whose declared aim was to substitute the burning of the dead for interment. The initial reaction was, however, hostile, not only among the general public, who had been scandalized in 1822 by the seashore burning in Italy of Percy Bysshe Shelley and his friend Edward Williams and who viewed cremation as an affront to their religion, but among the police and the medical profession, who believed that it would, as *The Medical Times* reported, prevent 'all possibility of discovering poison, if suspicions should arise at any future time'.

But people continued to die and something had to be done with their bodies. The problem was tackled in the short term by the construction of large cemeteries in city suburbs, which not only had room for tens of thousands of burials, but were made more pleasant by their garden layout, incorporating trees, flower beds, lawns and walkways, whose upkeep was paid for by the local council, not left to unpaid volunteers. Thus London, for example, saw the appearance around its borders of such now-familiar cemeteries as Abney Park, Camberwell, Hampstead, Hanwell, Kensal Green, Norwood, Paddington, and St Marylebone.

One effect of this was to separate inner-city dwellers from their deceased loved ones, who were no longer buried in the parishes in which they had lived. And visiting their graves often required a long journey by public transport, which the poor could ill afford or find time to make.

These difficulties curtailed the number of graveside visits and brought about a corresponding psychological distancing of the living from the dead. And this, allied with the fact that the Church was relieved by the Burial Acts of 1850 and 1852 of the responsibility of providing and maintaining resting places for the dead, produced a secularization of death. Indeed, many of the new cemeteries were non-denominational, and often mingled Christians with those born into other faiths, like Jews, albeit in separate areas.

But even though large new cemeteries were being opened, it was obvious to all who thought about the problem that with an average national death toll of over half a million a year, there would eventually come a time when even these would be full. And although deep burial prevented escaping odours, the gradual acceptance by the medical profession of the germ theory of disease brought home the fact that the pollution by microbes originating from rotting diseased bodies of underground water-courses, which fed wells supplying human drinking water, would be a continuing and ever-growing source of sickness and misery.

These health and space concerns helped promote the idea of cremation among the intelligentsia, who found a spokesman in the famous surgeon Sir Henry Thompson. He advocated the adoption of cremation in a hard-hitting and well-reasoned article that appeared in the January 1874 edition of the *Contemporary Review*, in which he asked how a dead body could be resolved 'into carbonic acid, water, and ammonia, and the mineral elements, rapidly, safely and not unpleasantly'. To which he replied: 'The answer may be practically supplied in a properly constructed furnace.'

It was technology that allowed cremation to gain a foothold, for it was obvious that bodies could not be burned in England on wood pyres as they were in India. Fortunately, experiments had already been conducted in Italy, where Dr Polli had burned the bodies of dogs at the Milan gasworks. These enabled him to determine the correct mixture of coal-gas and air needed to incinerate the animals completely. Professor Brunetti had also built a wood-fired furnace that carbonized a human body in two hours and conveniently dealt with the waste gases by absorbing them in charcoal and thus stopped them from polluting the atmosphere. This furnace was exhibited to the public at the Vienna Exhibition of 1873. Later, in a reverberating furnace fired by wood, Sir Henry Thompson reduced a 10 stone 4 pound human cadaver to 4 pounds of lime dust in fifty minutes. This burned off the gases by passing them through a second furnace.

Another important step was the founding, by Sir Henry Thompson and others, of the Cremation Society in 1874, which actively promoted cremation by publishing articles and books on the subject and by having its members address public meetings. The society bought land at Woking in 1878, and the following year a furnace designed by Professor Gorini of Italy was constructed there, and a horse successfully cremated. However, permission to incinerate a dead human body was not granted by the Home Secretary until 1885, when, on 26 March of that year, a woman became the first legally cremated corpse in the land.

These developments were assisted by the widespread fear of burial alive, which was based on the numerous cases that had come to light, and on the warnings of some physicians that the diagnosis of death was too often left to unqualified people like relatives, undertakers, and even creditors, who may have had a financial interest in the person's demise. Indeed, the laxness of the medical profession with regard to death and interment had prompted the founding of the Association for the Prevention of Premature Burial, which actively campaigned for changes in the law to make it illegal for doctors to sign a death certificate without having examined the dead person. They were still urging such changes as late as 1930.

The Cremation Society and the Association for the Prevention of Premature Burial were effectively two sides of the same coin, as it was obvious to members of each that cremation would prevent premature burial, although they conveniently ignored the fact that cremation might result in an equally horrible end, namely being burned alive.

Although cremation began in Great Britain in 1885, the numbers incinerated remained low for many years. There was, it is true, a small annual increase, yet cremations only reached 2,000 a year in 1919, spread among fourteen crematoria, out of a total of 579,352 deaths. This figure was something of a plateau, and remained steady for the following four years. But then, in 1924, there was a jump to 2,935, since when, almost without exception, there has been an inexorable rise each year. Almost 10,000 people were cremated in 1935, and sixteen years later, in 1951, the total first exceeded 100,000. In 1960, the figure topped 200,000, and by 1968 half of all British corpses were cremated. By 1996, the nation's 230 crematoria together incinerated 445,934 people, or 71.28 per cent of all deaths.

Because cremation is so final, reducing a body to a few handfuls of bone fragments which are then ground down to ash, the corpse must be examined by two independent doctors, who not only determine that the person is dead, but who also make sure that death has not resulted from violence, poisoning, or physical neglect. This double scrutiny naturally helps diminish inadvertent live cremation, but it does not entirely eliminating the possibility, as two doctors can still make mistakes. Fortunately, an extra safeguard is provided by those people, like ambulancemen, police officers, mortuary attendants and undertakers, who handle the dead and who, as we have seen, may often detect signs of life in those otherwise destined for the cremation furnace.

I must, however, relate a personal anecdote that still appals me. Many years ago, when I was a university student, I spent two summer vacations working in a large north London cemetery. People were not only buried there, but also cremated. Its furnace had been built during the second wave of crematorium construction in 1922.

Working in a cemetery in the summer must be one of the most pleasant jobs there is. One is outside, the tasks are physical yet not laborious, and the clients never complain. My tasks included weeding, clipping the hedges, mowing the grass, clearing away dead flowers, and generally keeping the place in order. But there were some bizarre sights, such as the morning a naked woman was discovered making obsesiance to a grave in the Greek section. The police were called to remove her, and it was eventually ascertained that she was missing from a mental institution, from which she had absconded the night before.

I had not been working at the cemetery long when the incident to which I am referring occurred. One of the full-time staff asked me if I had ever seen a cremation. When I replied in the negative, he slapped my shoulder and laughed, and took me through the side door that led to a coke-fired oven. The crematorium had two modern gas-heated Lockwood furnaces which handled the bulk of the cremation work, but it still possessed and operated an older coke-fired type, which was slower but none the less loved for its old-fashioned reliability. It was roaring away and cheerfully radiating heat. He bent and pulled open its iron door, motioning towards the burning, red-hot coke, amongst which, to my astonishment, I saw a person's skeleton, its skull nearest the door, the cranial suture lines clearly visible.

However, as we left the building afterwards, something

disturbing caught my eye. This was an open canister or tub placed just outside the door, which I had missed on going in. It stood about 2 feet high and was some 12 inches in diameter, and it was filled with bone fragments, most no more than an inch or so in width. I asked my companion what they were doing there, and he told me that they had come from the coke-fired oven and were on their way to be ground into ashes. I thought the amount of bone looked rather a lot.

'That's surely not all one person?' I commented.

'Oh no,' he replied. 'There are four or five people in there.'

'Four or five!' I gasped. 'But how can they tell the difference between them?'

He shrugged his shoulders. 'They can't.'

'So when someone comes to collect the ashes of his wife or relative, he gets a mixture of individuals and sexes!' I said incredulously.

'That's right.'

And that was the terrible problem with the old types of furnace. It took them too long to burn out and cool down, so that the bone fragments could be raked out, for it to be done after each cremation. So to save time several individuals were cremated one after the other, and then the furnace was left to go out and to cool overnight, the bone fragments being separated from the coke cinders in the morning. Stunned, I thought of all those people with ashes in caskets on their mantleshelves, who imagined that they only contained their loved ones, whereas the bulk of the contents was the remains of strangers.

Cremation in America followed a similar course to Britain, making a modest start at about the same time and struggling to gain acceptance. One of the first crematoria built was erected at Loudon Park, in Baltimore, Maryland, in 1885, which was the scene of a tragic accident that reportedly happened a quarter of a century later. The incident was brought to the British public's attention by Mr A.F. Jenkins, the Vice-President of the American

Association for the Prevention of Premature Burial, who attended a meeting of the AAPPB's sister organization in London on Thursday, 25 February 1909. At that meeting Mr Jenkins not only seconded a motion 'calling upon the Government to seriously consider the necessity of remedying the present unsatisfactory and dangerous state of the burial laws', but took the opportunity to describe what had apparently taken place at the Baltimore crematorium.

One day not long before, as a coffin was being drawn into the furnace by the mechanical pulley, a terrible scream or shriek was heard to emerge from it. 'But the machinery had put the coffin into motion, and it was hopeless to do anything to recover it,' Mr Jenkins told the shocked and dumbfounded audience. 'It was consumed in a few minutes.' The man inside, it seems, had been in a trance from which he had only woken moments before he was delivered into the furnace's flames.

However, this awful claim quickly brought denials from America, notably from Lewis Ehlers, a Loudon Park crematorium employee of many years standing, who said that no living cremation had happened there to his knowledge. Moreover, it was generally agreed that coffins were introduced into crematorium furnaces by means of an antechamber trolley, not by some unstoppable mechanical device. But perhaps most damaging to the story's credibility was the fact, mentioned by New York crematorium manager J.E. Carroll and others, that virtually every person cremated in America was first embalmed, and thus was most certainly dead. Mr Carroll noted: 'A sure test of death is the absence of blood from the arteries, and if one opened by the embalmer had blood in it he would know life was not extinct and act accordingly.'

Thus it seems that Mr Jenkins was probably misinformed, although such a live cremation could theoretically happen in Britain, given that embalming is carried out far less often. I therefore wrote to the superintendents of some of the oldest crematoria to enquire if any of them had come across a case of someone waking in a coffin prior to being immolated. They all replied that they had not. Mrs Carole Fenner, the General Manager and Registrar of Woking Crematorium, Britain's first establishment, built in 1885, said succinctly: 'I am pleased to report I have no knowledge of anyone reviving prior to their cremation.'

Mr Phillip Stephenson, the Chief Superintendent of Leeds's Lawnswood Crematorium, built in 1905, was slightly more forthcoming: 'I am not aware of any instances where cremations may have taken place where the person was found to be alive. The only instances I am aware of are a couple of nationally publicized incidents where bodies admitted to a mortuary have subsequently recovered.' Mrs Sheila Thompson, the Superintendent of Lodge Hill Crematorium in Birmingham, built in 1937, answered in a similarly reassuring manner: 'I would like to say I have never experienced any such happening. Personally I would be very sceptical of accounts of this nature, especially with the care taken with both burial and cremations today.'

Mr Andrew Helsby, the Superintendent and Registrar of Manchester's Chorlton-cum-Hardy Crematorium, built in 1892, told me: 'I have worked at the Crematorium since 1973 and have never experienced or heard of any situation where such a happening has taken place.' And he added why he thought this was so:

In the case of cremation the body is examined by two independent doctors and handled many times by the funeral director during the preparation for the funeral. It is most unlikely that any signs of life would pass unnoticed. As for earth burial, I have never worked in a cemetery but still have not heard of a 're-awakening' ever happening.

8 Premature Dissection

When I lived again,
The day was breaking – the grey plain
I rose from, silvered thick with dew.
Was this a vision? False or true?

From 'Easter Day' by Robert Browning

People have been cutting up corpses for a very long time and for a variety of reasons. Among cannibals it was always a necessary part of the culinary proceedings, whilst those well-known embalmers, the ancient Egyptians, routinely disembowelled their dead in order to preserve them.

Nowadays cadavers are still dissected by anatomy students, pathologists conducting autopsies, and – most hurriedly – surgeons wanting their organs for transplantation. Unfortunately, because the art of determining death is less than precise, not all those who are opened up are actually dead.

In the sixteenth and seventeenth centuries, hanging, drawing and quartering was a popular form of capital punishment, particularly for heretics. One live victim of drawing – or disembowelment – was an Englishman named Edmund Geninges, who, though born a Protestant, not only converted to Catholicism while staying at Rheims, in France, but went on to be ordained as a priest. He then took it upon himself to become a missionary in England, which was a treasonable offence. On 7 November 1591, he was arrested while conducting mass at the London home of a co-religionist named Swythune Wells, along with two other Catholic priests and four laymen, who were acting as helpers. They were all condemned to death, the three priests for high treason, the assisting laymen for felony. Geninges was executed, along with Swythune Wells, by hanging and drawing, on 10 December 1591, at Gray's Inn Fields, close to where he lived. His death is one of the most dreadful and remarkable on record.

The two men were pulled to the scaffold, close to which a fire was blazing, tied to hurdles. They were then released and hauled upright, and stripped to their shirts. Geninges was the first made to mount the scaffold ladder and to thus place his head in the hangman's noose. He was then called upon to confess his popish treason, with the promise of a possible royal reprieve if he did, but he would admit to no offence, only to professing his faith and religion. His perceived insolence so angered his interrogator, a certain Toplisse, that he told the hangman to turn the ladder. This was done, but Geninges had hardly swung in the air for half a minute when Toplisse caused him to be cut down; indeed, he was still conscious and able to stand when his feet touched the ground.

But Toplisse was not acting out of kindness, but rather, like so many of his kind, out of sadistic cruelty. For having 'hanged' Geninges in the strict letter of the law, he was now able to have him drawn. Geninges was therefore pushed to the ground and dragged to the dissecting block, where his abdominal wall was cut open. He cried out through the agonizing pain in a loud voice, 'Oh, it smarts!', while his shocked friend Wells could only shout to him that it was almost over. Geninges's stomach and intestines were then ripped from his abdomen and thrown into the fire, while the hangman, whose name was Bull, next opened his chest cavity and reached for his heart. As his hand closed around it and tore it out, the still-living Geninges cried out, '*Sancte Gregori ora pro me*' ('St Gregory, pray for me'). At which the disgusted hangman angrily exclaimed: 'God's wounds! See, his heart is in my hand, and yet Gregory is in his mouth; O egregious Papist!'

'And thus with barbarous cruelty,' wrote Geninges's brother, 'our thrice happy Martyr finished the course of his mortall life; and purchased no doubt a crowne of immortality in the glorious Court of heaven.'

A similarly grotesque demise, which was likewise brought about by religious intolerance, is reported in the Second Book of Maccabees, in the Apocrypha. Apparently one Razis, an elder at Jerusalem, showed more goodwill towards, and respect for, the Jews and their religion than Nicanor, the Governor of Judaea appointed by the Syrian king Demetrius, could tolerate. Nicanor therefore sent troops into Jerusalem to arrest Razis, hoping thereby to bring calamity on the Jews. But Razis had no intention of falling into Nicanor's hands, and when the soldiers were about to burn down the doors of the tower in which he had taken refuge, he tried to kill himself by falling on his sword. In the heat of the moment, however, the sword missed its intended mark and the wound it made in his abdomen was not fatal. Hearing the doors suddenly burst open, Razis next sprang up on to a wall and cast himself down among the troops outside. The fall injured him further, but again did not kill him. Razis therefore ran, bleeding profusely, through the troops and climbed on to a steep rock, where he pulled his intestines out through the hole in his body wall, and in a final act of defiance, shook them at the troops below. He then collapsed and died.

The ancients were generally forbidden to dissect human cadavers, and they had to rely for their knowledge of anatomy largely on animal dissections, although this knowledge was somewhat supplemented by seeing the internal parts of people who had been hacked to pieces in wars or in gladiatorial contests.

The earliest law to promote anatomical knowledge was passed in 1540, during the reign of Henry VIII, when the United Company of Barbers and Surgeons was given permission to dissect four criminals hanged at Tyburn each year. Any other human material they needed was made up by buying bodies stolen from their graves. As we have seen the nefarious trade in body-snatching flourished from about the middle of the eighteenth century to the passing of the Anatomy Act in 1832. Physicians were sometimes paid to perform an autopsy by a wealthy person's family, if they wished to know the cause of death. Nowadays, of course, post-mortem dissection is routinely carried out on those who have died suddenly. It is a gruesome procedure, which one surgeon described to me as 'the rape of a dead body', and which perhaps explains the reluctance of Jews and Moslems to allow their loved ones to be so desecrated.

An autopsy is usually carried out within a few days of a person's death, but in former times, when putrefaction was difficult to prevent, it always had to be done quickly, particularly in countries with a hot climate. However, speed of dissection combined with the fallibility of the signs of death led to some nasty accidents, when the dissector's scalpel roused a still-living person from a trance or catalepsy, only for him or her to die, ironically, from the cut or cuts received. And a mistake of this nature was a tragedy for both parties, as the following cases make plain.

The most famous physician of the sixteenth century was the Flemish anatomist Andreas Vesalius. He studied medicine at Louvain and at Paris, where he revealed a great interest in, and skill at, dissection, and he afterwards became Professor of Anatomy at Padua, Pisa, Bologna and Basel. He not only made many anatomical discoveries, but was able to show that the descriptions of human body structure given in the works of Claudius Galenus or Galen in the second century AD, which had become the standard reference texts of the day, were inaccurate and misleading, for they were based on the dissection of animals.

Vesalius corrected Galen's errors in his seminal work *De corporis humani fabrica* or 'On the Structure of the Human Body', published in 1543, whose text was supported by excellent diagrams. The following year he was appointed physician to Charles V, the German emperor, and several years later, in 1559, to his son Philip II of Spain. However, his human dissections, which were regarded as impious, and his criticisms of Galen made him many enemies. He also performed vivisection on dogs and other animals.

In 1562, a wealthy Spanish gentleman whom Vesalius was treating for a chest complaint, took a turn for the worse and apparently died. And the anatomist, always keen to examine any cadaver that came his way, took the rash step of asking the man's relatives if he might be allowed to dissect him, ostensibly to determine why he had died. What happened next is graphically described by Jacobus Winslow:

> But his request being granted, he had no sooner plung'd his Dissecting knife in the Body, than he observed the Signs of Life in it; nor could he be mistaken in this conjecture, since upon opening the Breast, he saw the Heart palpitating. The Friends of the Deceas'd, prompted by the Horror of the Accident, not only pursued Vesalius as a murderer, but also accus'd him of Impiety before the Inquisition.

In fact, he could hardly have made a worse mistake, for he had not only revealed himself to be apparently medically incompetent, but he then grotesquely compounded his error by inadvertently killing the man with his scalpel. His enemies were beside themselves with glee, and indeed when Vesalius was tried by the Inquisition, he was found guilty of murder and sentenced to death.

But thanks to King Philip, who thought highly of him and begged that he might be spared, he was reprieved from the gallows, on condition that he made an expiatory pilgrimage to the Holy Land. He willingly agreed to this, although as things turned out, it would have been far better for him to have been hanged.

He delayed his departure for as long as he could, but his hand was at last forced by the offer of a more prestigious job in Venice. He left for Palestine in June 1564 and after a safe voyage, visited Jerusalem and other holy sites. But the return journey, which he began in late September, was not so blessed by fortune. A violent storm blew up as his vessel sailed north through the Ionian Sea towards Venice, wrecking it on the rocky coast of the island of Zacynthus or Zante. Vesalius managed to swim ashore, but he then entered a nightmare, for 'having wandered some Days in the Deserts, and suffered the last Extremities of Hunger, he at last died in a deplorable manner for want of Relief, on the 15th of October 1564, and in the fifty-eighth year of his Age'.

Vesalius's patient evidently did not recover consciousness while being dissected, and therefore did not experience the agony of the scalpel cut. The medical author Dominicus Terilli, however, writing in his *De Causis Mortis repentinae* (On the Causes of Sudden Death) in 1615, describes how an unfortunate Spanish woman, who was thought to be dead from hysterical suffocation, reacted to the pain she felt:

> Upon the second stroke of the knife she was rous'd from her Disorder, and discovered evident Signs of Life by her lamentable shrieks, exhorted by the fatal Instrument. This melancholy Spectacle struck the By-standers with so much Consternation and Horror, that the Anatomist, now no less condemn'd and abhorr'd, than before applaud'd and extoll'd, was forthwith oblig'd to quit not only the Town, but also the Province in which the guiltless Tragedy was acted.

By fleeing, the anatomist managed to escape being murdered by the mob, but the error he had made and its terrible effect upon the woman so preyed on his mind that at last, in a fit of remorse, he took his own life.

The seventeenth-century French obstetrician Philip Peu, writing in *La Pratique des Accouchemens*, describes how at the start of his career he was called out to attend a heavily pregnant woman living near St Martin's Gate in Paris. When he arrived, he found her neighbours in a state of some excitement and distress. She was dead, they said, and they wanted him to perform an operation to save the child. Somewhat startled, Peu carried out the standard tests for death, using a mirror to see if she was breathing and feeling her chest for a heartbeat, but found no signs of life, although he admits that he was too ready to believe the opinion of the neighbours. He therefore decided to go ahead with the Caesarean section. What happened next shocked him terribly.

> It is certain that on using the scalpel to make my incision, the woman began to tremble and to grind her teeth and move her lips, which gave me so great a fright, that I swore never to attempt the operation again. And when, some days afterwards, a fellow doctor tried to get me to perform a Caesarean on the wife of a tiler living in Philippot Street, I flatly refused. He became increasingly angry and threatening, saying it is sometimes necessary to risk the life of the mother to at least save the child. In the end I told him that if he wanted an executioner, I wasn't the man for the job.

What makes the first incident even stranger is that the woman, despite evidently feeling the pain inflicted by Peu's scalpel, does not seem to have been wholly awake or in control of her movements. She did not raise a hand or scream, for instance, or even open her eyes. This suggests she may have been in a partial cataleptic state, and while she had doubtless felt Peu examine her earlier and had heard what he said, she was nevertheless unable to react either to his touch or his voice.

Another victim of premature dissection was the famous and prolific French author Antoine François Prévost d'Exiles who, having taken holy orders as a young man, is better known as Abbé Prévost. He wrote more than 170 volumes, including *Memoires d'un homme de qualitie* and *Histoire des Voyages*, although his immortal *Manon Lescaut* remains the most familiar.

In his old age, Abbé Prévost retired to his cottage at St Firmin, north of Paris. But on Wednesday, 23 November 1763, while walking through the forest of Chantilly, he had a sudden attack of apoplexy and collapsed at the foot of a tree. He was found by some peasants, who carried him to the house of a neighbouring parson. Believing Prévost to be dead, the parson contacted the local officer of justice to certify his death and to state its cause. This man, however, acted with undue haste by ordering that Prévost's body should immediately be opened and examined. His instructions were carried out, but the result was tragic, for Abbé Prévost was not dead, The *Biographie Universal* says, 'A heartrending cry came from the victim, which revealed his continued existence. The hand of the surgeon froze, but the murderous knife, thrust into his entrails, had fatally wounded him. The eyes of the unfortunate man flicked open to reveal the horror of his fate, and he succumbed almost immediately afterwards.'

Another tragedy in the dissection room is reported in the autobiography of the French chemist and statesman Jean Antoine Chaptal. Chaptal, who was made Comte de Chanteloup by Napoleon in 1811, in recognition of his chemical discoveries, became interested in human anatomy as a student, and on one occasion a male body was obtained by his college. Hearing of its arrival, he and his friend and fellow-student Pressine hurried to the dissecting room to take advantage of the opportunities it presented. On viewing the corpse, they estimated that it had been dead for about four hours. Overjoyed at having one so fresh to work on, they resolved to begin its dissection immediately, and Pressine politely allowed Chaptal to begin the procedure. What happened next took them both by surprise.

> I picked up my scalpel and made the usual incision through the breastbone, but even as I did so I thought I perceived faint signs of movement. I paused, scalpel suspended; we watched in horrified fascination, Pressine and I, as the 'cadaver' raised its right hand, brought it waveringly across his chest in a gesture of supplication, at the same time commencing to feebly shake his head. . . . The poor wretch was quite obviously begging us to cease our torment before it had gone too far.

Unfortunately, the man was too badly injured to survive and died soon afterwards. The shock of causing his death prompted Chaptal to abandon his medical studies and to opt instead for a career that did not involve living things.

This kind of ghastly error is more likely to happen nowadays to surgery patients who are given insufficient anaesthetic, which means that they either don't lose consciousness or they regain it before the operation is completed. Because they are also given a muscle relaxant, they find themselves in a somewhat worse situation than the above-mentioned victims, as they are unable to make any sound or movement at all to alert the surgeons to their agony.

On Tuesday, 24 May 1994, June Blacker, a 41-year-old mother of three, suffered the full horror of such a mistake when she underwent surgery at Prince Charles Hospital in Merthyr Tydfil, Wales. The operation to sterilize her should have been routine and problem free, but in the event it proved to be quite the opposite. She was first given a powerful muscle relaxant by injection, which completely paralysed her, so that she was unable even to move her eyes. An anaesthetic was then administered, but the dose was insufficient to put her to sleep. No one in the theatre noticed that it had not taken effect, and the operation went ahead as if she were unconscious. This is what she later said of her terrible experience:

I could still hear people talking around me, although I couldn't figure out what they were saying. The room felt like it was spinning. Suddenly I felt the worst pain I'd ever experienced in my life. At first I thought it was a needle being pushed into my arm, but suddenly it dawned on me that the acute pain was in my stomach. They were slicing my stomach open for the operation – but I wasn't even asleep. I tried to shout out. The words were forming in my head, but my mouth wouldn't move. . . . It was a living nightmare. I thought I was going to die. The unbearable pain lasted for a while before mercifully I blacked out.

June Blacker had had a heart attack after about fifteen minutes had gone by, and this finally alerted the slack medical team, who saved her with cardiac massage. The ghastly experience was not forgotten, however, and it has given Mrs Blacker nightmares and debilitating depression. She sued the Bro Taf Health Authority for negligence, and after they had arrogantly fought the case for more than four years, they at last admitted responsibility in August 1998. The amount of compensation had not been agreed at the time of writing, but is expected to exceed £100,000.

An increasing number of people are nowadays asking for their bodies to be embalmed or temporarily preserved. This typically happens if they wish to be displayed to their family and friends prior to being buried or cremated. Modern embalming on a large scale really began during the American Civil War, when families wanted their dead sons, who had often been killed many hundreds of miles away, returned home for burial. Their wish was satisfied by pioneers like Dr Thomas Holmes, who refined and made use of embalming techniques developed in Europe, to replace the ice-box, salting and other earlier, cruder methods. The practice of embalming has now gained such a hold on the American psyche that virtually every deceased citizen is so preserved.

Preventing bodies from decaying is difficult, and the methods used by the Egyptians, who were ardent and skilled embalmers, remained in vogue until about two hundred years ago. According to Herodotus, their most expensive and permanent method first required the pulling out of the brain through the nostrils with a hook, followed by the opening of the trunk and the removal of the internal organs, which were replaced by a mixture of aromatic and preservative spices, like myrrh, dragon's blood, and cinnamon. To complete the process, the body was next immersed in a solution of sodium carbonate or natrum for seventy days. Chillingly, Herodotus also records that the bodies of beautiful or notable women were only given to the embalmers after three or four days had passed, in order to prevent their corpses being violated.

A more recent case of the rape of a supposed corpse is reported, among others, by Dr Michael Ryan in his *Manual of Medical Juriprudence and State Medicine*. The date of the occurrence is uncertain, but it probably happened in the sixteenth century. A youthful monk who was on a journey stayed the night at a house where a pretty young woman had just died and was laid out for burial. He offered to mount a vigil by the bed and say prayers for her, but when they were left alone together, he could not resist the temptation of stripping the girl and admiring her feminine loveliness. Then, becoming excited by what he saw, he took the opportunity of satisfying his lust on her unresisting body.

The next day he continued his journey, and a few hours afterwards, much to everyone's astonishment, the girl spontaneously came back to life. She knew nothing of the sexual assault on her, although it eventually became clear that something odd had happened. For in due course she found out that she was pregnant, and nine months after the monk's visit she gave birth to his child.

On his return journey the monk stopped at the same house, where he learned that his nefarious act had made him a father.

Instead of slinking off, however, he owned up to the vile deed, offered to marry the young mother and, on gaining release from his religious vows, kept his promise. The pair, it seems, not only lived happily together but produced more children. So necrophilia can end happily for all concerned!

The embalming procedures of the Egyptians and other ancient peoples were simplified by the great Scottish anatomist William Hunter, who found that the easiest way to obtain temporary preservation was to replace the blood of cadavers with a preservative. Hunter had most success with a solution made of oil of turpentine, Venice turpentine, oil of lavender, and oil of camomile and vermilion, which was injected into the crural arteries of the thigh. However, if a permanent result was required, then some hours later, the internal organs were removed and separately injected with the preservative solution, and afterwards bathed in camphorated spirits of wine. On being replaced, the spaces between the organs were filled with a powder made from camphor, nitre and resin, which was also pressed into the mouth, nostrils, ears and other cavities. The skin of the body was then rubbed with oil of lavender and rosemary, and finally, the body was lain in a coffin on a bed of plaster of Paris, which gradually absorbed all the moisture from it.

In later years simpler and more effective preservative solutions were devised, such as arsenic in glycerine (which had the disadvantage of being dangerously poisonous), introduced via the femoral artery, and one made from water, alcohol, carbolic acid and glycerine, introduced via the carotid artery, which were sufficient to preserve the body against decay for several days. More recently formalin, a 40 per cent solution of formaldehyde in water, has been used. These solutions all replace the blood, which is drained from the body via one of the axillary veins.

The poet Robert Herrick (1591-1674) suggested a rather more pleasant method of preservation, although it's doubtful if it would work for everyone:

But, ah! by starres malignant crost,
The life I got I quickly lost:
But yet a way there doth remaine,
For me embalm'd to live again;
And that's to love me; in which state
Ile live as one regenerate.

Before William Hunter's time, the art of embalming, because of its great expense, had only been used to preserve those wealthy enough to pay for it. And such people, who included monarchs and members of the aristocracy, were therefore most at risk of being opened up while they were still alive.

This was the lot of 50-year-old William Herbert, the third Earl of Pembroke, following his apparent demise from apoplexy on 10 April 1630. His death was not unexpected, for while he had many virtues, 'he indulged to himselfe the pleasures of all kindes, almost in all excesses', according to the biographer and historian Lord Clarendon, adding, 'He was immoderately given up to women.' Yet Pembroke did not keel over in the bedroom, but rather, says Clarendon, 'after a full and cheerefull supper'.

What happened in the embalming room is described, albeit briefly, by the Reverend James Granger:

When his body was opened, in order *to be embalmed* he was observed, immediately after the incision was made, to lift up his hand. This remarkable circumstance, compared with lord Clarendon's account of his sudden death, affords a strong presumptive proof that his distemper was an apoplexy. This anecdote may be depended upon as a fact, as it was told by a descendent of the Pembroke family, who had often heard it related.

The *Annual Register* for 1773, in its review of a memoir entitled *On the Causes of sudden and violent Death*, written by the

French physician Jean Janin de Combe-Blanche, mentions the similar and terrible recovery of Cardinal Spinola during his embalming:

> He [fell] into a fainting fit, was thought dead, and his people were in haste to have him opened, in order to be embalmed. His lungs were scarce laid open, when it was perceived, that his heart did beat, and the unfortunate man, come to himself, had strength enough to stretch forth his hand towards the surgeon's scalpel that dissected him, and to push it back. But it was rather too late; he had received the mortal blow.

Such bad luck also afflicted the Italian Cardinal Giulo Maria della Somaglia, whose resuscitation during his embalming was strangely similar to that of Cardinal Spinola – surely one disadvantage of being a high-ranking churchman in a hot country. In 1830, at the age of eighty-six and following a period of intense grief, he became seriously ill. He gradually sank into a trance or coma, which was so profound and lasted for so long that it was mistaken for death. In order to stop his anticipated putrefaction and to prepare his body for burial in the family vault, he was embalmed immediately. But again, scarcely had the embalmer's scalpel opened his chest than his heart was seen to be beating, and the poor man, suddenly regaining consciousness, weakly lifted a hand to push away the dreadful instrument. But while the embalming was ended there and then, nothing could be done to save Cardinal Somaglia, whose lung had been fatally wounded, and he died not long afterwards, it is recorded, 'in a most lamentable manner'.

Someone else who returned to life while being embalmed was the French actress Elisa Felix, and like those I have already mentioned, the cuts that so painfully roused her also killed her. Under the stage name of Mademoiselle Rachel, Elisa Felix became celebrated for her leading roles in Racine's *Phedre*, Pierre

Corneille's *Horace*, Thomas Corneille's *Ariane*, Molière's *Le Misanthrope* and other great tragedies, in which she regularly brought audiences to their feet. But while she had a commanding presence on the stage, she was far less daunting in private. 'She is a very engaging, graceful little person,' wrote the actor William Macready, who met her in 1841, 'anything but plain in person, delicate and most intelligent features, a frank, a French manner, synonymous to pleasing.'

But the talented Mlle Rachel was unfortunate enough to contract the ailment that was the principal (and fashionable) cause of early death among the artistic set of her day, known as *la phthisie pulmonaire* by the French, which we call consumption or pulmonary tuberculosis. The disease followed its usual distressing course, with loss of weight, weakness, and the coughing up of blood-stained sputum, until its crisis came early in 1858, when the actress was at home in Canet, near Cannes. 'At ten o'clock on the night of 3 January,' says her English biographer Joanna Richardson, 'the choking returned more violently; after an hour, Rachel's flushed face turned pale, her head fell forward. . . . A few minutes later, holding Sarah's [her sister's] hand, Rachel died radiant, full of faith in the creed from which none had converted her.'

However, despite being certified as dead by two doctors, her demise was apparent, not real, a fact which was only discovered when she was embalmed. This operation began soon afterwards in preparation for transporting her corpse to Paris. However, the local embalmers were unfamiliar with the newer methods of temporary preservation by injection, and proceeded to slit open the actress's abdomen, in order to remove her internal organs. They were brought to a sudden and horrified stop when she suddenly screamed and opened her eyes. A violent trembling of her body accompanied these sounds and movements. A doctor was summoned, but it was too late, for despite receiving prompt medical attention, Rachel's injuries were too serious, and she too weak, to be successfully treated. She lingered on, but her end was inevitable. She died ten hours later.

Modern embalming, which can be performed quickly, has the advantage of ensuring that people in a trance or a cataleptic state cannot be buried or cremated alive. For they will either be killed, rapidly and painlessly, by the injection of the preservative, or their living condition will be noticed before by the embalmer, who will be able to take the necessary steps to have them resuscitated.

Just such an escape from death happened to an American serviceman, whom I shall call Homer Weisenstein, during the Vietnam War. He was injured and apparently killed by Viet Cong rocket and mortar fire. That he was teetering on the brink of death is indicated by the fact that he had what is known as an out-of-body experience or OBE, whereby his consciousness left his physical self and floated above it. From that vantage point he was able to look down at his body and at what was going on around it. He saw himself and his dead comrades robbed of money, jewellery and other possessions by the enemy soldiers, and then later he watched as his own and the other bodies were brought back to camp by an American recovery team.

'I looked dead,' Weisenstein said. 'They put me in a bag. We were transferred to a truck and then taken out to the morgue.'

There he witnessed his ripped and dirty clothing cut off him and his body afterwards washed clean of blood. The morticians next prepared to embalm him. One cut open a vein in order to drain out his blood, but fortunately, because his heart was faintly beating, the sudden flow of blood from the vessel warned the man that he was still alive. No preservative was therefore injected into him. Instead, his body was rushed to the camp hospital and given surgery, which was successful. He was afterwards transferred to the recovery room.

'The chaplain was in there saying everything was going to be all right,' recalled Weisenstein. 'I was no longer outside looking at the situation. I was part of it at that point.' And he went on to make a full and complete comeback from the dead.

About two years earlier, in 1967, another young soldier had a close encounter with an embalmer in Vietnam. On 16 July Private Jackie Baynes trod on a landmine while on patrol, and received serious injuries to both his legs. He was transported to a military hospital in Saigon, where he underwent twenty-six blood transfusions as doctors fought for hours to save his life. Yet despite all their efforts, Baynes's EEG reading finally went flat and stayed that way, apparently indicating that he had died.

His body was sent to the mortuary, and about four hours later the embalmers were ready for him. But as the team leader prepared to cut open one of his veins with a scalpel, he noticed a slight muscle twitch in his face. This suggested that Baynes might still be alive. The embalming team had him quickly returned to the hospital, and the doctors there, much to their surprise, detected a faint pulse. The dead man had spontaneously come back to life. And despite his terrible injuries, he stayed alive. He remained in hospital for several weeks, but eventually recovered sufficiently to be flown home.

In former times, when surgeons and anatomists found it difficult to obtain human cadavers for research and teaching purposes, they were obliged to enter into a devil's pact with body-snatchers who willingly supplied them with what they needed for cash.

One of the top body-snatchers was Jack Hall, whose day job as an undertaker gave him useful inside knowledge about where bodies had been freshly buried. Thomas Hood wrote a long humorous poem about him, which includes this verse:

> But long before they pass'd the ferry,
> The dead that he had help'd to bury
> He sack'd - (he had a sack to carry
> The bodies off in;)

In fact, he let them have a very
Short fit of coffin.

But while body-snatching was a despicable and much-hated trade, it none the less did result in the release from the grave of some prematurely buried people – although they then often had to face being dissected alive. The ones that made it through both processes were life's real lottery winners. Two astonishing cases are worth relating.

In 1824, a young medical student named John McIntyre, having worked himself into a state of complete physical and mental exhaustion, was put to bed, suffered a further deterioration that brought him to the brink of death, and developed catalepsy. He was examined by a doctor, who found no sign of life and certified him dead. He was laid out, and although he was fully aware of what was going on around him, he was unable to make any sound or movement to alert those who came to weep over him that he was still alive.

On the morning of the fourth day, the undertakers employed to conduct his funeral and burial forced him roughly into a coffin that was too small for him. He recalled later that when they nailed down the lid, 'each hammer blow rang through my head like a tocsin'. The coffin was conveyed to the local cemetery, a funeral service was said for him, and he was lowered into the grave. He remained conscious throughout the dreadful proceedings, yet he was still powerless to move. He recorded what happened next.

A jolt told me that I had reached bottom, and faintly, from far above, came the mournful voice of a friend, bidding me a most tender adieu. Next moment, and an appalling thunder of sound, like so many bolts descending upon my head, informed me that the grave was being closed, the earth packed hard above me: the light had gone, and I was alone.

Poor John McIntyre could not tell exactly how long he remained so uncomfortably buried, but it was probably for several hours. 'I hoped that my sufferings would be brief,' he comments, 'that lack of air would swiftly put paid to me, but yet I lingered on.' Then to his surprise he heard a noise above him, faint at first, but growing steadily louder, until at last he could distinguish the sound of digging and men's voices. Finally the loud scrape of shovels against the coffin lid told him that his wooden prison had been uncovered. He felt a surge of relief and hope as the coffin was hauled up and then placed on the ground above. Almost immediately there followed the deafening sound of crowbars being used vigorously and the splintering of wood. Suddenly, the lid of the coffin was wrenched open, and cool, fresh air flowed in around him. His heart leaped. He had been exhumed!

Unable to move or even to open his eyes, John could not see the men who had exhumed him, nor did he understand their unseemly haste and the unfeeling way in which they wrenched him from the coffin. But when they thrust him into a sack and carried him away in it, he realized to his horror that their hard work had not been carried out to save him, but to sell him to anatomists. He had been resurrected by body-snatchers!

They carried him for some way and then into a building:

I was ... finally taken into what was, from the echoes, a largish sort of room, possibly underground, and laid out upon a stone slab, damp and chill, with a cold that penetrated to the very bones. All about me I could hear voices: a veritable cacophony. Hands began prodding at me, fingers poking and pressing upon various of my organs; and then, one of my eyelids being pulled back. I was enabled at last to see – and wished almost, indeed, that I had not, for the sight that met my eyes was far from encouraging. I was in a dissecting room, stretched out like a fish upon a marble slab and surrounded on

all sides by numbers of young men, amongst whom I recognized several of my erstwhile colleagues.

Amazingly, John McIntyre had been sold to one of his own
teachers, who intended to carry out an electrical experiment on
him before he dissected him. To his alarm John felt wires being
attached to his body and then, as the current was switched on, 'a
million lights exploded before my eyes, and my body was almost
burst asunder with the shock'. The second electrical charge invol-
untarily contracted the muscles of his abdomen and made him sit
up; his eyes also flicked wide open. He saw those around jump
back in horror at the awful sight. Indeed, his fellow students were
so appalled at this treatment that some cried out it was enough.

The professor, indeed, thought better of repeating the experiment, but by carrying it out he may inadvertently have saved
John, for the electric current doubtless played a part in breaking
the hold of his catalepsy. This is what happened next:

Once more I was stretched upon my slab of marble – the
professor in charge approached me, knife in hand – made a
light incision down the centre of my chest – and in that
moment it was as if something inside me suddenly burst free.
A shrill cry tore its way out of my throat, to be answered by
echoing cries from those around me. The ties of death had
been broken: I had come back to life!

Although, as I have said, body-snatching was legal prior to
1832, those caught doing it were in danger of being badly beaten
or even lynched by angry mobs. There were also other dangers
associated with the profession which could injure or sometimes
kill the most careful resurrection men, including contracting fatal
diseases from the bodies they handled and being crushed by the
collapse of grave walls as they worked. And because grave-
robbing had to be done in darkness for fear of discovery,

accidents were common. Several body-snatchers' careers were ended by the onset of tetanus from wounds inflicted by a misdirected spade or pick-axe.

Perhaps the most bizarre fatal accident to befall body-snatchers, and one which has more than a whiff of divine punishment about it, occurred at Aberdeen in September 1784. A poor woman who had died in the city hospital was buried in a local churchyard. Hearing of her interment, some young surgeons, who wished to dissect her, bribed the grave-digger to mark the grave for them, in order that they might remove her coffin that night. When another grave-digger was informed of their designs he decided to frustrate them, and moved the mark to the grave of a woman who had been buried some three or four months earlier, and who would of course be too badly putrefied to be of any use to them.

That night, the group of surgeons went to the churchyard, found the marked grave, and after a good deal of labour lifted the coffin from it. They did not, however, open it there and then, as professional body-snatchers would have done but, perhaps fearing discovery, carried it straight from the churchyard to their residence. When they broke open the coffin lid, reported *The Gentleman's Magazine*, 'a vapour like a flame of brimstone came forth, and suffocated them in an instant'. The released gas, which was probably a combination of methane and hydrogen sulphide, also poisoned two women who happened to be passing the room, bringing the total of those killed to eleven.

Another close encounter with a dissector's scalpel took place some years after John McIntyre's. The man to whom the ghastly experience happened was George Hayward, a farmer's son, who was born in 1823 at Moreton-in-Marsh, Gloucestershire, and who later emigrated to America and settled in Independence, Missouri, where he became a well-known jeweller.

The incident that brought about his premature appearance on a dissecting table happened when he was a youth. Apparently, while working in his father's fields one day, he was accidentally stabbed in the cranium with the tine of a pitchfork wielded by a clumsy farm labourer. The injury did not appear to be very serious at first, but before long George was obliged to take to his bed. Two weeks later, his condition having rapidly deteriorated, signs of life apparently disappeared and he was pronounced dead by both his doctors.

But George Hayward was neither dead nor unconscious. He was aware of everything that was going on around him, although he was totally incapable of making any movement. This suggests that he, too, had been overcome by catalepsy. Thus he experienced the lamentations of his family, the visit made by the undertaker, who laid him out and measured him for a coffin, and later being placed in the long box. He also remained conscious throughout his funeral, and like John Mcintyre he also heard the thunderous sound made by soil failing on to his coffin, burying him alive.

However, as soon as he had been interred, the two doctors who had certified him as dead began arguing fiercely about the reason for his death, one claiming it was due to the penetration of the pitchfork tine into his brain, the other that it was the result of the pleurisy he had also developed. In the end they decided to settle the matter once and for all by exhuming George and dissecting him to determine the truth. The subject of their discussion had, in the meantime, thankfully lapsed into unconsciousness. He later wrote:

How long I remained in this condition I am not aware. The first sense of returning life came over me when I heard the scraping of a spade on my coffin lid. I felt myself raised and borne away. I was taken out of my coffin, not to my home, but to a dissecting room. I saw the doctors who had waited on me at my home, dressed in long white aprons. In their hands they had knives. Through my half-closed eyes I saw them engaged in a dispute. My sense of hearing was remarkably acute. Both approached the table and opened my mouth to take out my tongue, when by a superhuman effort my eyelids were slightly raised. The next thing I heard was:

'Look out, you fool, he is alive.'

'He is dead!' rejoined the other doctor.

'See, he opens his eyes,' continued the first doctor. The other physician let his knife drop, and a short time after that I commenced to recover rapidly. Instead of cutting me up they took me home.

The chances of something similar happening today are probably far higher than in the past. Bodies may no longer be stolen from graves by resurrectionists, but none the less a far greater number of people are routinely dissected. Post-mortem examinations have to be carried out on all those who die suddenly in order to discover the cause of death, but they are frequently also performed on people whose demise is no mystery. Indeed, many doctors prefer their patients to be dissected, for this enables them not only to verify the cause of death, but also, in the name of medical research, to find out more about associated diseases and abnormalities.

But while there may only be a slight danger of someone returning to life on an autopsy room table, and virtually none at all if the person concerned has been in a refrigeration chamber beforehand, the risk is much greater for anyone who becomes an organ donor, as the parts have to be alive when they are removed. In such 'grey area' cases, the patient is said to be dead when the EEG machine measuring brain activity fails to record any. The person then becomes 'brain dead', as doctors call it, a condition that by definition precludes any hope of recovery, although the rest of his body may still be alive and can often be artificially kept that way almost indefinitely. Indeed, our internal organs are remarkably tenacious of life, as the following two examples mentioned below demonstrate, and this in turn suggests that the brain may not be as easily put out of action as is commonly supposed.

The redoubtable Francis Bacon, writing in the *History of Life and Death* in 1623, records a curious incident at an execution he attended. 'I remember to have seen the heart of a man who was embowelled as a traitor, which, being thrown into the fire according to custom, leaped out at first a foot and a half, and then less by degrees for the space, to the best of my remembrance, of seven or eight minutes.'

John Bell, the eminent surgeon and anatomist, who perhaps knew more about the continuing life of removed internal organs than anyone, observes in *The Anatomy and Physiology of the Human Body*: 'A muscle cut from the limb, trembles and palpitates for long after; the heart separated from the body contracts when irritated; the bowels when torn from the body continue their peristaltic motion, so as to roll upon the table, ceasing to answer to stimuli only when they become stiff and cold.'

And although 'brain dead' has a sombre sense of finality about it, suggesting that all the brain is dead, this is something of an exaggeration. An EEG machine, for example, only records surface brain activity, not that which occurs at deeper levels, which is why it can make mistakes. And three cases that occurred in the 1970s reveal how untrustworthy diagnosis of brain dead can be.

In May 1972, a 23-year-old American named Russell Lee, a student at Long Beach City College in California, was seriously injured while out riding. According to eye-witnesses, his horse suddenly took fright and galloped under some low-slung power cables running alongside the Pacific Coast Highway. Russell struck his head against one of the cables, and the impact knocked him from the animal, causing severe damage to his cranium and spinal cord. He remained conscious as he was taken by ambulance to nearby St Mary's Hospital, however, although he reported difficulty in breathing.

At the hospital his condition steadily deteriorated. His breathing then stopped and he had to be resuscitated with a respirator. And twenty-five minutes later, when he was tested by a neurosurgeon, he was found to be brain dead. The Los Angeles County Coroner's office was notified of his death, and his mother, who was at his bedside, gave her permission for his eyes and kidneys to be removed for transplantation.

A notification of Russell's death was sent to Harbor General Hospital, where the transplants would eventually be carried out. The doctors there requested that his life-support equipment be kept operational in order to preserve the functioning of his kidneys. A specialist transplant team at Harbor General then left for St Mary's Hospital to carry out the organ removal.

But while the transplant team was on its way, something stirred within the supposed corpse. 'The patient developed brain life signs that he did not have before,' said Dr Paul Hildebrand, a hospital spokesman. Russell was not therefore quite as brain dead as the neurosurgeon had supposed. He was rushed to the intensive care unit, where he remained in a critical condition for some time. He eventually recovered, although he was left partially paralysed by the accident.

The following year a similar close encounter happened to an unnamed woman patient at the Queen Elizabeth Hospital in Birmingham. The incident was only disclosed in February 1976, when Mr Victor Brookes, a surgeon at the hospital, addressed a Birmingham Area Health Authority meeting. The woman had had no identifiable relatives, and Mr Brookes used her case to remind everyone that extreme caution was necessary when considering such people as possible organ donors. Indeed, after further discussion, it was decided that no organs should ever be removed for transplantation without the express consent of relatives.

The woman had gone into the Queen Elizabeth Hospital for a major cancer operation. But while it was in progress she underwent a respiratory arrest. 'She stopped breathing,' explained Mr Brookes. 'All the indications were that she was dead – her brain was dead and would not recover. We carried out the two types of investigation to determine cerebral death. Only then was the transplant team contacted.'

However, when the woman was examined by transplant surgeons she was rejected as a suitable donor, mainly because of the time it was likely to take to contact her relatives, who were unknown. Happily, she was kept attached to the life-support machine, and in due course, notwithstanding being classified as brain dead, she showed signs of life and was revived. She eventually made a complete recovery; indeed, Mr Brookes reported that he had seen the woman during an out-patient clinic only three months before.

The transplant surgeon's scalpel was actually used prematurely on 65-year-old Michael McEldowney, a resident of Selly Oak, Birmingham, after he was struck by a car on Saturday, 16 February 1974, and severely injured. Mr McEldowney was unconscious when he was taken by ambulance to Selly Oak Hospital. The accident could not have happened at a worse time for him, for he was due to retire in two months.

It was found that nothing could be done for him. A hospital spokesman later announced: 'He was operated on to improve his condition, but it was found that he had suffered extensive brain damage. On 19 February, his breathing stopped. He failed to respond to treatment and was believed to be dead.'

Mr McEldowney's family, who lived in Belfast, were informed of the accident, and permission was obtained from them to remove his kidneys in the event of his death. But as the spokesman revealed, the announcement of his death proved to be somewhat hasty: 'An operation for removal of his kidneys began,' he revealed, 'and after the first incision had been made, Mr McEldowney was found to be breathing. He was taken back to the intensive care unit and treatment was resumed. He died fifteen hours later.'

We do not know if Michael McEldowney was aware of any pain when he was cut open or if the incision hastened or maybe caused his death. But if the experiences of the other patients are anything to go by, we cannot be wholly sanguine about either. And certainly those who adjudged him dead were less than competent.

9   The Frankenstein
Experiments

I remained during the rest of the night, walking up and down
in the greatest agitation, listening attentively, catching and
fearing each sound as if it were to announce the approach of
the daemoniacal corpse to which I had so miserably given life.

From *Frankenstein* by Mary Shelley

The electric shocks given to John Mcintyre after he was stolen
from his grave and sold to an anatomist, which were described in
the last chapter, were among several electrical experiments that
were carried out on dead people in the early years of the nineteenth century. These somewhat gruesome investigations showed
scientists not only that electricity could cause muscle contraction,
but also that it had potential as a useful aid in resuscitation. And
indeed, the modern electric defibrillator, which is regularly used
to restart stopped hearts or to synchronize a disordered beating,
is a direct outcome of such work.

The generation of static electricity by rubbing amber against
silk was investigated as early as the seventh century BC by the
Greek philosopher Thales of Miletus, although his findings were
largely forgotten until Elizabethan times, when the English
scientist William Gilbert carried out further research into the
phenomenon. Indeed, it was Gilbert who first employed the term
'electricity' (from the Greek *elektron*, meaning 'amber'). He
showed that other substances, like glass and sealing wax, could be

used to produce a static charge by friction, and he even invented a way of measuring the strength of the charge.

Then, following the invention of mechanical devices for generating static electricity (known as electrostatic machines), and the Leyden jar, in which the charge they produced could be stored, it became possible to investigate the effect of electricity on living tissues. This research was pioneered in the eighteenth century by the great Luigi Galvani, Professor of Anatomy at Bologna University, who discovered that electric shocks caused muscular contraction in the limbs of dead frogs.

Galvani's most important finding was made when he quite by chance noted that a frog's leg muscles contracted strongly if a copper rod was inserted into its spinal cord, and the rod's other end bent into a hook and hung on an iron lattice against which the limbs lay. Such muscle contraction in the absence of a static charge not only meant that the spinal cord and the nerves leading from it were the pathways along which electricity travelled to the muscles, thereby causing them to contract, but it also suggested to Galvani that the animal tissue itself contained a previously unknown vital force, which he termed 'animal electricity'. This was most obviously present in electric eels and torpedo rays, and he postulated that it existed in addition to the 'natural electricity' of lightning and the 'artificial electricity' created by friction. Animal electricity, he believed, was produced in a dead animal when two metals formed a uniting bridge between the nerves and the muscles concerned. His experimental work and the conclusions he came to were announced to the world in a paper entitled *Commentary on the Effect of Electricity on Muscular Motion*, published in 1791.

Galvani's conclusions were investigated and ultimately challenged by the Italian physicist Count Alessandro Volta, who discovered that the electricity responsible for the contraction of the frog's leg muscles was actually produced by the two dissimilar metals (copper and iron) forming a circuit with the animal's nerves and muscles. He went on to show that one metal (copper) becomes positively charged, and the other (iron) negatively charged, and that a current of electricity spontaneously flows from the copper plate through the animal to the iron plate, and then from the latter back to the copper plate to complete the circuit. Indeed, Volta then went on to construct his famous 'voltaic pile', which consisted of several discs of copper and iron placed alternately one on top of the other to form a column or pile, and separated by moist pieces of towel. When the top copper disc is joined to the bottom iron one by a wire, a continuous current of electricity flows through them. This was the world's first electric battery, and its announcement in 1800 marked the start of the electrical age.

Later, it was found that an electric current is more efficiently generated if zinc is substituted for iron, and when plates of zinc and plates of copper are suspended apart and alternately in dilute sulphuric acid in a glass jar, and the first copper plate joined to the last zinc plate by a wire. This is the voltaic cell which, like the voltaic pile, works by turning chemical energy into electrical energy. The current so generated continues to circulate for as long as the plates remain connected – or until the zinc ones are eaten away by the acid.

We now come to the work of Luigi Galvani's nephew, Giovanni Aldini, who became Professor of Experimental Philosophy at Bologna. His electrical experiments on dead human beings, and on the potential of electricity to revivify them, may have inspired Mary Shelley to write her famous gothic novel, *Frankenstein, or The Modern Prometheus*, which was published in 1818. Indeed, Aldini certainly fits the bill as a model for the book's misguided hero, Victor Frankenstein.

'At Bologna, in the year 1802, the Government granted me permission to make experiments in galvanism on the bodies of two decapitated criminals,' Aldini says in his *General Views on the Application of Galvanism to Medical Purposes; principally in cases of*

Suspended Animation. The two executed men he eventually obtained were youthful brigands, both of robust physique, who lost their heads in January of that year. He had already done some electrical experiments on the decapitated bodies of animals, and he was keen to see if the same results would be obtained with human beings.

The decapitations took place in public, as was usual at the time, outside the Court of Justice, near which Aldini had rented a suitable room for his experiments. He had installed a dissecting table for the reception of the bodies, on which was placed a voltaic pile made from 100 alternating plates of silver and zinc, from which came two wire conductors, one from its top and one from its base. The anatomist Professor Mondini assisted him by performing 'all the dissections necessary, in order that the galvanic fluid might act in every part of the human body'. The work was begun as soon as the body and the separated head of the first felon were brought in. An invited audience of several dozen people was in attendance, none of whom had the slightest idea of the horrors they were going to witness.

'The head,' Aldini tells us, 'first underwent the action of galvanism.' It was stood upright on the table, its ears were moistened internally with a little salt water, and then the end of one of the wires from the voltaic pile was placed in the left ear, and that of the other into the right ear. It was crude stuff, but none the less effective. Aldini continues:

All the muscles of the face underwent frightful contractions. The motion of the eye-lids was very strong, though less sensible in the human head, than I had before observed in that of an ox which I had galvanised. I then placed a metallic wire in the form of a bow from the top of the pile, to the left ear, on one side, and a similar one from the base of the pile to the tip of the tongue, which was protruded about an inch beyond the lip; the face was again contracted, the tongue was drawn in on the first application, and the mouth emitted a little saliva. Strong contractions took place on applying the wires to the nose, to the forehead, to the eyebrows.

While this was going on the body and head of the second brigand were brought in, and Aldini carried out the same experiment on his head, with similar results. The table, hardly surprisingly, was now wet with the blood that had drained from each head, and this provided the intrepid experimenter with a suitable medium to carry out the most bizarre part of the entire proceedings. For Aldini now lay both heads sideways in the blood, facing each another but apart, and placed the end of one wire in the left ear of one head and the other in the right ear of the second. A circuit was formed by the electricity passing through the blood on the table.

It was surprising and even frightful to see these two heads making at the same time horrible contortions, as if at each other, so that some spectators who were not prepared for such results, were exceedingly terrified. I observed that the contractions excited in this situation were stronger than those produced when I made the experiments on each head separately.

These striking, awful, electrically induced contractions in the face muscles of decapitated heads show why defining death is so difficult. For muscles can only contract when they are alive, but whereas it is taken for granted that a beheaded man is dead, the muscles (and of course other tissues) none the less remain living for some time after decapitation. And if the muscles of the head and face can survive for an hour or more after decapitation, there is no reason to assume that the brain immediately dies either. For although brain cells are more sensitive to a lack of oxygen and glucose than muscle cells, they are not instantly deprived of these substances.

Nor need we suppose that the brain of a decapitated head immediately loses consciousness. Why should it? It is, after all, completely undamaged by the fall of the axe or guillotine blade, it receives no blow that would knock it out, and its tumble into the basket of sawdust below is more likely to jolt it into full wakefulness than lull it to sleep. This suggests that for a variable time after decapitation the head may be aware of its surroundings, of the pain from its severed neck, and of what is subsequently done to it.

In case this sounds too far-fetched and fantastic to be true, there are several recorded examples of apparent post-decapitation consciousness. These come mainly from France, where the guillotine was not only used to behead some 5,000 aristocrats during the Revolution, but continued to be used for the execution of murderers and traitors until as late as 1981.

The beautiful Charlotte Corday, the assassin of the revolutionary madman Jean Paul Marat, whom she stabbed to death in his bathtub on 13 July 1793, is one such example. She was guillotined a few days later, on Wednesday, 17 July. Shortly afterwards her head was lifted from the basket by François le Gros, the assistant executioner, and held up to the crowd. Not content with this indignity, he then slapped it once across the cheek with his hand. His action upset not only the crowd but evidently also Mlle Corday herself. Pierre Sue, a professor of medicine quoted by Alister Kershaw in *A History of the Guillotine*, states:

> Charlotte Corday's head showed in its countenance the most unequivocal signs of indignation. . . . Both cheeks reddened perceptibly. . . . It cannot be claimed that this flush resulted from the blow itself, for the cheeks of corpses may be struck in this way in vain; they never colour: moreover, this blow was only struck on one cheek, and it was remarked that the other cheek also coloured.

An even more remarkable and definite exhibition of awareness in a severed head was displayed by that of the murderer Henry Languille, who was guillotined in the early morning of Wednesday, 28 June 1905, and whose head was examined and experimented upon by Dr Gabriel Beaurieux. It had fallen upright on the sawdust, which meant that Dr Beaurieux did not have to handle it, and also reduced the amount of blood lost from the wound.

Dr Beaurieux noted that for about five or six seconds after decapitation the eyelids and lips of the head 'worked in irregularly rhythmic contractions', but that then the face gradually relaxed and the eyes half-closed.

It was then that I called in a strong, sharp voice: 'Languille!' I then saw the eyelids slowly lift up, without any spasmodic contraction – I insist advisedly on this peculiarity – but with an even movement, quite distinct and normal, such as happens in everyday life, with people awakened or torn from their thoughts. Next Languille's eyes very definitely fixed themselves on mine and the pupils focused themselves. I was not, then, dealing with the sort of vague dull look without any expression that can be observed any day in dying people to whom one speaks: I was dealing with undeniably living eyes which were looking at me.

Languille's eyes remained open and gazing at Dr Beaurieux for several seconds, but then, hearing nothing further from him, they slowly and evenly closed, as if he was somewhat bored with the proceedings.

It was at that point that I called out again and, once more, without any spasm, slowly, the eyelids lifted and undeniably living eyes fixed themselves on mine with perhaps even more penetration than the first time. Then there was a further clos-

Ing of the eyelids, but now less complete. I attempted the
effect of a third call; but there was no further movement - and
the eyes took on the glazed look which they have in the dead.

These findings may mean that one or other, or even both, of the
beheaded Italian brigands were aware of the shocks given to them
by Aidini.

Having completed his electrical experiments on the head of the
second brigand, Aldini then turned his attention to the same man's
body. He first asked Professor Mondini to bare the muscles of one
forearm and the tendons on the back of the hand. When that had
been done, he made a similar connection between them, the voltaic
pile and the spinal chord. The flow of electricity caused both arms
to rise from the table, much to everybody's surprise.

A more refined connection was then made between the biceps
muscle of the right arm and the spinal cord, which 'produced
such powerful contractions, that the arm which was placed hori-
zontally was raised in the fore part some six inches above the
surface of the table'. But what was achieved next was even more
astonishing. 'An hour and a quarter after their execution, I placed
in the palm of the hand a pair of iron pincers, weighing half a
pound; the hand was raised, and the fingers bent, as if they would
clasp them; but when arrived at the greatest height, the contraction ceased and the pincers fell.'

Aldini then had the heart of the brigand exposed. It had of
course stopped beating, and he was hoping that the electric
current would also prompt contractions in its muscular walls.
Much to his disappointment, however, the current failed in this
regard, perhaps because too much time had gone by. None the
less, he notes that in a similar experiment carried out at Turin
later the same year by Professor Vasilli-Eandi and others, 'strong
contractions of the heart' were produced. Thus the heart is just as
capable of being induced to contract by electricity as the voluntary muscles.

As the title of his paper indicates, Aldini was particularly interested in the potential of electricity for restarting hearts that have stopped and in thereby reanimating the apparently dead. He was encouraged by reports from elsewhere which suggested that this was possible, and he gives one example, which happened several years earlier, in 1774.

The case involved a three-year-old boy who had fallen out of a window on, to a pavement. He was unconscious and apparently dead, and indeed was declared so by a doctor. A gentleman living nearby, however, offered to try using electricity to reanimate him, and his parents agreed. As this was before Volta's discovery of his method for generating a continuous current, the anonymous gentleman presumably used a Leyden jar as his power source. And most remarkably, some twenty minutes elapsed before the electrical apparatus was obtained and set up. The first few shocks were directed without success into the child's stomach and related areas; a change for the better occurred, however, when his chest was selected as the target. 'On directing a few shocks through the chest, a small pulsation became perceptible, and soon after the child began to sigh, and to breathe, though with great difficulty; in about ten minutes, it vomited. A kind of stupor remained for some days; but it was restored to perfect health and spirits in about a week.'

This must be one of the first examples, if not *the* first, of electrically induced resuscitation, and is in essence exactly the same as that brought about by using an electric defibrillator today. When one realizes that mouth-to-mouth resuscitation was also first employed at about the same time, recovery techniques have not, it seems, advanced very far!

One year later Giovanni Aldini was invited to London, where in addition to giving some well-attended lectures, he organized a practical demonstration of the effects of electricity upon the human body, albeit this time with an entire corpse. The experiment took place at the College of Surgeons on the morning of

THE FRANKENSTEIN EXPERIMENTS

Monday, 17 January 1803, following the execution by hanging outside Newgate of a 32-year-old felon named George Foster, who 'conducted himself, in his last moments,' commented *The Times*, 'with becoming fortitude and resignation', and whose body was delivered to the College about one hour after he was declared dead. During that hour, Aldini records, Foster's corpse was exposed to a temperature of two degrees below freezing.

Foster, a journeyman coachmaker by trade, was hanged for the murder of his wife Jane and his twelve-month-old daughter Louisa by pushing them into the Paddington Canal, wherein they drowned, on Sunday, 5 December 1802. Although the evidence against him was largely circumstantial and he strongly protested his innocence during his trial, he broke down and confessed to the callous act immediately before he was hanged. Yet he gave no explanation for why he did it.

The Fosters had two other children, both of whom were in the care of the Barnet workhouse. Indeed, George Foster claimed that after having had a meal and a drink with his wife, from whom he was separated, that Sunday at the Mitre public house, which stood beside the Paddington Canal, he had proceeded from there on foot towards Barnet (which lay some 11 miles away), with the purpose of visiting the children, leaving his wife behind with the infant Louisa. He said that the onset of darkness prevented him from getting further than Whetstone, and that during his absence his wife must have somehow fallen into the canal, thereby drowning both herself and the child. Yet Foster's story of his long walk was shown to be false by the testimony of a witness, who said he had met Foster in Oxford Street at 6.30 that evening, as it would have been impossible for him to have walked all the way to Whetstone and back, a round trip of some 18 miles, in the two hours since his departure from the Mitre public house.

As before, Professor Aldini first applied the current from the voltaic pile to the felon's head, touching the wires to different parts of his face. When one wire was placed in an ear and the other in George Foster's mouth, 'the jaw immediately began to quiver, the adjoining muscles were horribly contorted, and the left eye actually opened'. And if that wasn't sufficient to alarm the audience, the next display certainly had the blood draining from their faces. In fact the entire event was so visually disturbing that it later caused the death of Mr Pass, the beadle of the Surgeons' Company, who was obliged to observe the experiment in an official capacity and who was presumably fairly used to grim sights, but who was so upset by what he saw that he collapsed and died of heart failure soon after returning home. 'On applying the arc to both ears, a motion of the head was manifested; all the muscles of the face became convulsed, and the lips and eye-lids were evidently affected. The action was increased by making one extremity of the arc to communicate with the nostrils and the other with the ear.'

The next test was somewhat more bizarre, for Aldini placed one electric wire in Forster's ear and the other in his rectum. 'Such violent muscular contractions were excited, as almost to give the appearance of reanimation.'

Following the delivery of shocks to the dissected arm muscles, producing a raising of the arm and clenching of the hand, Aldini turned his attention to the felon's heart. Forster's thorax was opened and the heart exposed, but the intrepid Aldini was again disappointed, for he found that no matter where he placed his wires, whether on the heart's ventricles, on the carneae columnae or on the nerves running to the coronary arteries, a contraction of neither the ventricles nor the auricles occurred. And although he afterwards obtained strong contractions in the muscles of the leg, notably when a circuit was made with the sciatic nerve and the gastrocnemius muscle, he must have been very puzzled by the lack of response of the heart, which is, after all, the key organ where resuscitation from apparent death is concerned. However, as he observed: 'From the preceding narrative it will be easily perceived, that our object in applying the treatment here described was not to produce re-animation, but merely to obtain a practical knowledge how far Galvanism might be employed as an axillary to other means in attempts to revive persons under similar circumstances.'

Further electrical research using a human corpse had to wait until 1818, when James Jeffray, Regius Professor of Anatomy at Glasgow University - and the inventor, interestingly enough, of the chain-saw, which he used during operations to cut through bones without damaging the associated soft tissues - obtained permission from the city authorities to carry out a similar electrical experiment on the body of a murderer. The convict selected for the gruesome test was Matthew Clydesdale (born about 1790), a powerfully-built weaver and part-time collier, who in August 1818 had beaten an old man to death with a pick-axe handle. When Clydesdale heard at his trial that after he was hanged, his body was to be used for some anatomical experiments involving electricity, he is said to have 'trembled excessively'. Later, while held in solitary confinement, he tried to commit suicide by cutting his throat with a broken bottle, but the attempt was thwarted by the quick action of the prison doctor.

He was hanged in the early afternoon of Wednesday, 4 November 1818, in front of the gaol, along with another felon named Ross. Clydesdale died almost immediately, but Ross took longer. The hangings were a tense affair, for the populace knew about the plan to dissect and electrify Clydesdale, and the authorities, fearing riot and disorder, and a possible attempt to free the condemned men, had called out a detachment of soldiers, who surrounded the gallows with fixed bayonets. But in the event there was no trouble, and Clydesdale, after being allowed to swing in the November breeze for about one hour, was cut down, placed in a coffin, and driven in a cart to Glasgow University's Department of Anatomy.

In the Anatomy Hall a low, stout table was ready for his body. At its head stood a 'minor voltaic battery, consisting of 270 pairs of four inch plates, with wires of communication, and pointed metal rods with insulating handles, for the more commodious application of the electric power. About five minutes before the police officers arrived with the body, the battery was charged with a dilute nitro-sulphuric acid, which speedily brought it into a state of intense action'. This description of the apparatus was written by Andrew Ure, a colleague of James Jeffray's and a chemist, who was Professor of Natural Philosophy at the University. He performed the actual electrification of Clydesdale, assisted by an anatomist named Marshall. Professor Jeffray's role was to direct the proceedings. Watching from the encircling galleries was a large, excited crowd of students, academics and interested members of the public, none of whom knew quite what to expect.

The popular account of what happened next is given by author Peter MacKenzie, who claims to have been one of the audience. He says that when Clydesdale's body was brought into the room, it was swiftly divested of its face covering and the cords that tied its hands and feet, and was then sat in 'an easy arm chair' (which is still apparently in the possession of the University), facing towards the audience.

A light air tube, connected with the galvanic battery, was soon placed in one of his nostrils. The bellows then began to gently blow into that nostril in solemn reality. His chest immediately heaved – he drew breath! Another tube was speedily placed in the next nostril. It made the executed body heave the more. A few other operations went swiftly on, which really we cannot very well describe; but at last the tongue of the murderer moved out to his lips; his eyes also opened widely – he stared, apparently in astonishment, around him; while his head, arms, and legs (at the same time, also) actually moved; and we declare he made a feeble attempt as if to rise from the chair whereon he was seated. He did positively rise from it in a moment or two afterwards, and stood upright.

The watching people, says Peter MacKenzie, were gasping with shock, horror or amazement at this incredible scene; but what happened next must have dumbfounded them, for MacKenzie relates that Professor Jeffray, aghast at what had been done, picked up a lancet, stepped forward, and then slashed through a jugular vein in Clydesdale's neck. The resurrected man immediately collapsed, and a few moments later was dead beyond revival in a pool of blood.

However, it is evident from MacKenzie's woolly description of how the electricity was used that his account is largely imaginary. To connect the battery with 'a light air tube' inserted into one of Clydesdale's nostrils would have been pointless, if not completely useless. And anyway, Clydesdale could not possibly have revived as rapidly as MacKenzie suggests, not least because he had been left hanging on the gallows for an hour. The felon might have been resuscitated by electric shocks delivered to his chest to restart his heart, combined with the inflation of his lungs by means of a bellows to simulate breathing. Yet even if this had been done and Clydesdale had revived, he would not have been able to stand up so quickly.

MacKenzie's account, which was not published until nearly fifty years afterwards, is also completely at odds with Andrew Ure's description of what he did, which he read to an audience at the Glasgow Literary Society on Thursday, 10 December 1818, a mere five weeks after the event took place. The latter records that remarkable things were induced in Matthew Clydesdale's body by electricity, but his revival from death was not one of them.

Ure recounts how the body of the murderer was brought into the Anatomy Hall and placed, not in an armchair, but on the table. Its resuscitation was then made virtually impossible by the fact that the anatomist Marshall immediately cut into the back of the neck, just below the skull, to allow him to remove the rear half of the atlas vertebra, thereby exposing the spinal chord. A second incision was made in the hip, cutting through the gluteal muscle, to bring the sciatic nerve into view. These exposures of nervous tissue were for the purposes of demonstrating that electricity has a greater effect on the muscles if it is conveyed to them by the nerves, than when it is applied to them directly. A small cut was also made in the heel of one of the feet.

That done, one of the rods from the voltaic battery was applied to the spinal cord, the other to the sciatic nerve. The effect was instantaneous and dramatic.

Every muscle of the body was immediately agitated with convulsive movements, resembling a violent shuddering from cold. The left side was most powerfully convulsed at each renewal of the electric contact. On moving the second rod from the hip to the heel, the knee being previously bent, the leg was thrown out with such violence, as nearly to overturn one of the assistants, who in vain attempted to prevent its extension.

The next experiment was, in its way, even more dramatic, for when Marshall had exposed the left phrenic nerve of the chest, Ure touched one electric rod to it and the other to the diaphragm, which had likewise been exposed by means of a small cut made under the seventh rib. 'The success of it was truly wonderful. Full, nay, laborious breathing, instantly commenced. The chest heaved, and fell; the belly was protruded, and again collapsed, with the relaxing and retiring diaphragm. This process was continued, without interruption, as long as I continued the electric discharges.'

Thus Clydesdale was indeed prompted to breathe, as MacKenzie maintains, but it was done by stimulating the muscles of his chest wall and diaphragm to contract, not by using a bellows. However, despite the fact that the electric shocks were entering the chest, no corresponding beating of the heart was induced. Andrew Ure believes that this was probably because the body had been drained of blood (presumably by the incisions made in the neck and thigh).

Next, one rod was applied to a nerve in the forehead, the supra-orbital, while the other was touched to the heel. By this means the 'most extraordinary grimaces were exhibited' in the face. Furthermore, by manipulating the battery, a series of shocks, each more powerful than the last, was sent into the head, and every muscle was 'simultaneously thrown into fearful action: rage, horror, despair, anguish and ghastly smiles, untied their hideous expression in the murderer's face. . . . At this period several of the spectators were forced to leave the apartment from terror or sickness, and one gentleman fainted.'

The fourth and last experiment was carried out by touching one rod to the spinal cord and the other to an elbow, which caused the fingers to move 'nimbly, like those of a violin performer'. When the rod was moved from the elbow to the tip of one of the clenched index fingers, 'that finger extended instantly; and from the convulsive agitation of the arm, he seemed to point to the different spectators, some of whom thought he had come to life.'

These four groups of experiments, each concentrating on a different part of the body, took about one hour to perform. And while they only brought about a semblance of life in the dead man, Andrew Ure was convinced that the corpse could have been resuscitated if they had been done somewhat differently. He writes:

We are willing to imagine, that if, without cutting into and wounding the spinal marrow and blood vessels in the neck, the pulmonary organs had been set a-playing at first, (as I proposed) by electrifying the phrenic nerve (which may be done without any dangerous incision), there is a possibility that life might have been restored. This event, however little desirable with a murderer, and perhaps contrary to law, would yet have been pardonable in one instance, as it would have been highly honourable and useful to science.

This work was truly remarkable for its time, offering as it did the real possibility that death itself might be reversed with the assistance of electricity, and the dead thereby restored to life. This was a truly awesome and exciting prospect, one that would seemingly place in Man's hands a power that had previously only belonged to God. And furthermore, if the dead could be reanimated, then perhaps life itself might one day be created. To achieve that would indeed mean acquiring God-like powers. But with such power comes danger, both to the creators and to the created, and it was this danger that Mary Shelley addressed in *Frankenstein*.

That she had probably heard about Aldini's electrical experiments, perhaps from her husband or one of his friends, is evident in the preface she wrote for the Standard Novels edition, published in 1831:

Many and long were the conversations between Lord Byron and Shelley, to which I was a devout but nearly silent listener. During one of these, various philosophical doctrines were discussed, and among others the nature of the principle of life, and whether there was any probability of its ever being discovered and communicated. . . . Perhaps a corpse would be reanimated; galvanism had given token of such things: perhaps the component parts of a creature might be manufactured, brought together, and endued with vital warmth.

However, the novel's hero, Victor Frankenstein, does not use electricity to animate his monster, although it figures prominently in the various films made of the novel. In these, the creature is brought to life during a thunderstorm, the lightning being directed down through conductors into the apparatus on which it lies, so providing the energy for its awakening. In the book, Frankenstein's method is altogether more subtle and sophisticated, although Mary Shelley had originally conceived of him inducing life in the creature by 'the working of some powerful engine'. Rather, by assembling the creature from the parts of both human beings and animals, Frankenstein is able to animate it by having discovered 'the cause of generation and life; nay, more, I became myself capable of bestowing animation upon lifeless matter'.

The Frankenstein monster is disadvantaged right from the start by its creator, for it is made very ugly and is given a gigantic stature – 8 feet high – although there is no mention in the book of it having a bolt through its neck. But it is well endowed with intelligence and sensitivity, neither of which favour it in finding happiness. It is shunned almost from the start by Frankenstein himself, who runs off and leaves it to its own devices. By hiding for many months in an outhouse attached to a family dwelling, which has an aperture in the intervening wall through which it peers, it is able to learn the German language and, because the family members read edifying books to one another, is able to acquire a tolerable knowledge of humankind. However, when it eventually presents itself to the father of the family, who is blind, hoping thereby to gain his confidence and assistance, it is attacked by his daughter's fiancé when he returns unexpectedly. The daughter herself, whom the creature cherishes, faints at the sight of him. This teaches him that he has no hope of ever being happy, finding love, or being accepted by ordinary people.

The remainder of the story is a ghastly tragedy, both for Frankenstein and for his creature, as each is the curse of the other. All those whom Frankenstein loves are murdered by his creation, and he himself dies while pursuing it through the wastes of the Arctic. The creature is made desperate by rejection and loneliness, and its anguish drives it to kill. For remarkably, it contained no innate malice, and it was originally as beautiful within as it was ugly without.

'I, the miserable and the abandoned, am an abortion, to be spurned at, and kicked, and trampled on. Even now my blood boils at the recollection of this injustice,' it cries when it stands beside the corpse of Victor Frankenstein.

The lament sounds a warning to all those modern descendants of Frankenstein, who are even now waiting to unfreeze the cryo-genically frozen, to clone people, to inseminate elderly women, or to fertilize young women with sperm taken from corpses.

10 Visions of the Hereafter

The Knell, the Shroud, the Mattock, and the Grave;
The deep damp Vault, the Darkness, and the Worm;
These are the Bugbears of a Winter's Eve,
The Terrors of the Living, not the Dead.

From 'Night Thoughts on Life, Death, and Immortality'
by Edward Young

As we have seen in the previous chapter many people have been brought to a state of apparent death, and have revived. And intriguingly, some of those who have done so report that, while lying in their death-like torpor, they left their physical bodies and were either taken to, or found themselves in, another realm of being. There they saw beautiful landscapes and buildings, and often encountered spiritual guides or loved ones and friends who had died before them. These out-of-body experiences were generally positive and uplifting, although sometimes a darker, less pleasant dimension was visited, which revealed that the hereafter is not all light and love.

These excursions into the beyond are today known as Near Death Experiences (NDEs), and are typically reported by those who are saved from death by modern resuscitative techniques. Indeed, since the publication in 1975 of a ground-breaking book entitled *Life Beyond Life* by Raymond Moody, many hundreds, if not thousands, of accounts of NDEs have been collected, which have together filled over a hundred books.

Thus far I have described only two cases of post-mortem recovery where those concerned mentioned that something extraordinary had happened to them at the moment of their death. The first of these was John Smith, who was hanged at Tyburn. You may recall that when he later spoke of what it was like to be hanged, he said: 'I felt my spirits in a strange commotion, violently pressing upwards: which, having forced their way to my head, I as it were saw a great blaze or glaring light, which seemed to go out at my eyes with a flash, and then I lost all sense of pain.' The second was the American soldier who was injured and brought to the brink of death in Vietnam. He suddenly found himself floating above his lifeless body, looking down at both it and the scene around. From that vantage point he not only saw himself and the bodies of his fallen comrades being robbed of their valuables by the Viet Cong, but later watched as they were all picked up and taken back to camp by American troops.

Dr Raymond Moody noted that most NDEs tend to follow a similar pattern, although the stages are sometimes different and by no means all went through the complete experience. Moody found that at the moment a dying person's heart stops beating, he (or she) typically hears the doctor pronounce him dead. He then becomes aware of a ringing or buzzing noise, and feels himself drawn out of his body through a darkness, as if he were moving down a tunnel. Then he suddenly finds himself outside his body, floating in the air, looking down on his still form and at the activity, if any, going on around him.

The person soon adjusts to his liberation and has no regret at having died. He may sense, however, that his form is quite different from his physical self. Yet when he next meets the 'spirits' of loved ones who have died before him, as usually happens, he recognizes them by their familiar human appearance. They form, in fact, a welcoming party.

He then encounters a very special spiritual entity, which manifests as a radiantly bright, whitish light, This 'being of light' is

216

totally warm, loving and welcoming, and he feels great peace and contentment in its presence. The light asks him non-verbally to evaluate his life, and to help him do so he may be shown significant scenes from it, which pass by in the form of a rapid and colourful playback. Watching them, he intuitively understands the consequences of all his actions, and feels within himself all the hurt and distress he has caused others. He may then be asked if he is ready to die.

The 'being of light' next leads him to some sort of barrier, which may be nothing more than a line on the ground, or more frequently a fence or a wall, and which symbolizes the end of earthly existence. He is given to understand that if he crosses over it, he cannot return to his physical body. Yet while he wants to continue on, he realizes that he has certain commitments and responsibilities in his earthly life, such as the care of young children, which he feels he cannot and should not avoid. Having made this decision, he immediately finds himself waking up in his physical body, having been resuscitated.

However, it sometimes happens that when a person finds himself outside his body at the moment of death, he does not necessarily leave the world. I mentioned two or three such examples in my book *Doubles: The Enigma of the Second Self*, of which one is sufficiently remarkable to make it worth recapitulating here. The man concerned was a German knight named Everadus Ambula, and his experience took place during the pontificate of Innocent II (otherwise Lothaire de' Conti di Segni), which lasted from 1198 to 1216.

Everadus Ambula fell sick and apparently died. He was accordingly laid out by his grieving relatives, but after some time had passed he suddenly regained consciousness and woke up. His family's astonishment grew when he told them that, while dead, his soul or wraith had left his body and had been taken on an extensive journey by 'evil spirits'. They had first carried him, he said, to Jerusalem, and afterwards to the camp of Saladin in

Egypt. From there they had gone to a wood in Lombardy, where he had met and spoken at length with a German friend of his; and lastly, he had been conducted to the city of Rome, whose buildings and scenes, as well as the appearance of several of its princes, he was able describe accurately, despite never having been there before. Even more remarkably, the friend whom he met in Lombardy, when contacted, not only recalled their meeting at the stated place and time, but said he and Ambula had talked of the very topics the knight claimed. He also thought he was talking to the real man!

While such a lengthy journey through the world is rare, the appearance of a dead person's wraith to one or more loved ones is quite often reported. One moving visit, which is recorded by the anonymous author of *Apparitions, Supernatural Occurrences, Demonstrative of the Soul's Immortality*, published in 1799, was made by a mother who had died in the night to her 9-year-old son. At the time of her death, the woman apparently came into the boy's bedroom.

> He heard the curtains undraw, and saw his mother stand by his bed-side: she put her hand upon his head, and said, Beal (that was his christian name), be a good boy, and fear God; – the child was not in the least frightened, having no suspicion of a preternatural appearance, his mother being in perfect health at the time he went to bed. Next morning he told a relation, his mother came to his bed-side and patted his face, and told him to be a good boy, and fear God; he was then informed of the loss of his parent, and that the hand of death was laid upon her.

I have had such visits in the night myself, so I can vouch for the authenticity of the experience. For example, at around midnight on the night in 1996 when my mother's brother died in a Luton hospital after a long illness, I was dozing in bed when I suddenly felt an arm being placed around my shoulders. It exerted a light but unmistakable pressure, and gave me what I can only describe as a comforting squeeze, which generated within me a mild, almost electric tingling. And then it was gone, having held me for no more than four or five seconds. I wondered at the time whether it was my uncle, and thus a sign of his death, but it was not until the next morning that I learned that he had passed away at about 11.15 p.m. I cannot be sure, of course, that it was him, but as it is the only phantom arm to have been placed around my shoulders in the night, I think the odds are that it was.

Another startling encounter with a wraith, which is also described in *Apparitions*, happened to a man named Wilson, a resident of Liverpool, who was one day walking at a place near the town known as St Domingo. Suddenly 'he thought he saw a relation whom he expected every day from Jamaica, in a field, near where he was; he directly went into the field, and came so near him, that he hailed him, but to his great surprise, he seemed to sink into the earth'.

This greatly alarmed Mr Wilson, and when he returned to the friends with whom he had been walking, they saw his distress and immediately asked him what was the matter. He told them he had just seen William James, whom they all knew, and said he believed they would soon hear of his death, explaining why. His friends, however, laughed at him, and said that he was imagining things. 'However, the next day the vessel came into the port of Liverpool, and brought the sad news, that this man, who was chief mate of a Guineaman, had at the time that Mr Wilson saw the apparition, tumbled down the hold of the ship, had fractured his skull, and expired within ten minutes.'

As these examples demonstrate, a wraith is the exact likeness of a person, and therefore his or her double. It differs from a ghost, however, in that not only does it contain the deceased person's consciousness, but it can also manipulate matter and thus move objects. This is why the dead mother's wraith in the example quoted above was able both to undraw the curtains around her son's bed and to apply a noticeable touch to his head. Indeed, a wraith possesses many of the properties of matter, which suggests that it may be, as the ancient Egyptians believed, quasi-physical. The arm that was placed around my shoulders certainly had sufficient solidity for me to feel both its presence and the squeeze it gave me.

I suggested in *Doubles: The Enigma of the Second Self* that this paranormal likeness, which can both interrupt and reflect light, and can thus be seen, normally resides within us during life, although it may on occasion leave the body and appear elsewhere. Such a separation typically happens when we are asleep, notably when we dream; or, if we are awake, during a period of emotional upset. At such times, this 'second self', emerging from a living person, is called a double, or doppelganger; the term 'wraith' is only used for it when it appears at or around the time of death. In fact, the function of a wraith is to provide a familiar boundary and setting for the consciousness, and travels with it into the next world after death.

In an essay entitled 'The Palimpset of the Brain' Thomas De Quincey records the experience of a close female relative of his, who, as a child of nine, was playing beside one of the deepest and most dangerous stretches of a country brook, when she fell into the water and sank.

> At a certain stage of this descent, a blow seemed to strike her; a phosphoric radiance sprang forth from her eyeballs; and immediately a mighty theatre expanded within her brain. In a moment, in the twinkling of an eye, every act, every design of her past life, lived again, arraying themselves not as a succession, but as parts of a coexistence. Such a light fell upon the whole path of her life backwards into the shades of infancy as the light, perhaps, which wrapt the destined Apostle on his road to Damascus. Yet that light blinded for a season; but hers

poured celestial vision upon the brain, so that her consciousness became omnipresent at one moment to every feature in
the infinite review.

This remarkable incident is similar, in its earliest stage, to that
of the hanged John Smith, who also saw a blaze of light depart-
ing as if from his eyeballs. But the drowned girl's 'phosphoric
radiance' was quickly followed by what Moody calls a 'life
review', in which she was shown every event of her existence.
This was particularly noteworthy in that events which had originally taken place in apparent succession, one after the other, were
seen simultaneously 'as parts of a coexistence', and that the girl
was able to comprehend them all at once.

The life review was ended, it seems, by the farmer who rented
the adjacent fields. He saw the girl fall into the water as he rode
his horse down a lane, and made his way to the spot as fast as he
could. He waded in and pulled her out, and then managed to
revive her. In *The Confessions of an English Opium Eater*, where the
occurrence is also mentioned, De Quincey adds the following
important rider, 'Forty-five years had intervened between the first
time and the last time of her telling me this anecdote, and not one
iota had shifted its ground amongst the incidents, nor had any of
the most trivial of the circumstantiations suffered change.' This
constancy of content attests to the account's truthfulness.

Writing in the Suffolk edition of *County Folk Lore*, Lady
Everline Gurdon describes the post-mortem experience of the
wife of Sir Richard Harrison, who resided at the oddly named
village of Balls, in Hertfordshire. Three months after giving birth
to her daughter Ann on 25 March 1625, Lady Harrison went
down with a fever and apparently died. She may in fact have been
the victim of plague, as there was a bad outbreak that year. After
having been laid out for two days, Lady Harrison was visited by a
mourner named Winston, a medical doctor, who suspected that
she was not really dead. He therefore sought permission from her

husband to make a small incision in the sole of one of her feet. When this was granted and the cut had been made, blood was seen to flow from the wound. Dr Winston therefore quickly set about trying to resuscitate her, and soon proved successful.

On opening her eyes, Lady Harrison first saw the wide sleeves of the gowns worn by two visiting ladies, which prompted her to say, 'Did you not promise me fifteen years, and are you come again?' This strange remark was explained when she later told her husband and their rector that when she died it seemed to her she was in a strange place impossible to describe, and a wonderful quiet was upon her, except that her mind was troubled about her infant. Suddenly two beings stood before her, clad in long white garments, who asked her what was the cause of her unhappiness. She fell on her face before them, crying out, 'Oh, let me have the same grant given to Hezekiah, that I may live fifteen years to see my daughter a woman!' Her prayer was evidently granted for not only did Lady Harrison return to life but she lived exactly fifteen years after the date of her singular vision.

A similar incident, which also took place in Hertfordshire, is reported by John Aubrey in *Miscellanies Upon Various Subjects*. He says that in 1670, a poor widow's daughter, who was in service, was brought close to death by a serious illness. When news came of her condition, her worried mother prayed to God that He would spare her daughter and take her instead. While she was praying, the daughter fell into a trance, which gripped her for an hour, and she was thought to be dead by the family for whom she worked. But she soon recovered, and she told of a remarkable experience that had occurred during her trance. According to Aubrey, she said:

That one in black Habit came to her, whose face was so bright and glorious she could not behold it; and also he had such brightness upon his Breast, and (if I forget not) upon his Arms;

and told her, That her Mother's Prayers were heard; and that her Mother should shortly die, and she should suddenly recover: And she did so, and her Mother died. She had the character of a modest, humble, vertuous Maid.

The figure who told the young woman that her mother's prayer had been heard is clearly another version of the 'being of light' described by Moody's subjects, although its black costume is unusual.

Another interesting, and fuller, seventeenth-century NDE happened to a 14-year-old girl named Anna Atherton. She was taken sick in November 1669 and her ailment, which resembled malaria, proved too difficult for her doctors to cure. In the following weeks she lost weight, and grew pale, listless, and despairing. Then in February 1670, her illness reached a crisis and she apparently died. Yet when she was being laid out, the women doing the job noticed that her body seemed warmer than it should. They opened the windows and extinguished the fire, in case the heat of the room was responsible, but the warmth, although only slight, persisted throughout the day. That evening the worried women held a mirror to her nose, which however did not mist over. Afterwards they placed live coals against the soles of her feet, which also brought no response. The failure of these tests seemed to confirm that, despite the puzzling warmth of her body, Anna was dead.

Her mother, however, maintained a faint hope that she might still be alive and ordered the funeral to be postponed. She left Anna lying in bed and kept a watchful eye on her. Seven days went by without any change, but then a sudden increase was noticed in her temperature. This prompted her doctor to use restorative techniques, which eventually had the effect of bringing her back to life and consciousness. As soon as she opened her eyes, she asked to see her mother, to whom she gave the following remarkable account:

> Oh Mother! Since I was absent from you, I have been in Heaven, an Angel went before me to conduct me thither; I passed through several Gates, and at length I came to Heaven's Gate, where I saw Things very Glorious and Unutterable, as Saints, Angels, and the like, in glorious Apparel, and heard unparalleled Musick, Divine Anthems and Hallelujahs. I would fain have entered that glorious Place, but the Angel that went before me withstood me, yet I thought myself half in; but he told me, I could not be admitted now, but must go back and take leave of my Friends, and after some time I should be admitted. So he brought me hither again, and is now standing at the Bed's-feet; Mother! You must needs see him, he is all in White.

Mrs Atherton, who could not see any such being at the end of the bed, said he was surely an illusion, and opined that she had doubtlessly dreamed of nearly being in heaven. But Anna protested strongly, saying that what she had seen was true, and to show that she was not imagining things, she mentioned the names of three or four other people who were also there. She had, she insisted, seen them pass by her when she stood at heaven's gate. 'One of those She named was reputed a vicious Person, came as afar as the Gate, but was sent back again another way. All the Persons she named, died in the time she lay in this Trance.'

Anna Atherton lived for two more years, 'enjoying perfect Health; and then died in great Assurance of her salvation; speaking comfortable words, and giving wholesome Instruction, to all who came to visit her'.

A similar out-of-body experience in wraith form occurred just over 250 years later to a 34-year-old Leicestershire man named Matthew Robinson. A resident of Market Harborough, he fell into a trance, much to his wife's alarm, at about 3 a.m. on Monday, 5 November 1821, after having returned home very late from a church service at Mount Sorrel. As far as I can ascertain, he was not thought to have died, but he remained worryingly unconscious for three days, until Thursday, 8 November.

In the pamphlet about his experience, Matthew says that on entering the trance 'I was immediately transported to a wide and fertile plain, where I saw no person near me'. This pleasant, seemingly outdoor scene is reminiscent of the 'beautiful green field' that John Hayes thought himself in after being hanged at Newgate in 1782, although he recalled nothing more when he revived on the dissecting room table. Matthew Robinson, however, did not remain alone for long:

After looking around some time, I observed an elderly and venerable person at a little distance, clad in a loose and flowing garment. He approached me with a cheerful smile, and waved a light silver wand for me to follow him. I instantly did so, and he conducted me by a narrow path into a delightful grove, where every air was balm, and every sound the most enchanting melody. 'This Son (said my guide) is the place where the souls of living saints meet in converse with God.'

The robed man then took him to another place that exceeded 'the force of language to describe'. At its centre stood a beautiful illuminated altar from which came a delicious, sweet-scented perfume which was, he explained, formed from the prayers of the righteous. The elderly guide then pointed upwards with his wand, and Matthew, following its movement with his eyes, saw to his astonishment another wonderful scene.

A diamond's blaze was darkness compared to the effulgent. beams that played around a throne, before which floated innumerable heavenly essences, that ever kept bowing in the most willing and grateful adoration. I felt confounded, and was about to throw myself on the earth, but my guide forbad me, and conducted me back in another direction, to the top of a

high mountain, from which I saw a multitude of persons, travelling in an open path, with the most riotous and intoxicated
joy. 'Son, (said my guide) I will shew thee the end of this
mirth.' My ears were instantly stunned with the most dismal
sounds of despair, and my eyes scorched with a prospect that
would have blasted any eye less than supernatural.

Matthew instinctively turned from this frightening view of the
nether world, and his guide, without hindering him, urged him to
remember what he'd seen and to let it help him work for good
when he returned to earth. And then, having uttered an involuntary 'Lord help me', he suddenly found himself back in his body,
'after three days' suspension of my natural powers'.

The experience of leaving one's body at the moment of death
and then being taken to a beautiful green field has in fact often
been reported. The following case, reported in the *Telegraph*
magazine, is a recent example. When 36-year-old Mrs Mary
Errington, of Washington, Tyne and Wear, clinically died
during a brain operation for an aneurysm, she first found
herself outside her body, floating up near the ceiling of the
operating room, and was then taken rapidly down a long tunnel
towards a bright, white light. She emerged from the light into
a meadow.

It was a vast meadow, with thick, luscious grass everywhere –
apart from this one tree which I could see in the distance. And
I could associate with it; I'd never really thought of trees
before, but this one was friendly, that's the only thing I can
say. I wasn't walking in the meadow; I was just floating gently
towards this tree at the far side of the meadow, And the quiet-
ness. . . . it can only be described as a heavenly silence. . . .
The branches of the tree were like outstretched arms. It felt
welcoming. And I felt that I had to go to the tree. I was nearly

there. I could almost put out my hands to touch it. And then suddenly I was coming back down the tunnel very fast, to the ceiling, and watching the doctors and nurses again, bringing me back to life.

Mary Errington's experience was wholly pleasant and non-threatening, although she is certain she could not have returned to life if she had reached the welcoming tree. Her failure to reach it, she believes, was caused by the fact that her family on earth still required her presence, and which accounted for her resuscitation.

Her description of the tree brings to mind a verse of the folk song 'All My Trials, Lord', which runs:

> There is a tree in paradise,
> A tree they call the tree of life.
> All my trials, Lord,
> Soon be over.

And like the other accounts of people finding themselves in a green field, it is also reminiscent of Psalm 23, which includes the words:

> He maketh me to lie down in green pastures: he leadeth me beside the still waters. . . . Yea, though I walk in the valley of the shadow of death, I will fear no evil: for thou art with me; thy rod and thy staff they comfort me.

The astonishing observation by Anna Atherton that there were several people at the gates of heaven, all of whom had died while she was in her trance and whose arrival suggests that she was actually at the place she describes, is not without precedent. There is a similar case which is worth repeating, not least because the principal character actually died.

The man in question was none other than the famous German

humanist and Hebraist Johann Reuchlin, who passed away at Ingolstadt on Monday, 30 June 1522. One of his oldest friends was a Franciscan monk, a man widely renowned for his holiness and piety, who lived in a convent at Tübingen. Ingolstadt and Tübingen lie just over 100 miles apart, and at that early time it took news several days to travel from one to the other.

Early in the morning of 30 June, just after the monk had celebrated Matins, he returned to his cell and lay back down on his bed, where he quickly fell asleep. According to the account in Erasmus's *Colloquies*, he suddenly found himself, as he believed, in another place, but one that is already familiar to us.

> Methought I was standing by a little bridge that led into a Meadow, so wonderfully fine, what with the Emrald Verdue, and freshness of the Trees and Grass; the infinite Beauty, and Variety of Flowers, and the fragrancy of all together that all the Fields and this side of the River lookt dead, blasted, and withered, in Comparison.

As he was gazing delightedly at this beautiful verdant scene, his friend Johann Reuchlin walked up to the bridge, giving him a blessing in Hebrew as he passed.

> He was gotten above half over the Bridge, before I was aware; and as I was about to run up to him, he lookt back and bade me stand off. Your time (says he) is not yet come; but five years hence you are to follow me. In the mean while, be you a Witness, and a Spectator, of what's done.

Reuchlin was dressed in a simple white robe, 'shining, like Damask', and when he gained the other side of the bridge he was met by none other than St Jerome, clad in a long gown that was 'as Transparent as Crystal', who said to him: 'God save thee, my most Holy Companion, I am commanded to conduct thee to the

Blessed Souls above, as a Reward, from the Divine Bounty, of thy pious Labours.' The saint then took out a robe like his own and put it on Reuchlin, whom he afterwards led into the meadow and climbed with him to the top of the hill at its centre.

And now the Heaven's open'd, to a prodigious widness, there appear'd a Glory so unutterable, as made every thing else that pass'd for wonderful before, to look mean, and sordid . . . . Out of this Overture, there was let down a great Pillar of fire, which was both Transparent, and very Agreeable. By the means of this Pillar, Two Holy Souls embracing one another, ascended into Heaven; a Quire of Angels all the while accompanying them, with so charming a melody, that the Franciscan says, he is not able to think of the Delight of it, without weeping.

The monk then awoke, 'but he started up like a mad man, and call'd for his Bridge, and his meadow, without either speaking or thinking of any thing else; and there was no perswading of him to believe that he was any longer in his Cell'. His behaviour reveals that what he saw was not something in a dream, for its reality was absolutely convincing to him. And further confirmation of this comes from the fact that the seniors of the monk's convent later learned that Johann Reuchlin had died at the time of his appearance beside the bridge.

Indeed, it is probable that the monk was fortunate enough to have had an out-of-body experience when he was asleep, and that his conscious double was projected to the border between this dimension and the next, where he witnessed the passing over of his friend and brother in Christ. We may also note that the monk died five years afterwards, just as Reuchlin had predicted!

Although this was overall a benign experience, like the others, the monk also said that he saw following Johann Reuchlin, 'a good way off', some large, grubby-looking birds the size of vultures, that 'would certainly have set upon him if they durst'. These were kept at bay by the dead man's wraith making the sign of the cross at them, and they were unable to fly into the glorious meadow. But several early NDEs took the wraith to places that were anything but pleasant.

One of the earliest of these is described by the Venerable Bede in his *A History of the English Church and People*. He writes of a man named Drycthelm of Cunningham, Northumbria, who, in about 695 AD, became sick, suffered a sad decline and eventually died at home 'in the early hours of the night'. But then, much to the astonishment and fright of his grieving family, he returned to life at daybreak, and told his stalwart wife, who had not fled from his bedside, what had happened to him when he was dead. He said he was met by 'a handsome man in a shining robe', with whom he walked in an easterly direction until they reached 'a very broad and deep valley of infinite length'.

The valley was distinguished by the fact that on one side were flames in which souls were roasting, while on the other was snow and bitter cold in which they were freezing. The souls could jump from one side to the other, in an attempt to escape their plight, but the benefit was only momentary, for those who had burned then froze, and vice versa. The number of souls thus tormented was 'countless', but the valley was not Hell, as Drycthelm had supposed, but rather a 'place where souls are tried and punished who have delayed to confess and amend their wicked ways'. They would be released, he learned, on the Day of Judgement. His guide then led him into the darkness at the far end of the valley, where there was a vast and deep pit from which 'masses of black flame' ceaselessly rose and fell. The tongues of flame contained the souls of men, which were thrown out like sparks, only to fall into the pit again. This awful place was the mouth of Hell, into which 'whoever falls . . . will never be delivered throughout eternity'.

From this dreadful spot, Drycthelm's guide led him along a

road branching to the right, which brought them back into the light and, in due course, to a wall of apparently infinite height and length, which lacked gates or other apertures. Then, to Drycthelm's astonishment, and without knowing how it happened, he suddenly found himself on top of the wall with his guide, from where he could see, lying within, a 'very broad and pleasant meadow', radiantly bright and filled with flowers, resembling in general form the grassy expanses mentioned earlier. However, in this field there were 'innumerable companies of men in white robes, and many parties of happy people sitting together'. And then, equally miraculously, the pair were down in the meadow, walking amongst its inhabitants.

But this delightful place was not the Kingdom of Heaven, for while those there, explained the guide, had done good in their lives, they 'were not so perfect as to merit immediate entry' into it. Drycthelm was then taken into another, even more wonderful light, one containing beautiful fragrances and the sound of delightful voices singing, which was close, his guide said, to the heavenly kingdom. He then told Drycthelm that he must now return to his physical body, adding that if from then on he lived simply and virtuously, he would in due course 'win a home among these happy spirits that you see'. Drycthelm did not want to go back to his body, but he suddenly found himself waking up in it.

Drycthelm paid heed to what his mysterious companion had said. He gave up life in the secular world and became a monk, spending the remainder of his days fasting and praying and, somewhat oddly, standing for hours up to his neck in an icy river, saying to any who questioned why he did it, 'I have seen greater austerity.'

An even earlier account of a journey after death is described by the Greek philosopher Plato in the tenth book of *The Republic*. The experience happened to a soldier named Er. The story of his return to life after being apparently dead for twelve days, just in time to avoid being cremated, was related in Chapter 7.

The tale he told when he regained consciousness was astonishing. He said that his soul had left his body and had 'travelled in company with many others until they came to a wonderfully strange place, where there were, close to each other, two gaping chasms in the earth, and opposite and above them two other chasms in the sky'. A number of judges sat between the two earth chasms, who judged those coming before them, directing the just to take the right-hand road that led up into the sky, while the unjust were ordered to take the left-hand path to the underworld. The good went into one of the sky chasms, which led to heaven, and the bad into one of the earth chasms, which led to hell.

From the other sky and earth chasms emerged souls who had already spent their allotted time in heaven or hell. They were now due to be reborn on earth, and when they had lingered together for seven days in the broad meadow surrounding the judges, they were first shown the structure of the universe and then went before Lachesis, one of the three Fates, to choose what their new life was to be. This was done partly by throwing lots. Men could opt to become women if they wished, and vice versa, or they could become animals, a choice that was often preferred by those who disliked the human race.

And to see the souls choosing their lives was indeed a sight, Er said, a sight to move pity and laughter and wonder. For the most part they followed the habits of their former life. . . . In the evening they encamped by the Forgetful River, whose water no pitcher can hold. And all were compelled to drink a certain measure of its water; and those who had no wisdom to save them drank more than the measure. And as each man drank he forgot everything. They then went to sleep and when midnight came there was an earthquake and thunder, and like shooting stars they were all swept suddenly up and away to be born. Er himself was forbidden to drink, and could not tell by what manner of means he returned to his body; but suddenly

he opened his eyes and it was dawn and he was lying on the
pyre.

Another glimpse of the nether regions was seen by the mother
of the French chronicler Guibert de Nogent, quoted in *Curiosités
Biographiques*, who had an out-of-body experience when she fell
asleep one summer night on a narrow grassy bank. She felt her
soul leave her body, pass across what seemed to be a gallery, and
then come to the edge of a dark pit. Her son describes what then
occurred:

Suddenly, there came from the side of the pit the shadows of
men, whose hair was like blown glass eaten to dust, and who
wanted to seize her with their hands and carry her into the
gulf. But there came a voice from behind my mother, who was
trembling and miserably agitated by their attack, addressing
itself to them. It commanded, 'Don't touch this woman!'
Chased away by the voice, the shadows dived back into the
pit. Thus delivered, my mother halted at its edge, whereupon
my father suddenly appeared from behind her, looking as he
had in his youth. Regarding him very attentively, she asked
him in a wavering voice if he was in fact Everard (which was
my father's name); yet he replied negatively.

It is uncertain why Guibert's father should have denied who he
was. Guibert somewhat oddly postulates that wraiths no longer
use the names they had in their earthly existence. If true, this
would certainly explain his father's denial. His mother's experience ended shortly afterwards, and she found herself waking up
back in her body.

These NDEs clearly reveal that the next world does contain
dark, terrifying regions where punishment is meted out to those
who pass evil and ungodly lives. Most religions maintain that
some form of judgement, followed by the punishment of

wrongdoers, takes place after death, and of course such NDEs support this belief. And while some people have claimed that the experiences are in fact subjective, being either dreams or fantasies, those who have had them say that they had a very real quality to them, that they seemed to be actual events, which doubtlessly explains why they not only remain in the memory but are recalled without alteration over the years. As such, they remain as stark warnings to all those who lack love and morality, and who think they can get away with anything. Such people will, in due course, get their just deserts.

However, to end this chapter on a more upbeat note, I shall recount the NDE of a Hastings man named Ken Harrison, who became very ill in 1988 following a hip-replacement operation that went wrong. His hip became infected and he developed a fever. His experience is sufficiently unusual to merit inclusion here, especially as it features a modern form of transport that one would not ordinarily expect to find in the next world.

At the height of his fever Ken suddenly became aware of a brilliant light in the doorway of his hospital room, and this seemed to absorb him and to gather him up, so that he was conscious of nothing except the light. Then, to his surprise, he found himself carrying a suitcase and apparently climbing up a railway embankment. When he reached the top, a train came along the line and stopped beside him, so he climbed aboard.

He found a seat inside the carriage, which contained many other passengers, although he did not know any of them. Then, when the train moved off, it entered a bank of thick fog, which completely obscured the surrounding countryside. While this was happening, a ticket collector came down the carriage and, noticing Ken, asked to see his ticket. When he sheepishly admitted to not having one, the ticket collector said sternly, 'Well, you shouldn't be on this train without a ticket, you'll have to get off.' Ken replied: 'You can't turn me off into nowhere. Look, I'm going to see my mother and father. They'll vouch for me when I get to the end of the journey.' And to his surprise, the ticket collector kindly agreed to let him remain on the train.

After travelling for some way, the train finally stopped at a station and the fog cleared, and Ken's heart leaped when he saw his father and mother standing on the platform. They greeted him delightedly when he stepped from the train, and embraced him warmly. Ken said to them, 'I've come to stay, but I've left Joyce and the girls at home.' His father smiled and replied, 'Yes, son, but I'm sorry, it's not time.' And to Ken's surprise they turned and walked away from him. At that moment everything disappeared, leaving a kind of space, he said, with a gate in the distance.

The next thing Ken knew, he was back lying in his hospital bed, feeling very unwell. He was told later that he had nearly died, and that it was touch and go for a while. It therefore seems that his dead parents had taken the opportunity to meet him during his brief sojourn in their world. But how strange and interesting that there was a train on hand to take Ken to where they were!

Ken has now made his final exit from this world, and he will doubtless have made another journey by train to the same station, although this time his parents will have known that he was stopping.

11   Preventing Premature Interment

The interval between the death and the interment is at present,
I believe, extended beyond what was usual at the time I refer
to: it was then two days and two nights, varying accordingly as
the demise took place in the early or later part of the day.

From a letter by J.B. about Cumberland funeral customs
to the editor of *Every-Day Book*, 1826

The awful fear of being buried alive reached its climax during
the nineteenth century, when ever more people realized that the
so-called signs of death were not infallible and that mistakes
could quite easily be made. Some well-publicized cases of
premature interment helped to foster and spread this concern.
As we have seen, even qualified medical practitioners can make
errors in diagnosing death, and these were far more likely to
happen at a time when doctors charged for their services and
when they were not required to be present to certify death,
which meant that the task of deciding if someone was dead or
not was frequently left to relatives and other inexpert parties.
Indeed, the founding of the Association for the Prevention of
Premature Burial in 1875, which quickly established branches in
the United States and elsewhere, reflected the growing public
anxiety and served as an effective, if somewhat hysterical, pressure group advocating changes in the law. The APPB not only
advocated the medical certification of death, but also fought for

the closure of overcrowded city churchyards, the opening of new cemeteries in the suburbs, the suppression of corruption amongst those dealing with the dead, and the use of cremation. Sir Henry Thompson, the great campaigner for cremation, was an active member.

The Association also urged the adoption of more immediately practical steps, such as delaying the burial of anyone who had died for up to seven days. To this end, it supported the concept of building properly supervised holding chambers or 'waiting mortuaries' in which the dead could be temporarily placed in open coffins until irrefutable signs of their death (meaning putrefaction) became evident. Such chambers had already been built in various towns and cities in Germany and Austria, and had the idea caught on here, waiting mortuaries would certainly have prevented many premature interments. But it seems that the general unsavouriness of the notion and the associated expense of constructing and maintaining these establishments weighed against it.

Prior to the nineteenth century the average person died at home, and the funeral was arranged by the family. This in effect meant that a coffin was knocked together by the local carpenter and a grave dug in the nearby churchyard, that relatives and friends carried the deceased to it, and that the local parson conducted a short graveside service. And no matter how upset a family might be at the passing of a loved one, most did not want to keep the corpse cluttering up a bedroom for several days on the off-chance that it might return to life. It was this desire to have the body removed as soon as was decently possible, without necessarily burying it immediately that the APPB hoped to satisfy by setting up waiting mortuaries.

The following short description by Colonel Edward Vollum of a Munich waiting mortuary, which appeared in a 1904 edition of *The Undertakers' Journal*, illustrates how anxiety was relieved there.

The waiting mortuary consists of a main hall where the bodies lie in open coffins, embowered by plants in the midst of light, warmth, and ventilation; there is also a laboratory, equipped with apparatus for resuscitation, post-mortem room, separate rooms for infectious cases and accidents; a chapel, quarters for the physician and attendants, and office.

Another commentator, writing a few years later, in 1908, added the observation that 'in some of these a bell rope is placed in the hands of the corpse, but as a distinguished authority had pithily remarked, "Since the institution of these chambers, no one had ever heard the bell ring." '

Indeed, it is ironical that waiting mortuaries are only needed, or at least can only be considered to be economically justified, when deaths are not certified by qualified medical practitioners, yet this certainly was not the case in Munich. For as Colonel Vollum points out, a dying person's doctor was obliged to be present during his or her 'death crisis', and although the doctor could pronounce him or her dead . . .

the law does not trust his unsupported opinion, however famous he may be. The inspector comes, and in the meantime nothing about the body must be touched by anyone. He makes his certificate, which covers every possible point in the case, and this is countersigned by the attending physician. Delay and resuscitation may be employed at this stage if the inspector sees fit. Ordinarily he allows from two to twelve hours' delay in the residence for ceremonies, etc., when the body must go to the waiting mortuary, where it remains for seventy-two hours, or longer, when the mortuary physician gives his certificate, if all goes without incidents, and the interment takes place in the adjoining cemetery.

In addition to these three experts, the corpse was also examined by a technically qualified woman known as a *leichenfrau*, who both laid it out and attended to its appearance, and made the funeral appointments. Thus each dead person was closely examined by four trained independent inspectors, which meant that there was scant chance of anyone who was still alive being placed in a waiting mortuary.

But in Britain the wheels of change turned slowly, shackled as they were by custom and vested interests, which explains why, as late as 1927, Mr J.R. Hurry, the secretary of the British Undertakers' Association, was lamenting the fact that 'over 60 per cent of the deaths in this country were certified by doctors without seeing the bodies after death had taken place'. And not even the Births and Deaths Registration Act which came into effect in January of that year made any difference to this situation, because it only specified that a body could not be buried until a certificate of death had been delivered to the 'person effecting the disposal'. Thus while it obliged a doctor to fill in a form certifying someone's death, it did not oblige him actually to view the corpse!

Hence it is hardly surprising that many people continued to be worried about being prematurely buried or cremated until well into this century, or indeed that a measure of concern still exists today. And hardly surprisingly, such anxiety led some people to include special clauses in their wills, stating what they wanted to be done to them when they died, to make sure they were actually dead.

One of the earliest instances of someone taking precautions to guard against premature interment happened on 1 February 1721, when Thomas and George Trigg, the brothers of Henry Trigg, a deceased farmer at Stevenage, in Hertfordshire, in accordance with the instructions of his will, from which they would thereby substantially benefit, placed his corpse in the special coffin that he had had made, whose lid had a lock that could be opened from the inside. A key to the lock was shut in with him. And because there was no chance of the farmer escaping if he revived after being buried, the coffin was then placed on a low beam in the barn, where it was to remain for thirty years, unless he unloosed himself in the meantime. The years rolled by until finally, on 5 February 1751, his brothers buried the dusty coffin in the local churchyard having left him for four days longer than the specified time, just to be on the safe side.

There was an interesting device put on display at the Washington Patent Office Museum in 1890, which recognized the fact that not everyone had a suitable beam on which to place a coffin. It consisted in effect of an escape hatch through which someone could climb from a buried coffin if he or she revived. Its inventor was a man who 'is said to have died and been buried in the usual way while his application for a patent was pending', which was not only bad luck but was hardly a good omen for the device's sales. The following description comes from *The Undertakers' and Funeral Directors' Journal and Monumental Masons' Review*:

A rectangular metal shaft extended from the head of the coffin, which was to be of a size to permit the reviving cadaver to move around in its shroud. Two panels of heavy glass close the respective plate ends of the shaft. The lower is so arranged as to drop out on the slightest movement within the casket. A bell at the upper end, which is supposed to project above the ground and form a sort of ready-made headstone, is sprung by the movement of the supposed dead person, and keeps on ringing for a space of time supposed to be sufficient to arouse the keeper of the city of the dead. This is a provision for such a condition of feebleness on the part of the recent corpse as to prevent its using the ladder that is available if the restoration is complete enough to leave an able-bodied man or woman as the result. The top plate is immovable from the outside, but falls before the approach of the party returning from the grave to the world.

One could of course be buried in complete confidence with such a shaft attached to one's coffin, although if it was bought and installed for someone who was really dead, it was a complete waste of money. So potential purchasers had to weigh the cost against the risk of being buried alive. Some obviously thought it was worth it. 'One newly-made bride,' the reporter observed, 'made her very fresh-looking groom solemnly promise to have her buried in that patent corpse-reviving contrivance, or she would go right back to ma. The promise was given.'

I do not know if farmers are more likely than most to suffer from premature burial anxiety (PBA), but in 1908, a wealthy Louisiana agriculturist named Mrs Pennord actually designed and built her own tomb. The coffin in which she was to be interred had air-holes drilled in it to allow her to breathe if she recovered after burial, and quite amazingly, considering the early date, it also had a telephone installed beside the headrest, which was connected to the house of the cemetery-keeper! Such an arrangement would be far cheaper and easier to arrange today, as once the holes in the coffin had been taken care of, one would only need to bury a corpse with his mobile telephone.

Premature interment can only be prevented by making sure that the person to be buried is really dead. In most cases, certification of this fact by one or more doctors is usually sufficient, although as we have seen doctors can make mistakes. But if you are worried about the possibility of being buried alive, you can arrange for your burial to be delayed for at least a week to give you a reasonable chance of reviving before your funeral. Alternatively, you can ask a willing party, such as your physician, to give your corpse a wound that would kill you if you were still alive, although whether or not this might be construed as murder if you were is a moot point.

It is interesting to note how one eighteenth-century clergyman became aware of the dangers of too hasty burial. The first wife of the Revd Mr John Dunton, the rector of Ashton Clinton in Buckinghamshire, fell seriously ill and was pronounced dead by her doctor, but recovered three days later. Knowing how close she came to being buried alive, Mr Dunton, who died in November 1777, specified in his will, 'that it is his desire, that his funeral might not be performed till five days after his decease'. His burial was delayed in accordance with his wishes.

Lord George Bentinck, the sportsman and politician who became MP for King's Lynn in 1826, was a champion of religious liberty and a staunch advocate of massive government aid for Ireland during that country's potato famine. When he suddenly died in September 1848, his will revealed that he suffered from PBA. A clause stated that 'so as to preclude the possibility of being buried alive, he directs that his coffin shall not be closed or covered up for three days and three nights after his decease, and that a daily and nightly watch shall be kept during this period'. Moreover, those who volunteered to sit by him were to be paid 50 guineas, an astonishing sum for the time, and one presumably calculated to ensure that they did not nod off while doing the job.

The April 1927 edition of *The Undertakers' Journal* reported that a wealthy Hove resident named Henry Lewis, who died in January of that year, had not only requested that his death should be certified by a doctor but said that he wanted to be 'placed in an open coffin for six full days, after which a different medical man should be called upon carefully to examine the state of his body, and if in his opinion death was absolutely certain *to sever an artery*'.

Similarly, the former actress Mary Wilde, who committed suicide at her Kilburn lodgings in 1909, said in the note she left that she wanted her doctor to cut through one of her arteries before she was interred. She desired this to be done, she explained, because she had once almost been buried alive and she did not want to find herself waking up in her coffin on this occasion.

Some people are more specific about which artery they want cut. For example, when Sidney Francis Bampfield Cogan, a wealthy Torquay resident, died in 1908, his will stated that he wanted Dr Hall, his trusted physician, to slice through one of his carotid arteries, for which act the good doctor would be paid £100. If for some reason Dr Hall was unable to perform this task, Mr Cogan's executors were instructed to hire another qualified physician to do it for him, although he was to be paid only £25.

Having a carotid artery severed is something of a favourite choice among sufferers of PBA. Miss Lucy Soulsby, the former headmistress of the Oxford High School for Girls, who died in May 1927, made this quite plain in her will and likewise explained why she wanted it done. 'Whereas I have always desired every precaution to be taken against being buried alive, I desire that at my death the doctor shall cut my carotid artery, and if by some mistake this be omitted, I desire that my body shall be exhumed and this be done.'

The celebrated feminist, philanthropist, and authoress Frances Power Cobbe, who wrote such searching volumes as *The Final Cause of Women* and *The Duties of Woman*, and who, it may be truthfully said, was the original Girl Power – and a vigorous campaigner against vivisection – was determined that she was not going to be buried alive. This much is evident from her correspondence with the President of the APPB, whom she graphically told: 'I have never made a will without inserting a clause requiring my throat to be cut before I am put underground.'

Miss Cobbe's awareness of the likelihood of premature interment derived from two personal experiences, the first of which, it seems, robbed of her of any confidence in either the sense or the competence of physicians. She wrote, 'One can have no reliance on doctors whatever, and I have known a case in which a very eminent one insisted on a coffin being screwed down because the corpse looked so life-like and full of colour that the friends could not help indulging in hopes.' The second case involved her great-grandmother, after whom she was named, who as a girl had once seemingly died, and for whom, being a wealthy heiress, a lavish funeral was arranged. But when the day of the funeral came, something extraordinary happened.

Among the guests came a young girl, who insisted she was not dead, and raised such a stir that the funeral was postponed, and time was allowed to pass till the marvel became that there was no sign of change. I could never ascertain how long this comatose state lasted before she recovered; but she did recover, so thoroughly that after her marriage with Richard Trench, of Garbuty, she became mother of twenty-two children.

The novelist and politician Edward Bulwer, Lord Lytton, who wrote over sixty works, several of which, such as *The Last Days of Pompeii*, *The Caxtons*, and *Richelieu*, have become part of the land-scape of English literature, was also concerned about a mistake being made at his death. This is why, to prevent himself from being immured alive, he left strict instructions that his heart was to be pierced by his doctor with a lancet.

This is a drastic course of action to take if the person is still alive, as was made clear by a case which happened in America. An old, well-established Virginian family's fears about premature burial had been roused in the middle of the eighteenth century, when the exhumation of a relative revealed that he had been buried alive. From that time on, whenever someone in the family died, the head of the house would take it upon himself to stab the corpse through the heart with a knife. All went well until 1850, when the paterfamilias's own daughter, who was by all accounts a beautiful young woman, died. In accordance with tradition, her father plunged a dagger into her breast. But to his horror the girl, who had merely been in a trance, screamed with pain and shock, and expired almost immediately from the fateful wound. The poor man was mortified by what he had done, and not long afterwards committed suicide.

But while the cutting of an artery is the preferred way of having someone make sure you are dead, there are those who are so fearful of being buried alive that they make outlandish demands to guarantee that they do not suffer such an end. Two examples will suffice to illustrate the development of PBA to a paranoid degree.

Francis Douce, the well-known English antiquary, book collector, and eccentric, who died in 1834, began his will in the following way: 'I give to Sir Anthony Carlisle £200, requesting him either to sever my head, or extract the heart from my body, so as to prevent any possibility of the return of vitality.'

James Mott, a retired Birmingham brass founder, was so determined not to be buried alive, that he bizarrely requested in his 1920s will that:

After my decease two medical men shall apply every test to prove that life is extinct, that a strong dose of prussic acid shall next be placed in my mouth, and that one of them shall then decapitate my body in the presence of the other, and that both shall certify that such decapitation had been done, or otherwise I direct that my body shall be dissected by post-mortem examination.

Such instructions are not really worth the paper they are written on, however. A doctor, after all, is only legally required to certify that a patient is dead. He is not obliged to cut off the person's head, slice through an artery, or do anything else in order to make sure that he or she is really dead. Indeed, any doctor who assaulted his patient in such a manner and who was unlucky enough to discover that he or she was in fact still alive, would get himself into serious trouble. He might even be accused of murder. So while I do not know if Sir Anthony Carlisle cut off Francis Douce's head, I rather doubt that he did, despite the promise of £200.

However, some people have requested that they be buried with a phial of poison, which they can swallow and so properly kill themselves should they awake in the grave, while others have asked to be interred with a firearm. Where the last is concerned, I must mention a woman resident of the town of Dux, in Bohemia, who was 'haunted by the dread of being buried alive' and in 1908 asked her husband on her death-bed to bury her with a loaded revolver. Her wish was complied with and the worried lady went to her grave with 'a crucifix in one hand and the revolver in the other'. Neither option is legally possible in Britain today, and indeed it would be asking for trouble if corpses were buried with loaded weapons, for they would certainly be dug up at night by criminals intent on stealing them.

So what can sufferers of PBA do to satisfy themselves that they will not be prematurely buried, cremated or dissected? The only straightforward, realistic choice they have is to request being embalmed. No one can survive having his or her blood replaced by preservative, so once this is done he or she (or you, for that matter) can then be certain of being dead.

Bibliography

Adams, David Morgan, 'My Heart Stopped, I Died', *Guide and Ideas* (May 1938)

Aldini, John, *An Account of The Late Improvements in Galvanism, with a Series of Curious and Interesting Experiments* (Cuthell and Martin, and John Murray, 1803)

Aldini, John, *General Views on the Application of Galvanism to Medical Purposes; principally in cases of Suspended Animation* (1819)

Annual Register, various issues

Arber, R.N. (ed.), *Directory of Crematoria* (The Cremation Society of Great Britain, 1997)

Aubrey, John, *Miscellanies Upon Various Subjects* (John Russell Smith, 1857)

Bell, Charles and John, *The Anatomy and Physiology of the Human Body, Vol. 1* (Longman, Hurst, Orme, and Brown, 1816)

Bell, Walter George, *The Great Plague of London* (Bracken Books, 1994)

Bell, Walter George, *London Rediscoveries* (The Bodley Head, 1929)

Biographie Universal Ancient et Moderne (Michaud, 1843)

Cheyne, George, MD, *The English Malady, or A Treatise of Nervous Diseases of All Kinds* (G. Strathan, 1734)

Cunningham, George, *London* (J.M. Dent & Sons, 1927)

Curiosités Biographique (Paulin, 1846)

De Quincey, Thomas, *Confessions of an English Opium-eater* (Henry Frowde, 1906)

De Quincey, Thomas, *Essays* (Blackie & Sons Limited, undated)

Derham, William, *Physico-Theology, or a Demonstration of the Being and Attributes of God, from his Works of Creation* (W. Innys, 1713)

Dickson, H.R.P., *The Arab of the Desert* (George Allen & Unwin, 1949)

Dictionary of National Biography (Oxford University Press, 1885)

Erasmus, Desiderius, *Twenty Select Colloquies of Erasmus*, translated by Sir Roger L'Estrange (Charman & Dodd, undated)

Fifty Strangest Stories Ever Told (Odhams Press, undated)

Forsyth, J.S., *The New London Medical and Surgical Dictionary* (Sherwood, Gilbert, & Piper, 1826)

Froude, J.A., *Lord Beaconsfield* (Sampson Low, Marston, Searle & Rivington, 1890)

Genninges, John, *The Life and Death of Mr Edmund Geninges*, (*Priest* 1614, reprinted by the Scolar Press, 1971)

Gentleman's Magazine, various issues

Goulart, Simon, the Elder, *Admirable and memorable Histories containing the wonders of our time*, translated by E. Grimeston (George Eld, 1607)

Granger, Reverend James, *Biographical History of England* (T. Davies, 1769)

Gurdon, Lady Eveline Camilla (coll. & ed.), *County Folk-lore, Vol. 1. part 2, Suffolk* (David Nutt, 1895)

Harrison, G.B., *A Jacobean Journal, 1603–1606* (George Routledge & Sons, 1941)

Howard, John, *The State of Prisons in England and Wales* (Warrington, 1784)

James, Dr J. Brindley, *Death and its Verification* (Rebman, 1908)

Jones, P. Herbert and Noble, George (eds), *Cremation in Great Britain* (The Cremation Society, 1931)

Jupp, Peter, *From Dust to Ashes: The Replacement of Burial by*

Cremation in England 1840–1967 (The Congregational Memorial Trust, 1990)

Kershaw, Alister, *A History of the Guillotine* (John Calder, 1958)

Keynes, Geoffrey, *The Life of William Harvey* (Clarendon Press, 1966)

Lady's Magazine (1813 and 1815)

Mackenzie, Peter, *Reminiscences of Glasgow* (John Tweed, 1865)

Marks, Alfred, *Tyburn Tree: Its History and Annals* (Brown, Langham & Co.)

McDonald, Stuart W, 'The Life and Times of James Jeffray, Regius Professor of Anatomy, University of Glasgow 1790–1848' (*Scottish Medical Journal*, 1995)

Montaigne, Michel de, *Essays, Vol. 3*, translated by Charles Cotton (George Bell & Sons, 1892)

N.H., *Ladies' Dictionary; Being a General Entertainment for the Fair Sex* (J. Dunton, 1694)

New Wonderful Magazine and Marvellous Chronicle, 1794

Notes and Queries, various issues

Pattison, F.L.M., 'The Clydesdale Experiments: An Early Attempt at Resuscitation' (*Scottish Medical Journal*, 1986)

Peckard, Peter, *Farther Observations on the Doctrine of an Intermediate State* (L. Davis & C. Reymers, 1757)

Peron-Autret, Dr, *Buried Alive* (Corgi Books, 1983)

Peu, Philip, *La Pratique des Accouchemens* (Jean Boudot, 1694)

Plato, *The Republic* (The Penguin Classics, 1959)

Poe, Edgar Allan, *Tales of Mystery and Imagination* (The New University Society, undated)

Pollock, Sir Frederick (ed.), *Macready's Reminiscences and Selections from his Diaries and Letters* (Macmillan, 1875)

Richardson, Joanna, *Rachel* (Max Reinhardt, 1953)

Rumblelow, Donald, *The Triple Tree: Newgate, Tyburn and Old Bailey* (Harrap, 1982)

Ryan, Michael, MD, *A Manual of Medical Jurisprudence and State Medicine* (Sherwood, Gilbert, & Piper, 1836)

Select Trials at the Sessions-House in the Old Bailey, for Murder, Robberies, Rapes, Sodomy, Coinage, Frauds, Bigamy, and other offences, Vol. 1 (James Hodges, 1742)

Stow, John, *The Survey of London* (Everyman's Library, J.M. Dent & Sons, 1960)

Taylor, Joseph, *The Danger of Premature Interment Proved* (W. Simpkin & R. Marshal, 1816)

Tebb, William, and Vollum, Col. Edward Perry, *Premature Burial* (Swan Sonnenscein & Co., 1896)

Terilli, Dominicus, *De Causis Mortis Repentinae* (Venetis, 1615)

Turner, William, *A Complete History of the Most Remarkable Providences* (John Dunton, 1697)

Ure, Andrew, MD, MGS, *An Account of some Experiments made on the Body of a Criminal immediately after Execution, with Physiological and Practical Observations* (Read at the Glasgow Literary Society, 10 December 1818)

Wanley, Nathaniel, *The Wonders of the Little World* (T. Basset, 1678)

Watson, Sir William, MD, *An Account of a Series of Experiments, Instituted with a view to ascertaining the Most Successful Method of Inoculating the Small-pox* (1768)

Whiter, Revd Walter, *A Dissertation on the Disorder of Death* (printed for the author, 1819)

Willughby, Percivall, *Observations in Midwifery*, edited by Blenkinsop (Warwick, 1863)

Wilson, Revd Thomas, *An Archaeological Dictionary* (T. Cadell, 1783)

Winslow, Jacobus Benignus, *The Uncertainty of the Signs of Death, and the Danger of Precipitate Interments and Dissections Demonstrated*, translated by J.J. Bruhier d'Ablaincourt (George Faulkner, 1748)

Dates of Persons Mentioned in Text

Adams, David Morgan, 1875–1942
Aldini Giovanni (or John), 1762–1834
Bathurst, Dr Ralph, 1620–1704
Bentinck, Lord George, 1802–48
Bernard, Jean, 1702–81
Boccaccio, Giovanni, 1313–75
Chaptall, Jean Antoine, 1756–1832
Churchill, Arabella, 1648–1730
Churchill, John, Duke of Marlborough, 1650–1722
Cibber, Caius, 1630–1700
Cobbe, Francis Power, 1822–1904
Combe-Blanche, Jean Janin de, 1731–?
Corday, Charlotte, 1762–93
De Quincey, Thomas, 1785–1859
Disraeli, Benjamin, Earl of Beaconsfield, 1797–1882
Douce, Francis, 1757–1834
Duns, John Scot, *c.* 1265–1308
Fabrizi, Girolami, 1530–1619
Felix, Elisa (Mademoiselle Rachel), 1821–58
Fracastoro, Girolamo, *c.* 1478–1553
Galenus, Claudius, 103–93
Galvani, Luigi, 1737–98
Geninges, Edmund, 1567–91

Gilbert, William, 1540–1603
Hayward, George, 1823–1904
Howard, John, 1726–90
Hunter, William, 1718–83
Jeffray, James, 1749–1848
Koch, Dr Robert, 1843–1910
Lancisi, Giovanni Maria, 1654–1720
Laurens, Henry, 1724–92
Leclerc, Jean, 1657–1736
Macready, William, 1793–1875
Manning, Owen, 1721–1801
Martin, St, 316–97
Maynard, Sir John, 1602–90
Misson, Francois Maximilian, 1650?–1722
Monstrelet, Enguerrand de, c. 1390–1453
Montaigne, Michel de, 1533–92
Nashe, Thomas, 1567–1601
Petty, Sir William, 1623–87
Pius IX, pontificate 1846–78
Plato, 427–347 BC
Prevost, Abbe, 1697–1763
Reuchlin, Johann, 1455–1522
Shirley, Laurence, 4th Earl Ferrers, 1720–60
Somaglia, Giulo Maria della, 1744–1830
Thompson, Sir Henry, 1820–1902
Vesalius, Andreas, 1514–64
Volta, Count Alessandro, 1745–1827
Wanley, Nathaniel, 1633–?
Watson, Sir William, 1715–87
Webster, Benjamin Nottingham, 1797–1882
Willis, Dr Thomas, 1621–73
Willughby, Percivall, 1596–1685
Winslow, Jacobus Benignus, 1669–1760

Index